# Advance Praise

Tom has a passion for patient safety and in this book he brings to light evidence-based, effective plans that work. We have a lot to learn from the science of positive psychology, including how we can, literally, rewire our brains to be better at problem-solving—particularly in times of crisis—and how we can consistently work together in ways that enhance the care we provide. At the same time, you'll find that what you'll learn from this book will support your growth as a professional *and* as a human being.

**Peter J. Pronovost, MD**
*Author of* Safe Patients, Smart Hospitals
*Director of the Armstrong Institute for Patient Safety and Quality*
*Senior Vice President for Patient Safety and Quality at Johns Hopkins Medicine*

I worked with PROPEL for years at the Johns Hopkins Hospital, Baltimore, Maryland. It's amazing to me what these principles can do to engage a multidisciplinary healthcare team. The units that used PROPEL saw results such as increased employee engagement scores, decreased falls, and decreased turnover. People started coming to work were happy to be there, instead of dreading the issues that were bound to come up. PROPEL changed the way that our teams viewed and solved problems. Problems became an opportunity to improve and collaborate rather than a way of bringing the team down. The staff started supporting each other and work became more like a family. I'm now the senior vice president of Patient Care Services and chief nursing officer at the Greater Baltimore Medical Center (GBMC) HealthCare, Baltimore, Maryland and have already brought PROPEL to this organization because I know about the positive changes it creates.

**JoAnn Z. Ioannou, DNP, MBA, RN, NEA-BC**
*Senior Vice President—Patient Care Services and Chief Nursing Officer, GBMC*
*HealthCare*

A must-read for healthcare leaders desiring enhanced teamwork and improved outcomes. The PROPEL principles artfully distill essential positive psychology research and offer efficient implementation techniques for converting theory to action.

In this enjoyable read, Thomas Muha, PhD unlocks the pathway to peak performance, accessible even to the busiest professional.

**Brooke Buckley, MD FACS**
*MedChi, The Maryland State Medical Society, President 2015–2016*
*Chief, Division of General Surgery*
*Medical Director, Acute Care Surgery*
*Anne Arundel Medical Center*

Muha has written a very important book that should be mandatory reading for anyone involved in healthcare. It combines scholarly research findings with practical advice and strategies for both personal flourishing and organizational success. Given the importance and centrality of healthcare in our society and around the world, this work is sure to make a significant impact for the better.

**Kim Cameron, PhD**
*William Russell Professor of Management and Organizations*
*Ross School of Business*
*Cofounder, Center for Positive Organizations*
*University of Michigan*
*Author of* Practicing Positive Leadership

# PROPEL to Quality Healthcare

# PROPEL to Quality Healthcare

## Six Steps to Improve Patient Care, Staff Engagement, and the Bottom Line

Thomas M. Muha, PhD

with Martha Murphy

Foreword by Peter Pronovost, MD
Author of *Safe Patients, Smart Hospitals*

CRC Press
Taylor & Francis Group
Boca Raton  London  New York

CRC Press is an imprint of the
Taylor & Francis Group, an **informa** business
A PRODUCTIVITY PRESS BOOK

CRC Press
Taylor & Francis Group
6000 Broken Sound Parkway NW, Suite 300
Boca Raton, FL 33487-2742

International Standard Book Number-13: 978-1-1382-1504-7 (Hardback)

**Library of Congress Cataloging-in-Publication Data**

Names: Muha, Thomas, author.
Title: PROPEL to quality healthcare : six steps to improve patient care,
staff engagement, and the bottom line / Thomas M. Muha.
Description: Boca Raton : Taylor & Francis, 2018. | "A CRC title, part of the
Taylor & Francis imprint, a member of the Taylor & Francis Group, the
academic division of T&F Informa plc." | Includes bibliographical
references.
Identifiers: LCCN 2017006431 | ISBN 9781138215047 (hardback : alk. paper) |
ISBN 9781315116846 (ebook)
Subjects: LCSH: Health services administration. | Medical care--Quality
control.
Classification: LCC RA971 .M73 2018 | DDC 362.1068--dc23
LC record available at https://lccn.loc.gov/2017006431

**Visit the Taylor & Francis Web site at**
**http://www.taylorandfrancis.com**

**and the CRC Press Web site at**
**http://www.crcpress.com**

# Contents

## SECTION II   A TALE OF TWO UNITS

## SECTION IV    TOOLKITS FOR INDIVIDUALS AND PROPEL TEAMS

# Foreword

In addition to my work as a critical care physician, as an improvement science researcher, and as an executive of a large health system, I have seen the miracles healthcare can perform and how much better it can be: for patients, for clinicians, for healthcare provider organizations, for employers, and for us all.

I've found that one of the most effective steps we can take toward improving care and reducing harm is to collaborate—across job titles, across disciplines, and with patients themselves. This finding has been confirmed in numerous studies, including a 2015 National Academy of Medicine Report, "Improving Diagnosis in HealthCare," in which "teamwork" is cited as a highly effective yet underused solution to reduce diagnostic errors and provide safe, quality patient care and outcomes. Teamwork, the report shows, achieves much more than an improved work culture; its biggest benefit is to patients. Effective treatment is based on an accurate diagnosis, which is far more likely to occur when teams take a collaborative approach.

Collaboration also engenders a sense of purpose, of "belonging." There is enormous power bestowed by an atmosphere of belonging. In healthcare, I've observed that such an environment enables professionals to push beyond what they think their limits are. Bolstered by connections based on trust, humility, and a common desire to redefine what is possible, we are able to do our best work and derive more joy from our work.

Love, the love of our patients, the love of our fellow healthcare professionals, underlies improvement. The response to this statement is often raised eyebrows. Yet the more we learn about how love and other emotions work, the more we recognize the immense power of love over the quality of care we deliver and over our efforts to improve that care. We also understand that this form of love is indeed practical and attainable in our hospitals and clinics. Biomedical and social scientists alike are helping us understand how love is based upon micro-moments of positive connection between people. These positive emotions help open ourselves to others, whereas negative emotions can break the bonds between people and even harm the performance of clinical teams.

That is why I am delighted to have made the acquaintance of Tom Muha, PhD, and why I am glad to help spread the word about *PROPEL to Quality Healthcare*, a six-step program for healthcare professionals that can improve patient care, staff engagement, and the bottom line. Dr. Muha's work is based on decades of research in the science of positive psychology (if you are unfamiliar with the specialty, you'll learn about it in Chapter 2), as well as his 15 years of field work in major hospitals and medical centers across this country—including my hospital, Johns Hopkins, Baltimore, Maryland, where we have seen incredible results from adopting the principles and tactics of PROPEL.

Dr. Muha has a passion for patient safety, and in this book he brings to light evidence-based, effective plans that work. We have a lot to learn from the science of positive psychology, including how we can, literally, rewire our brains to be better at problem solving—particularly in times of crisis—and how we can consistently work together in ways that enhance the care we provide. At the same time, you'll find that what you'll learn from this book will support your growth as a professional *and* as a human being.

Through my work we have learned that the secret sauce of improvement and patient-centered care—and life in general—is not simply a technical solution or a checklist. These are helpful, yet they are not the mojo of life. We need to create positive resonance not only between clinicians and patients but also among clinicians. To quote Avedis Donabedian, the father of quality improvement in healthcare, "Ultimately, the secret to quality is love." And, as Dr. Muha knows, it's contagious.

Thank you, Dr. Muha, for your important work and for this book. You truly help us "propel" ourselves to be deserving of the honor it is to work in healthcare.

**Peter J. Pronovost**
*Author of* Safe Patients, Smart Hospitals
*Director of the Armstrong Institute for Patient Safety and Quality*
*Senior Vice President for Patient Safety and Quality at Johns Hopkins Medicine*

# Acknowledgments

I am eternally grateful to my wife, Carole, for her loving support and encouragement through many years of perfecting the use of the PROPEL Principles in healthcare settings. I am also grateful to my literary agent, Jeanne Fredericks, and my coauthor, Martha Murphy, who believe in the value of this work and have been instrumental in finding a publisher and creating the book. I thank my editor, Kristine Mednansky, at Taylor & Francis Group for having the vision to take on a work dedicated to making a difference in the lives of healthcare professionals.

I extend a special note of thanks to Diann Snyder, Administrator and Director of Nursing of the Department of Gynecology and Obstetrics, and to Debbie Dang, Director of Nursing Practice, Education, and Research at the Johns Hopkins Hospital, Baltimore, Maryland. They are courageous leaders who have led the effort to study the effectiveness of the PROPEL Principles in healthcare settings. I also thank other innovative leaders who supported the development of PROPEL through the years: Jim Walker, former Chief Executive Officer at University of Maryland Baltimore Washington Medical Center, Glen Burnie, Maryland; Diane Johnson, Director of Nursing at Sinai Hospital, Baltimore, Maryland; and John Spearman, former Vice President at R. Adams Cowley Shock Trauma Center, Baltimore, Maryland.

I want to express deep appreciation to the PROPEL coaches—Linda Burton, Janet Ladd, and Corrine Lears—whose hard work with healthcare providers has helped their units, clinics, and leadership teams create healthier workplace environments. Working together, we have learned a great deal about how to improve the well-being and performance of healthcare teams. I am grateful to PROPEL coach Sue Knight for being a wonderful source of insight and inspiration to me while writing this book.

To the thousands of leaders, healthcare providers, and staff members who have embraced the use of the PROPEL Principles, thank you for making a meaningful difference in patient care, staff engagement, and your organization's ability to flourish. Because you were willing to learn and grow—and teach others to do the same—healthcare delivery is improving.

Finally, I am indebted to Lola, my Portuguese water dog, who was literally by my side as I wrote this book. She was always happy to provide the playful breaks that allowed my weary brain to rejuvenate. Lola is living proof that having more love and joy in your life improves productivity.

# Author

**Dr. Thomas M. Muha** is director of The PROPEL Institute. As the science of optimal human functioning has emerged, he has become a leading practitioner of positive psychology. His mission is to be at the forefront in the study of how people involved in healthcare systems can achieve the highest levels of success and satisfaction.

More than 15 years of research at Johns Hopkins Hospital, R. Adams Cowley Shock Trauma Center, and Sinai Hospital, Baltimore, Maryland, has enabled Dr. Muha to prove the efficacy of the PROPEL program. *PROPEL to Quality Healthcare* provides the six-step formula that more than 100 units, clinics, and leadership teams have used to improve patient care, staff engagement, and a healthy bottom line.

Teaching the leaders and the staff to use the PROPEL positive psychology principles has also been shown to significantly counter the effects of stress and burnout. Medical professionals report enhanced life satisfaction, loving relationships, job enjoyment, and work–life balance.

Dr. Muha has been a keynote speaker and a workshop presenter at some of the world's top healthcare organizations, including the Institute for Healthcare Improvement, the Sigma Theta Tau, the American Organization of Nurse Executives, the Magnet Recognition Pathways to Excellence, and the HealthStream's Healthcare Summit.

Dr. Muha earned his doctoral degree in psychology from the California School of Professional Psychology, Los Angeles, California. He is the founder of The PROPEL Institute, LLC. He has written a weekly newspaper column focusing on positive psychology for the *Capital Gazette* newspaper chain for more than 25 years.

# Introduction

When I learned I needed an invasive major surgery to save my life, it was a wake-up call. What I didn't anticipate, however, was that my subsequent intersection with healthcare would be life-changing in other ways. Yet, that's exactly what happened. After barely making it out of the hospital alive—yes, I came close to being one of those statistics in the "preventable medical errors" database—I became impassioned to join the efforts to improve healthcare in the United States. Although I didn't have a medical background, I did have years of experience helping individuals and teams to function at their best.

I resolved to research, design, and launch a performance improvement program. It's now been used in major hospitals and medical centers for more than a dozen years, and it's proven highly effective in addressing the biggest issues in healthcare today: patient safety, staff engagement, and a healthy bottom line. That program is called PROPEL, and it's the basis of this book.

The six principles of PROPEL—Passion, Relationships, Optimism, Proactivity, Energy, and Legacy—have provided thousands of healthcare providers the tools they needed to make significant change, get past formerly impenetrable roadblocks, and achieve positive outcomes—for themselves, their teams, and their organizations.

Healthcare today is in crisis. Administrators are under mounting pressure to make the numbers work to generate enough money to keep the doors open. Nearly three out of four nurses report symptoms of stress and overwork due to long hours and mounting demands, with more than 50 percent of critical care nurses intending to leave their jobs within 1 year. More than 45 percent of physicians report having at least one symptom of burnout. But there is a fix. There are proven performance improvement strategies based on solid science and tested in real-life healthcare settings. Understanding those strategies will give you hope. Implementing them will improve your life, personally and professionally. And these strategies lead to improved patient care.

You may have already participated in efforts in your workplace to find solutions. However, since two-thirds of change initiatives in hospitals *fail to meet expectations*, your experience trying to achieve significant improvements has probably left you discouraged.

Take heart. I've written this book for you. The six-step PROPEL plan works, and the tools you will find here were made possible thanks to scientific research into how human beings can change their behavior. This book can help:

- Executives trying to maintain staffing engagement and retention levels capable of delivering good patient care while their budgets shrink every year.
- Nurse managers overloaded by the demands from executives in the C-suite, staff members, patients, and their families.
- Bedside nurses feeling powerless to take care of patients because the pharmacy doesn't deliver medications on time, a doctor won't return pages, and support staff members can't get rooms cleaned in a timely manner.
- Physicians who are overloaded with patients, paperwork, and perfunctory meetings.

In the chapters that follow, you will get an up-close-and-personal look at struggles in real hospitals, outpatient clinics, and other healthcare facilities. You will discover how—in diverse settings and facing a range of problems—individuals and teams made the PROPEL Principles work for them. Based on true stories, the characters you will meet serve as illustrations. Identifying information and specific interactions have been modified to protect confidentiality for the people and organizations involved. However, the remarkable results achieved by the PROPEL team in each story are real.

In Chapter 1, I share my own story to illustrate how challenging circumstances can become the inspiration for improving our life and our world. In Chapter 2, you'll learn about the science behind positive psychology—the study of people who are most satisfied and successful—which forms the foundation of the PROPEL Principles. In Chapter 3, you'll get a glimpse at a top-rated hospital and how exploring the interface of reality and research led to the development of the PROPEL performance improvement program. Chapters 4 through 6 use real stories (modified to preserve confidentiality) to demonstrate how PROPEL addresses problems in healthcare settings, overcomes the setbacks that arise, and provides specific steps that lead to success.

In the next six chapters (Chapters 7 through 12), I take you through each of the PROPEL Principles, one at a time, using a "before and after" look at a real-life healthcare setting populated by real executives, nurses, and physicians—showing you how they struggle and how they succeed—and I introduce you to the science behind each of the six PROPEL steps. I demonstrate how teams of dedicated professionals attain amazing improvements.

I thank you for the work you do in healthcare, and I'm honored that you will be taking the PROPEL journey. I'm humbled to have an opportunity to be part of the solution to improve healthcare, both how it's delivered and how it's received. By the time you finish reading this book, I hope your professional and personal life will have changed in ways you never thought possible. And, I hope you'll contact me at The PROPEL Institute to tell me about it. I'd love to hear your story.

**Thomas M. Muha, PhD**
drtommuha@propelinstitute.com

# WHY POSITIVE WORK ENVIRONMENTS MATTER

Negativity has disastrous consequences for healthcare providers and their patients. Positivity is a prerequisite for optimal functioning. You are about to discover why—through stories that illustrate and research that illuminates.

# Chapter 1

# Modern Times in Healthcare: From the C-Suite to the Bedside

"Barbara?" It was 3:30 a.m. and she knew it was the hospital switchboard as soon as she looked at her cell phone. "I'll connect you to the night supervisor," the operator said. "There's something happening on the cardiac floor."

"Sorry to call at this hour, Barbara, but wanted to give you a heads-up." The calm voice of Steve J., a veteran RN perfectly suited for the lonely job of managing staff members on three floors while patients slept, was even but serious. "You're probably going to have to meet with risk management and then a family when you get in. We had an open-heart patient make it up to the floor without pain med orders and it's taken a while to track down the on-call doc." He paused. "The patient has been awake the whole time."

Over the course of 30 years, Barbara had worked her way to the highest position a registered nurse can attain: hospital vice president and chief nursing officer (CNO). Responsible for oversight of all inpatient and outpatient services at a 900-bed acute care medical center, she had paid her dues to get there—from a scared, fresh-out-of-school 22-year-old slogging through the trenches of the ER, then obstetrics, intensive care, pediatrics, telemetry—caring for patients who would heal and go home and for patients who never would.

Barbara's passion for the work had kept her going, giving her the drive to go to school at night for advanced degrees. Now, she had arrived. The hours were long (11-hour days were not uncommon), but the pay was good (six figures) and she had always wanted to have a greater influence on patient care. Finally, she could. Or could she?

Her schedule is filled with back-to-back meetings in conference rooms far from patients, and those with the chief executive officer (CEO) always begin and end with discussions about money. She is constantly being asked to justify expenses, to find ways to increase revenue. To help with this goal, the hospital has hired a consultant (whose expertise, by the way, is improving manufacturing assembly-line processes) who recommends reducing staff members. Certified nursing assistants (CNA) (a nurse's "right hand") were let go right away, and RN schedules were "flexed." Some of the most senior nurses left, and human resources replaced them with *per diem* staff members. Barbara wants enough staff members to provide safe patient care. The CEO wants to keep the hospital out of the red. Welcome to American healthcare today.

Back to Barbara's story. She was roused at 3:30 a.m. regarding the open-heart patient's pain management incident. By 7:00 a.m. she had met with the patient's nurse, questioned the floor's nurse manager, reviewed notes from the operating room's (OR's) hand-off team, and had a brief, unpleasant phone conversation with the patient's surgeon. A meeting with the head of risk management would be required, but first she had to sit down with her counterpart, Jim, the equally busy Chief Medical Officer. Their conversations never seemed to go well, and this one was no exception:

*Barbara:* This incident poses a serious risk for the hospital. Why did it take over 4 hours for one of the on-call doctors to answer the charge nurse's multiple pages?

*Jim:* We were short-staffed that night because one of our physicians called out. There was a patient in the intensive care unit (ICU) who had coded and the doctor who was covering that floor was tied up trying to save her life.

*Barbara (becoming irritated):* How many times have we talked about your staffing issues? Why does this keep happening? Why can't another doc be called in to help?

*Jim (on the defensive):* You know damn well why this happens! I can't get budget approval from the chief financial officer (CFO) to hire another doc for the overnight shift. What do you want me to do, answer the page myself?

*Barbara (sarcastically):* Maybe you ought to. I do.

Stalemate. Animosity. Once their frustrations had boiled over into the open, it was only harder for them to work together. Two highly successful healthcare professionals, dedicated to helping people, feel stuck and feel they have failed—themselves, their staff members, and patients. They cast blame but no process changes are made. And the patients continue to suffer. Sound familiar?

Oh, that open-heart patient who had not received pain medication after surgery? That was me. That terrifying experience was the impetus for the launch of a new stage in my career as an organizational psychologist. It was the turning point at which I became dedicated to helping find answers to the complex challenges facing healthcare systems.

## My Story

After undergoing open-heart surgery—at a prestigious medical center, I should add—I awoke in my hospital room to experience a pain that can only be described as stunning. Eventually, a nurse responded to the frantic buzz of my call bell. Flooded with relief at the sight of someone who could help, tears streamed down my face. The moment was short-lived.

"I'm waiting for the doctor's orders," she told me. She explained that she could not give me anything to relieve the "discomfort" (hospital-speak for agony) until a physician saw me. "He'll be here soon," she assured me as she headed to the door. "Just rest."

The pain, unfortunately, wasn't interested in rest. It progressed.

I wanted to be a "good" patient, compliant. The wailing, the nonstop grip on the call button—they were involuntary reactions, beyond my control. The noise caught the attention of the charge nurse and, God bless her, she had guts. She picked up the phone in my room. "Get Dr. Graham NOW," she shouted. "Well, page him. We've got a big problem here. We have an open-heart patient with no post-op pain med orders."

She sat with me, wiping my brow with a cold washcloth until the student nurse she had summoned arrived to take her place. Powerless to alleviate my suffering, the young woman could only hold my hand, while tears streamed down both of our faces.

It was now the middle of the night. The on-call doctor did, finally, respond and wrote the orders for oral and intravenous analgesic drugs. More than 5 hours had gone by since I'd been wheeled out of the OR. I was outraged that the doctor had taken so long to respond and demanded to know what happened. "I was dealing with patients on another unit," he said, explaining himself with an air of indifference and a shrug of his shoulders.

As a result of this medical error, I suffered serious complications: the agitation of my uncontrolled writhing resulted in fluid accumulation in my chest. This led to my readmission to the hospital within 30 days of discharge. I spent 10 days in the ICU at a cost of over $2,000 per day. That one preventable medical error cost more than $20,000, which, under the Affordable Care Act, was an expense slated to be absorbed by the hospital.

Later, I sent a letter to the head of the hospital complaining about the doctor's indifference and commending the nurses for their efforts to take care of me. In response I got a call from the CNO and the charge nurse, both of whom offered formal apologies. The charge nurse added, "I'm sorry, that was the best I could do that night." I heard the despair in her voice, a tacit acknowledgment that there were times she was powerless to get patients on her unit the pain relief they required.

I wanted to know if anything was going to happen to prevent problems with unresponsive doctors in the future. What would be done to deal with the doctor's indifferent attitude? The CNO said those issues were out of nurses' hands and that the matter would be dealt with by the physician group. "Please ask them to let me know what they intend to do differently," I requested. But I never got another call from anyone at the hospital. I did, however, get a bill for more than $40,000.

## The Scope of the Problem

Was my experience a freak occurrence? Sadly, no. As soon as I recovered enough to research the topic of preventable medical errors, I discovered I was among millions of people that year who suffered from a preventable medical mistake while in a hospital. At least I was not one of *the hundreds of thousands* of documented deaths that year resulting from a preventable medical error.

These astounding statistics, first revealed in 1999 when the Institute of Medicine published its report, "To Err Is Human," have only gotten more shocking over the past 17 years. A September 2013 article in the *Journal of Patient Safety* estimated that more than 15 million patients are harmed and over 400,000 patients die every year from *preventable* medical errors.[1] That's equivalent to killing every resident in the city of Miami, Florida, this year, then the population of Sacramento, California, next year, and so on.

As I looked into the scope of medical errors, I became aware of and somewhat overwhelmed by the magnitude of the problems in healthcare. How could I (or anyone else, for that matter) ever tackle such a massive challenge? But there's an old saying that when the student is ready, the teacher appears.

On one of the days I was recovering in the hospital I heard the renowned psychologist Martin Seligman being interviewed on *Good Morning America*. He was announcing a new science devoted to understanding optimal human functioning. Dr. Seligman, known as "the father of positive psychology," explained how he had brought researchers from around the world together to study individuals and organizations who had achieved an extraordinarily high level of functioning.

I had an epiphany that morning. I knew in my healing heart that this emerging science might hold the key to transforming healthcare. Rather than studying dysfunctional individuals, teams, and organizations, positive psychology explored the *other* end of the continuum—human beings who had achieved satisfaction with their life and success in their workplace. I committed then and there to using this new form of research to learn how the best hospitals, most respected healthcare providers, and outstanding administrators attained remarkable results. I wanted to teach those lessons to healthcare professionals and organizations who desire to experience that level of success as well.

Unfortunately, many healthcare providers have given up trying to change their workplaces. According to Gallup research, 50 percent of hospital employees report being "disengaged" (doing the minimum to get by) and nearly 20 percent identify being as "actively disengaged" (voicing their unhappiness and bringing everybody down).[2] These numbers are reflected in outpatient clinics, rehabilitation centers, and nursing homes, too. That leaves about one in three employees engaged in their jobs. No wonder healthcare is struggling—only 30 percent of people are aligned with their organization's goals and working diligently to achieve them.

There is a perfect storm brewing in healthcare. The typical healthcare organization is underperforming, according to *Becker's Hospital Review*, due to the fact that 70 percent of staff members are doing the minimum to get by or sabotaging their leader's efforts.[3] But the need for effective healthcare will continue exploding as more than 77 million baby boomers hit their sixties and seventies. Add to that the staffing reductions caused by reimbursement cuts and you have a recipe for disaster—and a desperate need to turn things around.

How desperate? Nationwide, there are

- More than 3 million registered nurses. Three out of four cited stress and overwork as causing major health concerns in 2011 survey by the American Nurses Association.[4]
- More than 900,000 physicians—46 percent of whom reported they had burnout on a 2015 Medscape survey.[5]
- More than 6,000 hospitals and medical centers that, according to a 2015 NSI Nursing Solutions report, had a 17 percent average RN turnover rate. With an average cost of $48,000 to replace just one nurse, the typical hospital loses more than $6 million per year due to turnover.[6]

## The Pilot Studies

I began my journey by immersing myself in positive psychology research and conducting appreciative inquiries at top-tier healthcare organizations. I wanted to create a program based on a combination of what the scientific studies were showing as well as what I observed in real-life situations from superb healthcare systems.

**Appreciative inquiry** (commonly abbreviated as AI) is a "change management approach" that focuses on identifying **what is working well**, analyzing **why it is working well**, and then **doing more of it**. The basic tenet of AI is that an organization will grow in the direction the people within it train their attention.

By taking a deep dive into a high-functioning hospital that enabled people to work together to take great care of their patients and their coworkers alike, I discovered six recurring principles I refer to as PROPEL, an acronym that stands for Passion, Relationships, Optimism, Proactivity, Energy, and Legacy.

Following my AI, two pilot studies using the newly discovered PROPEL Principles were conducted on hospital units with histories of "poor performance" ("abominable performance" would have been more accurate), where leaders and staff members struggled with a dysfunctional work environment. The Director of Nursing for these units had tried numerous training programs and consultants for nearly a decade, all to no avail. In desperation, she decided to try an approach based on the newly emerging science of positive psychology.

After a year-long initiative during which the leaders and staff members on one of the units learned to use the PROPEL program and its six positive psychology principles, that unit was performing at such a high level it garnered an outstanding performance award. Independent assessments found job satisfaction and staff members engagement had both increased by more than 80 percent, and patient satisfaction had improved by 50 percent.

Beyond the external measures of success, the inside story is that the people involved in learning to use the PROPEL Principles became happier—at work and at home. The nurse manager went from spending her days arguing with her staff members about their misdeeds to offering kudos for the great teamwork the staff members demonstrated almost every day. She had been on the verge of resigning because she was miserable but instead transformed her job from spending 80 percent of her time catching people doing things wrong to 80 percent of her time appreciating what they were doing right. And her marriage improved significantly when she came home with stories about how staff members worked together to take care of patients rather than angry that someone else had lodged a complaint.

In the pilot study, newly minted nurses had a 100 percent turnover rate within the first year, largely because they felt bullied. At the end of the PROPEL initiative, almost all of the new RNs stayed because they loved the mentoring they were receiving from the more experienced staff members. And those senior staff members were extremely proud that they were making a meaningful difference in the lives of new nurses coming into the profession.

*Comradery, Teamwork, Professionalism.* This became the mantra on the unit that had embraced the PROPEL Principles, and every day people were recognized for having done something to live by those values. Even the doctors and patients began to write compliments on the "kudos" whiteboard that had been installed near the nurses' station.

With more positive feelings between the doctors and the nurses on the unit, the director of nursing and the medical director had far fewer complaints to resolve. This allowed them to direct their time and attention to how their respective staff members could work together on improving the patient experience. The culture on the unit had changed, as witnessed by the improvements in patient satisfaction and safety measures that were sustained for the 5 years that postintervention follow-ups were conducted.

In addition to improved patient care, learning to use the PROPEL Principles had other significant benefits, ones that are particularly important in today's healthcare environment. By reducing staff turnover, PROPEL was saving money. By improving care, outcomes, and patient satisfaction scores (now tied to reimbursement), PROPEL was increasing revenue. Improved patient care, lower operational costs, and higher reimbursement revenue. A trifecta of sorts—a win–win–win situation.

---

### By the Numbers:
### Pilot Study Results on a Unit with 150 Full Time Employees:

- Hospital Consumer Assessment of Healthcare Providers and Systems (HCAHPS) scores improved by 43 percent over 2 years
- RN Satisfaction and Engagement improved by 84 percent and 81 percent, respectively
- RN Retention improved by 49 percent
- Rand Patient Safety: Teamwork up 17 percent, Safety Climate up 10 percent, Job Satisfaction up 19 percent
- National Database of Nursing Quality Indicators (NDNQI): RN/RN Interaction up 21 percent, RN/MD Interaction up 14 percent, Job Enjoyment up 22 percent
- RN Call Out/Sick Leave down 75 percent
- **Total annual cost saving = $816,000**

---

Scores of initiatives have now shown that, across a range of healthcare contexts, PROPEL enables individuals and teams to perform at their best. People who have learned to live by the six PROPEL Principles say they

- Look forward to coming in each morning because they know they'll have far more good than bad exchanges with other staff members.
- Take care of each other so they'll be able to take better care of patients, who frequently express their gratitude for their efforts.
- Feel appreciation in their working relationships.
- Leave work tired but satisfied they made a difference that day.

■ Arrive home with a positive attitude rather than emotionally exhausted.

■ Generate more caring connections in their most important relationships.

■ Set off upward spirals of rejuvenation that enable them to be extraordinary.

This is how we all want healthcare providers to describe their work. It is the life you can learn to create for yourself.

But there is a cautionary tale to be told as well. Another unit had also been invited to participate in the PROPEL program. However, I encountered stiff resistance from their old-school nurse manager and one of her senior nurses. The two of them sneered at incorporating positive psychology principles into their daily operations, stating that what was needed was more discipline rather than coddling.

A nurse working temporarily on this troubled unit wryly observed that the nurse manager's philosophy was tantamount to "the floggings will continue until morale improves." This unit did not make any improvements at all, although the staff members did master the art of making excuses. Their vacancy rate remained at nearly 50 percent because they couldn't recruit and keep staff members in their toxic environment.

The nurse manager would go home filled with irritations from the day. It made for a bad night's sleep. Fatigued the next morning, she drove to work thinking about all the "problem people" she would have to contend with during the day. The closer she got to the hospital, the more she armored her mind to defend herself and prepared to attack the problems she knew she would encounter with her staff members. This unit's story provides important insights about how dysfunction and distress are created and maintained.

There are no mistakes, however, only lessons. The PROPEL Principles also help leaders with the tough choices they must make in their jobs. When leaders develop an understanding of how to enable the vast majority of people to learn and grow, they find it unacceptable to have a few staff members stubbornly refuse to change behaviors that lead to poor performance. You will read about managing these extraordinarily difficult situations in order to eventually achieve a successful transformation in Chapter 5.

Using the six PROPEL Principles to create a positive work environment has now been thoroughly researched on more than 80 units at one of the country's most renowned academic medical centers. And the program is still in use there today, over 12 years later, continuing to produce remarkable results. In addition, numerous outpatient centers and community hospitals have also discovered that implementing PROPEL can dramatically improve performance and contain costs.

## What You Will Get Out of This Book

You may be thinking, *how can I become an effective change agent capable of achieving results like this?* Read on! You will learn the essential skills that extraordinarily influential people use to inspire and influence others.

The first principle for improving performance—yours as well as your staff members—is to ignite *Passion*. When you envision a positive outcome that you have a passion for achieving, you will activate the "executive functioning" part of your brain. Once the left prefrontal cortex has a vision of a positive outcome, it recruits other parts of your cerebral cortex to help it create solutions and strategies for getting there.

The next principle, *Relationships*, focuses on enabling people to remain resilient during the change process by garnering support from other people. You'll discover how to cultivate positive relationships with key individuals who share your vision and forge them into a highly effective team. They will need to be *Optimistic* thinkers (the third principle) to persevere through the trial-and-error process required to make incremental improvements.

The fourth principle, *Proactivity*, enables people to convert their negative reactions into positive actions. Numerous studies show that achieving success comes from knowing what personal qualities empower people to be at their best. Twenty years of research has proven that proactive people attain the highest level of success because they know and use their strengths when facing challenges.

Change rarely happens quickly or easily. You will need to be able to continually replenish your *Energy*, which you will learn how to do when you read about the fifth PROPEL principle. Developing habits for renewing your energy will give you grit, the ability to persevere toward the outcome you passionately desire to attain.

Finally, to feel deeply gratified with the results of your change efforts, you will need to feel that you have left a *Legacy*. Living by this last PROPEL principle means learning how to empower other people to make a lasting and meaningful difference.

## Optimal Functioning Can Be Learned

As we ask doctors and nurses to do more than they've ever done, and with sicker, more acute patients, the stage is set for mistakes, burnout, and turnover. The cost is high: in dollars, time, and lives. A fix is desperately needed. PROPEL initiatives have brought hundreds of healthcare teams together to solve problems *themselves*, empowering people to be at their best consistently over the course of their career. PROPEL teams have figured out how to cut their turnover rate in half, reduce fall rates by 70 percent, and buddy-up to get lunch breaks on 12-hour shifts to reduce burnout on their unit from 37 percent to 3 percent.

Whether you're a doctor or a nurse, a CEO, or a clinical technician, you have ideas about what needs to happen to make improvements. *That's ridiculous*, you may be thinking, because you have a hard time getting anyone to even listen to you, much less act on your ideas. Keep reading and I'll show you how that can change.

Being aware of what you believe needs to improve is the first step of the change process. But you can't accomplish anything by yourself. You will need to join forces with people from every level—from the C-suite to the bedside—whose participation in a multidisciplinary PROPEL team will lead to real improvement.

Importantly, this team is not made up of the usual formal leadership group. Instead, they're the most positively engaged and socially connected people from a wide variety of roles.

Solutions that produce significant, sustained improvements almost always incorporate ideas from the people who have to make the change. For example, bedside staff members know the practical considerations and downside aspects entailed in making changes. Getting their input before proceeding is essential. My research reveals their contributions provide crucial insights into the underlying factors that must be considered in a successful performance improvement initiative.

You, too, can learn to use "smart team" technology to create a "tipping point," joining forces with the 30 percent of engaged staff members to influence the 50 percent of employees who are in the disengaged category. Finally, you will discover how to sustain your gains and take on the next challenge.

You are now one chapter into this book. Ahead, you will find real examples from diverse settings and data from extensive research that lay out a clear step-by-step approach proven to work in a variety of healthcare settings. The following chapters will take you from a basic understanding of positive psychology and how it can be used in the workplace, to actively using my six-step evidence-based PROPEL plan to transform team dynamics and the cultural environment of virtually any healthcare setting.

Most importantly, this book will *motivate* you. My goal is to supply you with everything you need to proceed on the path to better staff satisfaction, engagement, and retention, which leads to a higher performing workplace and improved patient care and safety. These fundamentals form the foundation of quality healthcare. PROPEL can also fulfill your desire to be part of a high-performing team providing the best possible patient care. And the bottom line matters, too, which is why CFOs should also be encouraged to support a PROPEL initiative. Implementing the six positive psychology principles can significantly improve a hospital's fiscal health as well.

Ready to PROPEL? Let's get started!

*Chapter 2*

# Positive Psychology: The Science of Optimal Human Functioning

Human beings are hardwired to fire off fight or flight reactions in stressful situations. When we feel threatened, our brain discharges stress chemicals. A surge of adrenaline is released, which enabled our ancestors to attack a foe or flee from danger. An accompanying flood of cortisol kept people on edge for hours afterward so they could guard against a return of the enemy. During this time of high alert, it's nearly impossible to use logical and sequential thought processes to solve problems. Our attention is riveted on defending against the immediate threat, and we ruminate on how the problem could escalate into a full-fledged catastrophe.

We've all been there. We have felt the surge of anger associated with the fight instinct and the heart-pounding anxiety that drives flight.

## But What about People Who Shine in Stressful Situations?

Everyone has seen individuals who quickly regain their wits in high-stress situations. Somehow, they set aside their negative emotions and think clearly about solving the problem. In the midst of a bomb threat—or earthquake or train wreck or other extreme event—the brain of this kind of person can conjure up actions that achieve the best possible outcome.

These individuals acknowledge the gravity of the situation, but believe they will ultimately prevail. These kind of cool-headed thinkers move quickly to rally support from allies. Their reactions include recognizing and harnessing the best qualities of others as their brain works to orchestrate success. And when they are not in the crisis mode, these folks are able to relax and enjoy life. Wouldn't it be wonderful to know how these extraordinary people have mastered the skills necessary to achieve this level of functioning?

There is a new brand of psychologists studying these individuals. They are called *positive psychologists*. They have found that people who deal with problems in a more effective manner are able to quickly shift their thinking from worst-case scenarios to envisioning positive outcomes. And when the threat has subsided, they engage in satisfying activities and relationships to renew their body, mind, and spirit.

## The Birth of Positive Psychology

About 20 years ago, psychologists began to question the traditional research approach of focusing on how to fix dysfunctional individuals and organizations. As late as 1998, there was a 17-to-1 ratio of studies examining people with problems versus high-functioning individuals.

That same year Martin Seligman became president of the American Psychological Association (APA). Troubled by the fact that for 100 years the profession had devoted almost all of its attention to the disordered and dysfunctional, with disappointing outcomes for society, he advocated for a new approach. He noted that although the goal of alleviating human suffering by studying people with problems was noble, the results were disturbing: the rates of divorce, depression, and anxiety had all *doubled* from 1965 to 1995!

He used the platform of the APA to start a revolution in the field of psychology; he challenged researchers to study "optimal human functioning." Seligman orchestrated a seismic shift by advocating for the scientific study of people who were at the *other* end of the continuum—those who were most satisfied and successful. He obtained a massive grant from the late billionaire philanthropist Sir John Templeton to fund research into optimal human functioning. Positive psychology was born.

"Flourishing" is the word positive psychologists use to describe the combination of attributes characteristic of people who live within an optimal range of human functioning—one that connotes goodness, generativity, growth, and resilience. In the mid-range of human functioning, is languishing—feeling that life is missing something. At the far end is dysfunction, which signifies a life of suffering with depression, anxiety, and loneliness.

In his 2011 book *Flourish*, Seligman distilled data from thousands of positive psychology studies and identified five factors shown to be essential for achieving authentic happiness and optimal functioning.[1] In the PERMA model, he identifies the core ingredients of flourishing, which are as follows:

- Positive emotions
- Engagement
- Relationships
- Meaningfulness
- Accomplishments

## How Well Are Americans Doing?

Most people in United States have not learned how to flourish at home or at work. According to a 2016 Harris Poll, fewer than one-third of Americans described themselves as "very happy," an all-time low.[2] The survey showed that life satisfaction improves once people retire, with 41 percent of adults over the age of 65 reporting low-stress and high-happiness levels. However, only 28 percent of people aged 30–40 years said they were very happy with their lives.

In a 2013 white paper "The American Workplace: Employee Engagement Insights for U.S. Business Leaders," Gallup reports that employee engagement has not changed substantially since they started measuring it nearly 15 years ago (as shown in Figure 2.1).[3]

Gallup reported that 52 percent of American workers described themselves as "not engaged"—emotionally disconnected from their workplaces. These employees no longer cared about the organization's mission or their leader's goals. That attitude translated into minimal motivation, disengagement from coworkers and customers, and lackluster performance. People in this group described living lives of "quiet desperation." Disengaged workers were "clock watchers" who were doing the minimum to get by until quitting time. They were missing key ingredients essential for flourishing, such as finding ways to have meaningful engagement in their work and enjoying the positive emotions that come from significant accomplishments.

Here is the truly disturbing data. Another 18 percent of workers admitted to being "actively disengaged," which, according to Gallup, means that they are "more likely to steal from their companies, negatively influence their coworkers, miss workdays, and drive customers away."[3] This segment of the population is suffering from—and spreading—some serious unhappiness in life.

The Gallup report estimated that disengaged and actively disengaged employees cost the United States between $450 billion and $550 billion each year in lost productivity. Absenteeism, high turnover, shrinkage, employee safety incidents, patient safety incidents, work quality, customer satisfaction, productivity, and profitability were all linked to low engagement.

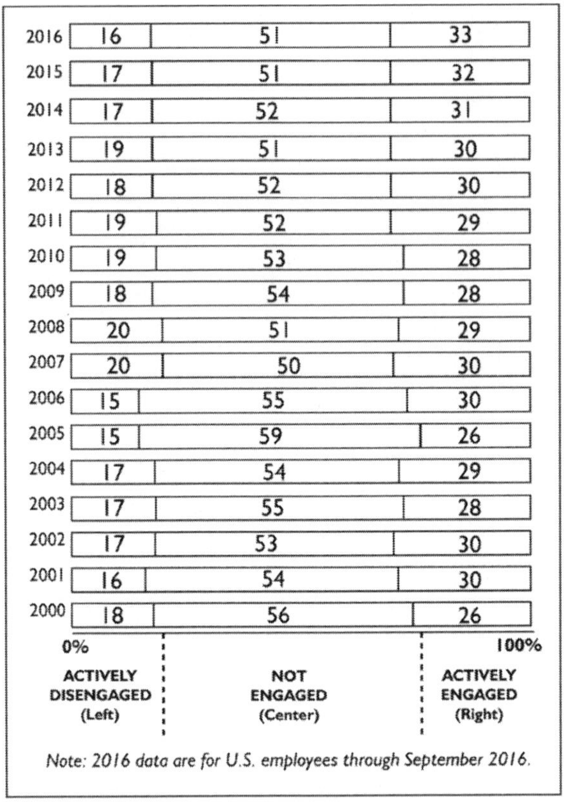

| Year | Actively Disengaged (Left) | Not Engaged (Center) | Actively Engaged (Right) |
|------|------|------|------|
| 2016 | 16 | 51 | 33 |
| 2015 | 17 | 51 | 32 |
| 2014 | 17 | 52 | 31 |
| 2013 | 19 | 51 | 30 |
| 2012 | 18 | 52 | 30 |
| 2011 | 19 | 52 | 29 |
| 2010 | 19 | 53 | 28 |
| 2009 | 18 | 54 | 28 |
| 2008 | 20 | 51 | 29 |
| 2007 | 20 | 50 | 30 |
| 2006 | 15 | 55 | 30 |
| 2005 | 15 | 59 | 26 |
| 2004 | 17 | 54 | 29 |
| 2003 | 17 | 55 | 28 |
| 2002 | 17 | 53 | 30 |
| 2001 | 16 | 54 | 30 |
| 2000 | 18 | 56 | 26 |

0% ⋮ ⋮ 100%

**ACTIVELY DISENGAGED (Left)** ⋮ **NOT ENGAGED (Center)** ⋮ **ACTIVELY ENGAGED (Right)**

Note: 2016 data are for U.S. employees through September 2016.

**Figure 2.1   Employee engagement among the U.S. working population.**

Only 33 percent of the American workforce say they are "engaged"—defined by Gallup as people who are involved, enthusiastic, and committed to their work. These are the individuals who make significant contributions. Engaged employees drive innovation, growth, and revenue by generating new ideas, building new products and services, and creating new customers.

As seen in Figure 2.2, Gallup reported in a 2009 survey of more than 30,000 business units that high levels of employee engagement were strongly connected to an organization's financial success, including productivity, profitability, and customer satisfaction.[4]

## How Well Are You Doing?

Where are you on the continuum that extends from suffering to languishing to flourishing? Are you exhausted most of the time? Often irritated (and occasionally angry) with other people? Prone to procrastination and lateness? Dissatisfied

---

**Employee Engagement:**
**Top-quartile units outperform bottom-quartile units by:**

- 12 percent in customer loyalty/engagement
- 16 percent in profitability
- 18 percent in productivity
- 25 percent in turnover for high-turnover companies
  (those with 60 percent or higher annualized turnover)
- 49 percent in turnover for low-turnover companies
  (those with 40 percent or lower annualized turnover)
- 49 percent in safety incidents
- 27 percent in shrinkage
- 37 percent in absenteeism
- 41 percent in patient safety incidents
- 60 percent in quality

---

**Figure 2.2   Gallup performance comparison of 32,394 business units.**

with your life and pessimistic about it ever improving? Feeling contempt for people in your workplace? Generally cynical about where the world is headed?

Maybe you feel you're living a life of quiet desperation. Are you feeling a lack of real connection in your relationships? Do you have trouble sleeping because you worry about things? Do you feel like an imposter who's ultimately going to be seen as a failure? Do you comfort yourself with too much food or drink? Are your credit card bills out of control? Do you find yourself frequently watching the clock at work? These are the characteristics of people who are languishing.

Perhaps you're someone who makes lemonade out of lemons. Are you remarkably resilient during tough times? Do you feel you have the right stuff to overcome the challenges you face? Do you love discovering something new? Are you eager to get up in the morning? Are you supported by people at home and at work? Do friends and family often come to you when they need some nourishing? Are you secure in your loving relationships? Do you believe that you're making a meaningful difference in the world? The more of these elements you have in your life, the closer you are to flourishing.

## Is Positive Psychology Fluff or Financially Beneficial?

Some healthcare leaders dismiss teaching employees the principles of positive psychology as "fluff," insisting that their focus must be on hardcore business results. The evidence shows when staff members create more positive engagement in their workplace, they also generate solid financial results. In hospitals, the cost of turnover on units has been carefully studied, making it a good metric to use when conducting a cost–benefit analysis of creating a positive work environment. According to the 2016 National Healthcare Retention & RN Staffing Report[5]:

> "In 2015, the turnover rate for bedside RNs increased to 17.2%, up from 16.4% in 2014. Registered Nurses (RNs) working in Pediatrics and Women's Health continue to record the lowest rate, while nurses working in Behavior Health, Emergency and Med/Surg experienced the highest. Certified nursing assistant (CNA) turnover exceeded all other positions at 23.8%."

> "The cost of turnover can have a profound impact on the already diminishing hospital margin and needs to be managed. According to the survey, the average cost of turnover for a bedside RN ranges from $37,700 to $58,400 resulting in the average hospital losing $5.2M–$8.1M. Each percent change in RN turnover will cost/save the average hospital an additional $373,200."

Gallup research has revealed that improving employee engagement reduces turnover between 25 percent and 49 percent, depending on the severity of the problem. Turning over 17 of every 100 RNs employed by a hospital costs between $640,900 and $992,800 per year. Cutting the turnover rate by 25–49 percent could result in cost savings of $320,000–$496,400 annually *for every 100 nurses* employed by the hospital.[5]

Turnover is only one metric that has been improved by teaching staff members to use positive psychology. Other areas of financial gain have come from improved Hospital Consumer Assessment of Healthcare Providers and Systems (HCAHPS) scores, enhanced patient flow increasing productivity, fewer workmen's comp claims, less absenteeism and family leave, and a decrease in patient safety incidents.[6]

## How Do Positive Workplaces Make a Difference?

Whether you are successful and satisfied in your job depends on how you respond to the challenges you face. If you respond the way the average employee does, you've given up trying to improve things. After concluding that nothing will ever change, you've stopped beating your head against the wall. The acute headaches subsided as you disengaged because you don't care as much. You do what you must to get through your day without making a mistake that will lead to being fired. The best part of your day is quitting time. You watch the clock, eagerly awaiting the moment that you can get out of work and go do something that makes you feel good.

Or maybe you're among the nearly 20 percent of employees who have become deeply dissatisfied with the workplace. The frustration and resentment has built up within you to the point that you can't contain it. You feel compelled to criticize people who you see "screwing up." You blame your boss for allowing the problems to plague your unit. Coworkers seem inept at best and downright incompetent at times. And you're not shy about sharing your feelings. You tell everyone within earshot—coworkers, patients, and neighbors—about the terrible conditions and incompetent coworkers. You feel you're "telling it like it is."

## What Does the Research Reveal about Flourishing?

People who flourish are not simply people who are happy or have the material trappings of success. They're people who function at an extraordinarily high level in their relationships. While it's true that people who flourish frequently feel happy and have a high level of life satisfaction, they derive that positivity by being actively engaged in doing good. Whether it's encouraging their kids while getting them off to school or sharing the goodness of the day with their spouse in the evening, they're purpose driven. They know how they want to feel at the end of the day, and they savor the steps they took toward generating those emotions. They're deeply appreciative of others who help them each day on their journey to their best possible future.

In her 2009 book *Positivity*, Barbara Fredrickson reveals the results of her research into positive emotions.[7] In a seminal finding, she uncovered a cornerstone necessary for humans to survive and thrive: the principle of "broaden and build." She discovered that the purpose of positive emotions is to broaden people's perspectives and build their capacity to respond to challenges. Only by generating enough positivity have humans been able to innovate their way to the top of the food chain. Negativity narrows our focus to what threatens us; positivity expands our attention to new possibilities for building a better future.

Fredrickson's studies have uncovered six vital facts that illustrate how positivity broadens and builds our ability to flourish:

1. *Positivity gives you good days.* When you read the descriptions of the three levels of human functioning, you undoubtedly felt better reading about what it's like to flourish. You instinctively know how good it would feel to have that kind of life. You yearn for the positive emotions that accompany flourishing: joy, gratitude, serenity, interest, hope, pride, amusement, inspiration, awe, and—most importantly—love.

2. *Positivity changes how you think.* More than simply swapping out bad thoughts for good ones, positivity broadens your perspective and builds your capacity to see new possibilities. It enhances your ability to see other people's point of view and to empathize with their feelings. A large reserve of positive emotions allows you to stay calm enough to understand how to support a coworker who is reacting negatively to a problem. Rather than focusing narrowly on who is to blame, you are able to see all the factors that contributed to the problem and are able to see solutions that can improve the situation.

3. *Positivity fuels your best possible future.* As your mind becomes better able to see that positive outcomes are possible, it automatically begins to look for the pathways to get there. Because you relate well to people, for example, you will garner support from friends who will help you overcome challenges. You put yourself on the upward spiral of flourishing.

4. *Positivity counteracts negativity.* Negative emotions are automatically aroused when you are in a stressful situation. Knowing how to shift your mind to positive thinking will calm you, which is the secret to being resilient. With practice, you'll develop the capacity to remain optimistic, set specific goals, take decisive action, learn from your mistakes, and persevere until you reach a positive outcome.

5. *Positivity creates tipping points.* The results achieved by people with high positivity are exponentially greater than those attained by negative people. Positivity is nonlinear, meaning that seemingly small steps produce disproportionately large changes. When the distressed coworker presents his or her problem and you change the course of the conversation from criticizing others to seeking solutions, you will create a new trajectory that will lead to a much different outcome. When you rally support from other positive people, the sum of the combined positive energy will be greater than the total of each individual contribution. Tipping points occur when the positivity of a few infects the whole team.

6. *You can increase your level of positivity.* You were not born knowing how to flourish, although suffering was automatically included in the price of admission. Positive psychologists have discovered the forces that enable flourishing. You will learn in this book the steps that others have taken in their quest to create a tipping point in their personal life as well as their workplace. The lessons and exercises in Sections II and III will teach you how to unleash *your* ability to flourish.

## Can You Really Become a More Positive Person?

Positive psychologist Shawn Achor discusses the methods for creating positivity in his book, *The Happiness Advantage: The Seven Principles of Positive Psychology That Fuel Success and Performance at Work.*[8] This Harvard professor states that you can learn how to bring out the best in yourself and others when responding to problems. Here are his seven suggestions:

1. *Retrain your brain to be more positive.* Biologically, people who increase positivity are better able to improve productivity and performance.
2. *Manage how you experience the world.* How you explain challenging situations leads your brain to activate stress circuits or success pathways.
3. *Learn to stop dwelling.* Rather than ruminating on the catastrophic consequences of failure, teach your brain to see possibilities for achieving positive outcomes.
4. *Deal with setbacks.* Discover how to cope effectively by shifting your mindset from suffering to learning lessons that will enable you to succeed in the future.
5. *Overcome being overwhelmed.* Respond to your challenges and regain control by setting and accomplishing small goals. Rebuild confidence with a series of "wins."
6. *Sustain your gains.* Manage your energy so that you rarely allow your willpower to fail and old habits to resurface.
7. *Invest in the greatest predictor of success.* Maintain mutually supportive relationships with coworkers, friends, and family.

## Does Positivity Help Organizations Be More Successful?

Positive organizational psychologists have dedicated the last decade to conducting research to determine if positive work environments affect performance. The core questions they investigated were as follows:

1. Can positivity in the workplace be defined and measured?
2. Can positive organizations be shown to have significantly better outcomes?
3. What specific positive practices are most effective in enhancing performance?

The results are in. Positive practices produce good outcomes in organizations by increasing productivity, quality, customer satisfaction, employee retention, and profitability. In *Practicing Positive Leadership*, Kim Cameron reveals research that supports these results across 16 different industries that include both for-profit and nonprofit organizations.[9] The big firms studied included General Electric, OfficeMax and National City Bank. Smaller nonprofit organizations such as educational institutions and hospitals were also shown to be significantly more effective when they had high marks for using positive practices. Moreover, hundreds of studies show that positive practice workplaces benefit employees' physical health, emotional well-being, brain functioning, interpersonal relationships *outside of work*, and their ability to learn.

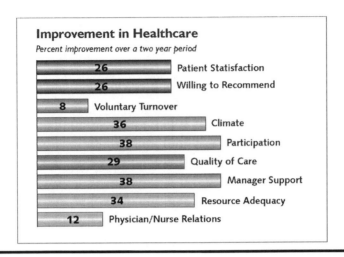

**Figure 2.3   Results of implementing positive leadership practices in 30 hospitals.**

## Creating a Positive Climate

Cameron found four characteristics that create positive work environments: positive climates, positive relationships, positive communication, and positive meaning. When all four elements are present, employees can "achieve their highest potential, flourish at work, experience elevating energy, and achieve levels of effectiveness difficult to attain otherwise."[9]

But do more positive work environments produce results in healthcare settings? One study Cameron conducted involved 30 healthcare organizations. It demonstrated that positive leadership practices differentiated performance between high- and low-functioning hospital units on a number of metrics, as shown in Figure 2.3.[10] Topping the list of those positive outcomes were improved workplace "climate," increased manager support, more staff member participation, higher patient satisfaction, and an elevated quality of care.

## The PROPEL Principles: Six Steps for Applying Positive Psychology

For decades, people interested in improving organizations have focused on putting problem employees into "performance improvement" plans. The traditional approach has held leaders responsible for poor performing employees and provided remedial training in how to hold their employees accountable. However, a quick review of the Gallup longitudinal data from Figure 2.1 demonstrates that these approaches have not had a significant impact on employee engagement or organization performance.

However, positive psychology studies have shown that engaging employees in the process of learning how to create a more positive and productive life is an effective strategy for improving workplace performance. PROPEL uses a different methodology, which has produced some big improvements. I have found it far more effective to engage employees, as well as leaders, in the change process. But not any employee, at least not in the beginning. PROPEL studies show that the best way to change the culture and performance on a unit is to create a "tipping point."

Consider the impact on the climate of a unit with a few BMWs (blame, moan, and whiners). When a BMW starts spewing forth negativity by pointing out what is wrong, who is to blame, and why it will never change, everyone on the unit can quickly become deflated and discouraged. Even when the manager or others attempt to curtail the negative comments, the atmosphere on the unit has already been poisoned.

If a few "actively disengaged" employees can have that kind of impact, then doesn't it seem possible that a group of positive people could affect the opposite outcome?

Bringing the most highly engaged staff members together and teaching them to use positive psychology strategies creates a team capable of getting the people in the middle 50 percent to join forces with them. As the middle group begins to experience the benefits of a positive working environment, a tipping point is achieved. The case studies included in all of the chapters that follow show how this shift in numbers allows staff members to make high performance possible. PROPEL teams are able to generate a wellspring of innovative ideas, abundant energy for implementing them, and ample amounts of resilience for overcoming setbacks.

Learning to use the PROPEL principles enables people to harness the power of positive psychology. By translating the scientific findings into a series of specific steps, healthcare professionals can win the trifecta: high staff engagement, excellent patient care, and cost containment.

# Chapter 3

## It's the Culture, ~~Dummy~~ Darling: A Look at a Top-Rated Hospital

### The Chicken and Egg Question

There are a multitude of positive psychology studies that illuminate the elements that foster optimal functioning. But what comes first—high performance or happy people?

As I was starting my journey to help healthcare professionals, I wondered what positive psychology looked like in a real-life setting. What did an optimally functioning healthcare organization do to create a satisfying and successful model?

I was privileged to spend a year in a hospital that was ranked as a top 100 U.S. hospital by several independent organizations. Clearly, this highly ranked hospital had created an optimally functioning healthcare organization. Patient safety and satisfaction scores as well as nurse satisfaction and retention statistics were excellent. The hospital had one of the lowest RN vacancy rates in the country. Surveys of nurses, physicians, and administrators pointed to an incredibly collaborative practice environment.

Every year firms such as Thomas Reuters and HealthGrades, national leaders in hospital quality improvement research, rank hospitals by evaluating the overall performance—to include patient care, operational efficiency, and financial stability. A select group makes it onto the list of the "Top 100 Hospitals," which is published annually and serves as a resource for further study of what makes a top quality healthcare organization.

According to Thomson Reuters, if all patients received the same level of care as those treated in the top 100 facilities, the benefits would be enormous[1]:

- More than 186,000 lives could be saved.
- Approximately 56,000 patients could be complication free.
- More than $4.3 billion could be saved.
- The average patient stay would decrease by nearly half a day.

If the same standards were applied to *all* patients, the impact would transform healthcare. Imagine.

I had a burning desire to understand how this hospital had achieved this elite status. That knowledge, I believed, would open the possibility that its success could be replicated. And, I wondered, how much of what positive psychology research claimed was essential for success would show up in a real-world example of optimal functioning.

Robert, the Chief Executive Officer (CEO), was understandably proud of the transformation that had occurred under his leadership. In our conversations, I discovered that Robert had learned from his predecessor's mistakes. He had devoted himself to systematically creating a culture that turned a poorly regarded hospital into a top-ranked institution.

This chapter shows the far-reaching effects of an organization's culture and the distinct "gotta-have-it" components that allow every employee from housekeeping to the executives to achieve a high level of success—saving lives, saving money, and saving talented staff members.

## In the Beginning

In his former position as Chief Operating Officer, Robert had spent years observing the ill effects of the command-and-control style of his predecessor. Power was concentrated at the top with communications flowing down; it was a trickle-down formula that made it impossible for anyone else to make a contribution for improving the workplace. As a result, Robert believed, the hospital's performance languished.

When Robert was appointed the new CEO, his top priority was to create a "people-oriented culture." He began his tenure by addressing issues he believed affected the employees' ability to do a good job. He made it clear that the values he was going to bring to the organization would become the cornerstone for a culture capable of providing the best patient care.

When notified he would be ascending to CEO, Robert immediately took out his "what I will do differently" file. Over the years when Robert had seen something occur that he thought was a mistake, he made a note of it along with his thoughts about what he would do differently.

The first change Robert wanted to make was how he would engage with employees. "The previous CEO would tell them what to do and hold them accountable. He didn't care why his deadlines weren't met. People would fail and be punished even if they had been put into impossible situations. What he thought was the best thing to do often wasn't practical or even possible. I learned how important it is to ask those who need to make things happen for their input about how to do it successfully."

Robert decided his top priority as the new CEO was to build the best possible human resources (HR) department. At his first meeting with the executive team, he announced the approach he would take with employees: emphasizing learning from honest mistakes rather than using HR policies to punish people who were trying their best. His goal was to have the staff members feel free to offer their ideas about how to make the hospital work well.

The head of the HR department, who had worked for years with the previous CEO, objected, stating that employees were only motivated if there was a tough system of discipline in place. "It focuses their attention," he proclaimed, "and motivates them to do what they're supposed to do." Robert responded, "If you really feel that is the only way to motivate employees, please have your resignation letter on my desk by the end of the day." And that is what he got.

## It's All about the Family

Maria was appointed the new Vice President (VP) of HR. She shared Robert's value of creating a people-oriented culture and was dedicated to recruiting and retaining the right people. Maria believed it was critical to "get it right from the beginning" with new employees. Her recruiters made every effort to find the right person to fill the right position. That fit included more than job skills—applicants had to demonstrate the personal traits that would allow them to be a part of the "family."

Maria would tell new employees that the recruiters' job wasn't over once a person was hired. Her theme was "We'll do everything we can to help you succeed." She encouraged employees to contact the recruiters at any time to discuss issues that affected their ability to adjust to their new role, including how to be "adopted" by their new work family.

The hospital's new employee orientations were structured to teach the values that were important for doing well in their jobs. First and foremost, Maria said, is that the staff members care about each other.

## What's Most Valuable?

Robert would almost always clear time in his busy schedule to meet with new employees at the group orientation. He handed each person a card that attached to their ID badge, saying, "Everyone here is expected to live by these six values":

1. To set a positive example in all that we do
2. To respect all associates, promoting unity, trust, pride, and teamwork
3. To accept and promote positive change, take risks, accept responsibility, and be accountable for our actions
4. To achieve a high quality of work life through effective communication and through the involvement of all associates in an environment of openness and fairness in which everyone is treated with dignity, honesty, and respect
5. To promote a dedication to the hospital's commitment of achieving excellence in services rendered to all of its customers
6. To create a culture that emphasizes constant learning and development

"The mission of the hospital can only be achieved by employees living these values," Robert explained. "Our performance evaluations include a rating in each of these values. So, when you see me walking around the hospital, please stop me if you have a concern or a suggestion that you believe would help us provide excellent patient care."

Maria supported Robert's point: "Good communication is the cornerstone of understanding what each person on a team needs to provide the best patient care. Ask for what you need and always be willing to assist others. When someone speaks up and asks for help in our hospital, the answer is always 'yes'."

## Talk to Me

True to his word, Robert made it a habit to walk around the hospital nearly every day, seeking insight from the staff members, asking, "What do you think would make things better here?" It was a simple question he posed over and over. Then he listened. And learned. And took action. Results: patient safety and satisfaction improved tremendously, as did the satisfaction of the doctors and nurses. The culture—that mysterious intangible composed of specific behaviors, policies, and processes—had changed.

It was readily apparent that collaboration was a top priority the moment that you entered Robert's office. Prominently displayed on the CEO's wall behind his desk was a large frame containing a Vince Lombardi quote:

> "Build for your team a feeling of oneness, of dependence upon one another and of strength derived by unity."

Nursing leaders told us that they feel a true sense of collaboration with Emily, Vice-President for Nursing. "Emily sets target goals," Donna, a nurse manager, explained, "and then gets out of the way. That brings out the best qualities in her team because they become intensely focused on figuring out how to get to the goal. People appreciate the vote of confidence from the VP that they'll be able to do it."

"Vital to this collaboration process is the fact that managers are allowed to take risks without fear," echoed Dianne, Director of Emergency Nursing. "The hospital allows us to try different approaches to find out what works best. We work in a non-punitive environment where we're rewarded for innovation and excellence."

## It's All about Teamwork

Joy, Director of Perioperative Services, was describing her relationship with her boss Emily, the VP of Nursing: "The expectation from Emily is that everyone will figure out how to cobble together the best possible solution. When people work together to successfully implement a solution they come to trust one another."

When collaboration broke down, Robert would bring the parties involved into his office and tell them, "This isn't how I expect things to be done. Those who can't cooperate don't last long at this hospital." That clear expectation forced people (who wanted to keep their jobs) to step out of their entrenched positions and find mutually agreeable solutions.

Robert explained, "I don't listen to each person's arguments and tell them what to do. And I don't pick sides. I believe that the best answers surface when people have to forge agreements. Then they have a vested interest in making their side of the commitment work so they're not seen as the problem."

Joy cites as an example the hospital's struggle to ensure implementation of the Joint Commission's standards. "When finger pointing started, Robert brought all of the department heads together to address potential problems. He wanted to know what each one of them was going to do to straighten out their own department. By redirecting the focus to our own responsibilities rather than the shortcomings of others, we were able to change course. The directors took their concerns to the staff members on the units and asked them to address the issues. Everyone worked in their own domain to correct issues, and the hospital passed the inspection with flying colors."

## Don't Blame Me

Joan, the nurse manager in the operating room (OR), maintains that "the greatest strength of our hospital is that blame is unacceptable at any level. It kills collaboration. Leaders here assume that everybody is trying to do a good job, so errors are viewed as a learning experience. When troubles flare, it's because nurses blame others rather than taking responsibility for making things work well."

## This Is Crazy

Many hospitals lament the chronic problem of getting psychiatric patients out of the ER. When these patients would have to wait hours for a bed to open up, they were using precious space needed to treat people arriving with life and death emergencies. The financial impact of psychiatric boarding in the ER is significant. According to one study, the problem accounts for a direct loss of $1,198 per patient compared to non-psychiatric admissions. Factoring the loss of bed turnover for waiting patients and opportunity cost due to loss of those patients, psychiatric patient boarding typically costs $2,264 per patient. The study concluded that psychiatric patients awaiting inpatient placement remain in the ER 3.2 times longer than non-psychiatric patients, preventing 2.2 bed turnovers (additional patients) per psychiatric patient, thereby decreasing financial revenue.[2]

Another success story from the top 100 hospitals involves two of their best collaborators, Chris on the psychiatric unit and Laura in the ER. They became incredibly efficient at keeping psychiatric patients from backing up in the ER, occupying much needed trauma beds. Their success is based on constant communication, giving them an awareness of what's going on in the other's unit. By understanding that situation, they continually make adjustments to accommodate one another's needs.

"Early in our employment, our immediate supervisor, David, made it perfectly clear that as intelligent adults we were expected to work out mutually acceptable solutions. As a result, we have mastered the art of compromise," Chris told us. "We'll make trade-offs to take care of each other," Laura said, "because we've learned to turn to each other for help. That way only one of us gets crazy at a time."

Chris and Laura revealed that over time they came to realize "getting recognized for having done a good job means more than money." They attribute their success to the leadership style of the people for whom they work. "From the beginning," they told us, "we have felt our problem-solving capabilities were valued and respected. We thrive in our jobs," they added, "because we get positive reinforcement from someone almost every day."

Laura lives much closer to other hospitals, but she drives past them every day to commute to her high-functioning hospital. "It's worth the trip," she shared, "because of the close, collaborative connections I have with the other staff members."

## What Difference Does It Make?

Chris, a new nurse, also feels that personal connections are the glue that creates a bond among the staff members. "When I first started my internship as a student at the hospital, a woman walked through our unit most mornings. She made it a point to say hello to me. After a few days I asked who this person was, and was shocked to hear that it was the chief nursing officer (CNO), Emily."

Later when Chris was finishing school, Emily paid her a visit to extend a personal invitation to come work at the hospital. After she'd been in her position for a while, Emily called her to tell her she was proud of how incredibly well she was doing. That extraordinary behavior on the part of the CNO who took a couple of extra minutes out of her busy morning schedule, eventually saved her untold hours of aggravation trying to straighten out costly throughput problems in the ER.

Kathleen, Director of Psychiatry, believes that collaborative relationships such as Chris's and Maria's are contagious. Her unit costs the organization money every year rather than producing revenue. Kathleen challenged her staff members to bring added value to the organization: "You can make an important difference to the hospital. What kind of difference do you want to make?"

Her staff members responded with an idea based on their skill for making people feel better. "They decided to make an extraordinary effort to respond to the requests of staff members on any unit that asked for help to manage a difficult patient. They went out of their way to calm distressed patients to take the burden off the doctors and nurses."

Kathleen was her team's biggest fan. She was fantastic at catching people doing things right and making sure their efforts were recognized and reinforced. As emotions are contagious, her team found themselves doing the same for other staff members. And what a difference it made. The mental health team needed to ensure that the other departments would champion their cause every year during budget negotiations. In fact, the other departments had to contribute a part of their budget each year to make sure the psychiatry services would remain viable. They gladly did so because they saw the value that the mental health team brought to increasing the well-being of patients and staff members alike.

## Whether You Think You Can or Can't—You're Right

The optimism in the staff members at these top 100 hospitals was palpable. And, once again, it emanated from the top. Robert's optimistic style of thinking was apparent when asked how he accounts for having such a high-functioning staff. The three factors he identified are the definition of optimism.

"The first factor," he said, "is maintaining the belief that everybody is good and wants to do their best. The second is having high expectations, which involves inviting people to speak up and take responsibility for figuring out the best way to accomplish their goals.

"The third factor is developing trust that when problems arise people will bring not only a description of the issue, but some ideas for a solution." Robert explained, "Much of our success can be attributed to asking our staff members to think of long-term solutions. We tell them it's important because we intend for them to stay with our organization for a long time."

A good example of optimism in action can be seen in the work of the Director of Hospital Learning. Lisa often serves a vital role in resolving problems wherever they arise. She described working with a team that had become bogged down in figuring out how to handle a sentinel event. Here's how she described helping them find a solution: "It was a process of give and take, getting them to be honest in putting out the issues in a way that was striving for a win-win. They had to develop trust that everyone would snap out of their defensiveness and start to search for solutions. Everyone was encouraged to be active in the discussions, to think of other possibilities, and to have empathy for other's positions.

"It was a rewarding experience," she said, "because the dynamic teamwork that developed ended up producing great results. The team was able to develop a new protocol to prevent similar problems in the future." Lisa was also able to save the career of a staff nurse who had wanted to resign because she had felt so badly about the incident.

## Who Do You Think You Are?

Robert encouraged his new leaders to become proactive when they first came on board. A couple of weeks after Curt took over as director of environmental services, Robert strolled into his office. Poor Curt must have been asking himself what he could possibly have done so wrong in his first few weeks that it would warrant a visit from the CEO.

But that was not what prompted Robert to stop by. First of all, he wanted to learn more about Curt and his family. He discovered that Curt was an encouraging father who looked at his children's missteps as growing pains. "No mistakes, only lessons" was the way Curt described his parenting style.

Robert asked Curt how he could apply that philosophy to the staff members in his department. "What have you observed in your first few weeks here that you believe are crucial 'lessons' that the people you lead need to learn?"

Curt suggested, "We could impose some stricter standards as well as clear consequences for failing to adhere to them." But he was stunned by Robert's response: "We have to have high standards, of course. And I'm wondering what you've learned about your staff members that enables them to do their best work?"

Curt was encouraged. "Are you asking me to find ways that the environmental services team could make improvements by building on what the staff members are already good at doing?"

"I'm concerned that cracking down on what they were doing wrong would only focus them on their mistakes," Robert cautioned. "And even worse, I fear that 'cracking down' would put you in a position of policing your team's performance. I'd rather see you helping them figure out how to be at their best to consistently achieve good results."

## To Tell You the Truth

At his next staff members meeting, Curt asked his team, "What do you believe enables you to be at your best when cleaning patient rooms?" Staff members told him, "It's discouraging to walk into a room that hasn't received a deep cleaning for a long time."

"We don't have time to do a really good job, so we do just enough to get by to get the room ready for the next admission," one worker told Curt. "The nurses are pressuring us to get the room done as quickly as possible because they have a patient being transferred from the ICU," another added.

"And no matter what we do, we catch hell from somebody," a staff member commented with obvious dissatisfaction. "If we take too long because we're trying to do a good job, the charge nurse complains. But if we get the room cleaned quickly, our supervisor writes us up for poor performance." Nearly everyone in the room grumbled in agreement.

Curt realized that he was discovering a problem, but not really learning what it would take to solve it. So he circled back to the question of what happened on those occasions when the staff members felt the cleaning went well.

One of the more senior members of the group spoke up: "Well sir, we used to have some time set aside to do a top-to-bottom cleaning. When we needed to turnover a room quickly it was possible to make that happen and still have the patient's room up to snuff."

A younger team member added: "If we were walking into rooms that had been cleaned properly in the first place, it would be much easier to do what's necessary to keep the room in good shape."

Finally the most respected person on the team spoke: "We can all work quickly when we have to, but there are a few of us who can really get rooms cleaned up the way they should be when we're given the time. Fact of the matter is that we can clean rooms fast or we can clean them right, but we can't do both."

## Getting an Earful

"The challenge," Curt said, "is to accomplish a deep and thorough cleaning of all the patient rooms and still be able to admit a new patient in a reasonable amount of time." Curt followed up on the names of people referenced by his other staff members as being particularly adept at doing a comprehensive cleaning. He spoke to each one of them individually to learn what they thought might work to restore the rooms to top-notch condition.

Alan offered a plan for getting the job done expeditiously. He thought that a small team could tackle one empty room at a time. They could work through the night when there were far fewer distractions and have the room refurbished by noon the next day when the new admissions started arriving. Alan was clearly a strategic thinker.

Rose had ideas about how best to work together as a team. She told Curt that there were two or three staff members who were friends who tended to help each other out when one of them got overwhelmed. Put these people on a team, she told Curt, and they will figure out how to work together to get the job done right.

Shirita suggested a way to influence other people to support the project. Since the crew would need to put up a barrier to block off the room receiving the deep cleaning, adorn it with signs telling the staff members, "We are enhancing our patient's experience—and yours too!"

Curt decided to speak with Donna, a veteran nurse manager his team really liked. "I'd like to get your take on what we could do about the difficulties with getting rooms cleaned properly when we have quick patient turnover. Seems like the priority has been 'speed' over 'quality'. But the downside is that we've created conditions that are no longer tolerable. My staff member tell me that you're someone who usually has good ideas. What do you believe would work to get us enough time to do a deep cleaning of the patient rooms and still maintain the patient flow?"

"Most of our discharges and admissions come in the late afternoon and early evening," Donna told Curt. "That's when I speak to the bed assignment team so I have an estimate of how many people are in the pipeline. I could include you in that conversation so you'd know when we're most likely going to end up with an empty bed."

Donna liked the idea of sprucing up the rooms on her unit, even though she knew it would cause some difficulties. She worked with Curt's team on a pilot study to perfect the system for refurbishing rooms with minimal disruption to discharges and admissions. Once they had made the process as seamless as possible, they took their program to Robert, who approved the plan for all of the other units in the hospital.

Patient satisfaction scores for cleanliness of rooms rose quickly from 51 percent to 68 percent as his staff members' initial success fueled their motivation. Curt achieved the hospital's target goal of 80 percent in just a few months. The team's success also helped improve the satisfaction level of his environmental services employees, helping him cut his turnover rate by 50 percent.

When the project had been successfully completed, Robert held a town hall meeting to honor those who had contributed to achieving such positives outcomes with minimal disruptions. There's nothing like getting a standing ovation. For that matter, the staff members said it felt great to be giving their colleagues a standing O. "It was kinda like being a fan in the stadium cheering the home team," one person told us.

## Caring Is a Behavior, Not a Slogan

Being interested in taking care of people extended well beyond the CEO. We found the culture of caring for one other permeated every level of the organization. One of the most often repeated phrases we heard was, "we genuinely care about one another."

Although we doubt it was in his CEO job description, Robert went to extraordinary lengths to encourage people to take care of themselves and one another. He would often eat in the cafeteria, showing up before the lunchtime rush started.

He positioned himself at the entrance so he could greet people as they arrived, thanking them for their hard work and telling them to enjoy their lunch break.

When he finally did sit down to eat, Robert would grab a seat at a table filled with staff members. No work talk, he would tell them. "I want to hear about what's going on in the rest of your life." People would talk about everything—their kids, vacations, engagements, a husband's deployment, an impending divorce, or a struggle with an illness. Robert would respond with delight when people shared their good stories and was empathetic when they were struggling.

"Life can be hard," Robert told us, "and the best we can do is help each other through it. I like to ask people what they're doing to take care of themselves during the tough times. And I'll look over at the friend sitting next to them and ask how they've been helping out. We have to be as committed to taking care of ourselves as we are to taking care of our patients." A perfect illustration of his commitment occurred on the holidays when Robert and his wife made it a tradition to show up at the hospital, bringing food and treats for the staff members worked those dates.

The custom of checking in on the well-being of coworkers was not exclusive to the CEO. Employees routinely wanted to know how their coworkers were doing in their personal life as well as on the job. The OR staff members put it this way, "When one of us hurts, we all hurt. If someone has a problem, we step up and help. We'll take their kids to school or bring over dinner. We're always talking about who needs help and we're proud of the fact that we always step up."

The bedside nurses echoed the same sentiments. "If someone is really ill, we put up a sign-up sheet to work for them, donate our vacation hours and contribute money to help them out." The staff members told us that their nurse manager set the example of taking care of people's personal needs, and the rest of the staff members follows suit. "She goes out of her way to accommodate her staff members' requests to be able to do things for their family, such as going to their children's sporting events. We never need to use agency nurses because our own staff always volunteers to cover openings in the schedule."

One of the units we interviewed told us that patients request to be assigned to a bed on their floor. "Typically, someone in their family had been well treated in the past and raved about our unit, so they request a bed here. When we meet people out in the community," they said, beaming with pride, "they tell us what a good job we did taking care of their grandma."

## You've Got Quite a Reputation

How did this unit develop such a great reputation? They developed a buddy system to ensure that the staff members are able to take care of themselves and their coworkers on every shift. "We have the previous shift assess patient acuity and assign buddies. Nurses with patients requiring extra attention are paired with nurses who have a lighter load," they explained.

"When a new shift starts, we huddle up, including our tech, to discuss our plan for the day. Throughout the shift we're checking in with each other to be sure our buddy is getting breaks, drinking enough water, and has time for lunch. We answer call bells for each other and get meds for patients when our buddy is tied up in another patient's room. Our goal is to walk out of the hospital together so no one is left behind trying to catch up."

The OR team is another great example of what happens when employees take care of one other. These highly trained and hard-to-replace OR nurses said, "We're routinely recruited by other hospitals, and some pay even more money than we're making. But we turn down their job offers because we truly love the people we work with."

The OR staff continued: "We want everybody to succeed because we know we need each other. So we treat everybody like a good friend. We want to give each other the best day possible. When problems do occur in the OR, no one even has to ask for help. Everyone automatically jumps in." The OR nurses reported that the people-oriented culture has permeated over to the MDs who have stepped up to help out when the nurses really needed it.

This energy for taking care of each other is translated into how they take care of their patients. The OR staff says, "We work as a team to take care of patients because we know they are our neighbors, friends, or parents of our coworkers. So we treat everybody like they're family members."

## Making a Mark in the World

The same sense of engagement and excitement that the OR staff brings to their work can be seen outside of the hospital as well. A few years earlier, they had decided to contribute a holiday dinner and gifts for one needy family, but their generosity quickly multiplied into taking care of several families who were struggling during the holidays.

With an increased awareness of the needs of poor families in their community, the staff members started making neighborhood rounds to the local schools, taking supplies for children of families that couldn't afford them. One of the oncology nurses described the evolution of their giving to those in need this way: "We discovered that there were a large number of students who would come to school hungry on Monday mornings because they had not had enough to eat over the weekend. So we partnered with a local foodbank to collect food that could be stuffed into backpacks that the children take home with them when they leave."

## Eating It Up

We encountered a unique method for making a difference when we spoke to Lynn, Assistant Director of Nutritional Services. She wanted to create a new diet for diabetes patients. "I felt too many patients were coming back into the hospital because their blood sugar would get out of control, frequently because they we not managing their diet well.

"I spoke with the chief dietician, the medical staff and nursing to learn about the best meal plans for diabetics," Lynn explained. "And I reviewed the Nutritional Services department surveys we conduct on 50 percent of our hospital patients every week. I scoured the reviews looking for feedback on improving the food and service, paying particular attention to the input from diabetes patients."

Then Lynn tested recipes with patients, and let the nurses sample the food themselves. Only then was approval sought to change the existing menu. To take her work to the next level, Lynn created recipe cards to give to patients so they could make healthful meals at home.

Lynn says, "My staff members and I see our work as a calling, not just a job. Food is such an important part of making a patient's stay in the hospital a positive experience. And helping to keep people healthy when they leave the hospital is the best gift of all." Lynn treasures the letters and e-mails she gets from patients who tell her how terrific her food tasted, and how easy it is to make at home.

Employees at this top 100 hospital were happiest when they were taking care of one another, working together to provide the best possible patient care, and feeling like they personally contributed to the success of the hospital. Their passion for caring about others and for being at their best clearly made a major contribution to creating the outstanding outcomes this hospital had been able to achieve.

In fact, rather than burning out over time, we found that employees who had been with the hospital for many years demonstrated the most passion for their work. This happened, they said, because their leaders were excellent at continually making people aware of how important their contributions were to their coworkers, patients, and the organization.

## Lessons Learned

The top-rated hospital in our appreciative inquiry contended with the same number of serious problems that all healthcare organizations face. But they used a different set of tools to fix their system when it broke down or needed to be renovated. During our wrap-up discussions, we all reflected on the key ingredients that enabled them to be a high-functioning hospital.

"Put down passion as the first and most important ingredient of our success!" I was told with absolute certainty that passion was the foremost factor contributing to this hospital's extraordinarily high level of functioning. Every member of the executive and nursing leadership teams was adamant about how crucial it is to have a passion for your job, your staff members, and your patients.

"But," I tried to argue, "your teamwork at every level is outstanding, so wouldn't that be the first ingredient of success?" "No," the leaders insisted, "teamwork would not be the same without a passionate commitment to the values of the organization."

Where does your passion originate? "From a crystal-clear vision of what it looks like to live up to the organization's values," I was told. "At our hospital, people know why they're here," said Dianne, Director of Emergency Nursing. "We tell our employees what our values are on their first day and show them what it means to live those values every day for as long as they work here. And they see the results. Our staff is intensely interested in having their neighbors say good things about our hospital.

"Our staff constantly shares ideas about how to achieve our vision of being the best possible community hospital," Dianne continued. "They have a deep desire to be a part of a team that is passionate and proud about providing the best possible patient care."

To that end, Dianne cultivates her staff members' passion for being the best by teaching them that their unit is their own small family business. "Then they run the ER like a family business where everybody pitches in to do whatever is necessary to get the job done. They fuss with each other occasionally, but they love one another like family." Encouraging employees to treat their unit as if they own and work in a successful small family business proved to be a monumentally effective method for generating extraordinary teamwork.

Another key ingredient we discovered was that leaders in this high-functioning hospital set goals and then get out of the way. They believed their staff members are capable of figuring out the best way to achieve the objective: "We believe that our staff is able to see solutions that will work best at the bedside," Emily, the CNO told us. "We encourage people to try innovative approaches and accept that not everything will work as planned. But that's part of the process of learning how to improve."

"But aren't you afraid of failure?" I wanted to know. Debbie, Director of Acute Care Nursing, told us that the key to mitigating the risk of failure is "listening to the ideas from staff members and colleagues when seeking solutions to complex problems. Bringing people who will be impacted by a change into the decision-making process enables us to find solutions that have a high probability of working well for everyone involved. Over time we've developed the belief that together we can figure out how to overcome whatever challenges we're facing."

Another factor that made this a top 100 hospital was that the staff members were able to find the courage to act because they believed in themselves and their colleagues. They were able to achieve remarkable results because they used their best qualities when striving for positive outcomes.

Curt, Director of Environmental Services, put it best, "Because I'd been able to help my kids do well in school, I believed I could help my staff perform well in their jobs. I listen. Learn. I persevere until I succeed. And I see how others can be successful as well."

And the final ingredient for maintaining their ability to perform at a high level was their commitment to taking care of themselves and their coworkers. "Making sure your coworkers are able to take care of themselves is essential," the staff told us, "if you expect them to be able to take good care of the patients."

The extraordinary people we met in our yearlong appreciative inquiry were the happiest healthcare team I have ever encountered. They certainly made a difference in my life, and in the lives of thousands of healthcare professionals with whom I have shared the strategies they use to achieve the highest level of satisfaction and success.

# A TALE OF
# TWO UNITS

This section tells the story of Carol, Director of Women's Services at a large hospital, her Assistant Director Karin, and her two Nurse Managers Maureen and Jan. Over the space of Chapters 4 through 6, you will learn the appalling details of the problems the department faces. By applying the PROPEL Principles, Carol, her leadership group and a team of staff members learn to work together to transform the broken system.

These stories are based on actual situations, but identifying information has been changed and dialog has been created. The stories are illustrations. The results are real.

# Chapter 4

---

# Stuck: Between a Rock and a Hard Place

---

Albert Einstein is attributed with defining insanity as "doing the same thing over and over again and expecting different results." In my years of working with hospitals and healthcare systems troubled by poor patient outcomes, staff disengagement, and hemorrhaging budgets, I have observed a lot of insanity.

The people I've met while working in healthcare have been smart. They have expressed a heartfelt desire to provide good care to patients (well, they all started with that attitude). They chose healthcare as a career because they wanted to take care of people. But the bedside staff members complain that they have been assigned to so many other tasks—from documentation to tracking down a prescription— they don't get to spend enough time with their patients.

Managers quickly learn they are caught between a struggling staff and demanding directors. Senior leaders spend so much of their time in meetings trying to address the organization's high-level issues that they lose touch with what's really going on at ground level. Many providers find that when they voice their concerns—even over unsafe and unhealthy conditions for patients or staff members—their input goes nowhere.

After years of trying to make the system work, many healthcare professionals become stuck in a downward spiral that makes it impossible to do the good work that got them into healthcare in the first place.

In recent times, many people feel the focus is on finances. These smart folks recognize that the bottom line is important but know other elements receive too little attention: staff satisfaction, employee engagement, patient satisfaction, and patient safety. And they are right. These are the factors that truly affect the bottom line, as the research presented in Chapter 2 demonstrated.

## A Department Director's Perpetual Problems

Carol's boss was disturbed by the turnover rate of nurses in her department and had charged her with presenting a written plan to solve the problem. "What am I going to do," she asked herself, "to retain the new RN staff members who are quitting after 12 months of employment, year after year?"

Carol felt a sense of anxiety so great she was certain it was damaging her health. Jan, the new labor and delivery (L&D) nurse manager, hadn't turned things around and had lost all 20 of the new nurses she'd hired in the past 2 years. Maureen, the experienced nurse manager of the women's cancer unit, was filling half of her RN positions with expensive agency nurses. Seeing the budget-busting payroll numbers left Carol worried about her own future.

Carol kept replaying the problems in her mind. "Why can't Maureen attract and retain long-term staff members? I've met with her repeatedly to work on solutions. Every time, she pretends she had everything under control when clearly the payroll numbers tell a different story. It's not my leadership style to become confrontational but our meetings never lead to any new ideas or approaches. It doesn't take long for Maureen to be insisting, 'I've got it figured out, Carol! I know what I'm doing after all these years!'"

Deep into ruminating, Carol's thoughts continued to pull her into a dark, paralyzing place. "What am I going to do to help Jan who's become totally exasperated with her staff members? I've engaged every resource I know—HR consulting, Nurse Manager Academy, peer counseling, and my own coaching. I see Jan trying to rectify the problems, but it's 'whack-a-mole management.' No sooner has one problem been whacked away than another pops up."

As if she didn't have enough on her plate, Carol spotted an e-mail with a subject line that automatically caused her heart to start pounding. The latest staff satisfaction survey results had been posted for her department. She had a lot riding on seeing improvements over the survey that had been done 2 years earlier.

Even though the issue of improving staff satisfaction had been a pressing concern for years, the scores for the nurses in her department had been among the lowest in the hospital for nearly a decade. Year after year her boss made the matter one of her top priorities during her performance evaluations. Disappointing survey results would bring even more pressure into Carol's already stressful life.

She opened the attachment and stared in disbelief at the numbers. The staff members in her department had indicated once again that their satisfaction with their job was well below the institutional average. Carol teetered on being overwhelmed by despair, which was in sharp contrast to her usual optimistic approach to solving problems.

Her mind raced: "I've spent 25 years in this profession because I care about my staff members and patients. Lately, though, all I can focus on are the staff vacancy problems, personality conflicts, and budget over-runs. The pressure from executive leadership is almost unbearable. I've brought in some of the top consulting firms to help, but they simply told me what I already knew. None of their 'scripts for staff' or 'hold them accountable' strategies have worked. Staff members scoffed or quit. The problems keep getting worse. My head is going to explode."

## Becoming a Champion for the PROPEL Initiative

Carol and her assistant director, Karin, were apologetic for being late for our initial meeting. "It's the time of the year when we have our budget meetings," Carol explained with a smile that made it impossible to be upset with her. "I'm glad you're here," she continued. "I've heard about the work you've been doing." There was that smile again. "I was at a conference with their senior VP who shared a story of how you turned one of their units around. We could use that kind of help here."

"Sometimes staff members get stuck in situations they don't know how to change," I acknowledged. "To be fair, it was the doctors and nurses whose efforts got such great results. They're a team of highly talented individuals who needed some help learning how to work together to achieve positive outcomes. Tell me about the problems your team is having and how you've tried to fix them."

Carol looked at Karin as if to prompt a response, but the blank look on the assistant director's face gave the appearance that she had something else on her mind. Carol redirected her attention to me and launched into an executive summary of the issues that plagued her Women's Services Department, starting with one of two nurse managers, Maureen, a 20-year veteran:

- Maureen has a 50 percent RN vacancy rate on her cancer unit.
- She doesn't get along well with the younger staff members.
- Her staff satisfaction is low and her turnover rate is high.
- The cost of agency staff members is breaking the budget.
- She works 70–80 hours a week.

Carol took a deep breath and continued, this time recounting the situation with Jan, the nurse manager on her other unit, L&D:

- L&D hasn't had an effective nurse manager for nearly 10 years.
- Jan has been managing the unit for the last 2 years.
- It's her first leadership position and she's struggling.
- She's been trying to hold staff members accountable, but that's been a real battle.
- The turnover rate among new RN hires has been 100 percent within their first year.
- The staff satisfaction level on her unit is the lowest in the entire hospital.

"I've worked here for over 25 years, beginning as a bedside nurse. It breaks my heart to hear how bad it's become on our units. Not to mention that the President and

CFO repeatedly remind me that it costs over $50,000 to replace one RN, and we're replacing over 20 every year in our department."

Carol's smile had vanished. "I tried bringing in our HR specialists, who told me to 'hire the right people and strictly adhere to the hospital's performance improvement process' to weed out the poor performers. When I ask how their recruiters could help find the right people, they told me that wasn't their job; they only forward resumes that meet the minimum standards to qualify for employment here. To say they were not helpful would be an understatement."

"What about the performance improvement process? How does that work?" I inquired.

"It doesn't," Carol stated flatly. "We go through all the steps to discipline an employee when she doesn't adhere to our standards. The person will comply for the 90 days they are on probation and then revert to their old ways on day 91. Jan spends an inordinate amount of time following the HR counseling guidelines about how to talk to an employee about improving performance. She tells me that those conversations quickly devolve into the employee justifying their behavior and arguing that the punishment is unfair. Maureen's good at cracking the whip to keep people in line, but she ruffles a lot of feathers in the process."

"Do you ever ask the staff members what they believe would work to fix these problems?" I probed.

"Oh, yes," Karin finally chimed in, "the staff members take a lot of surveys that measure their satisfaction level, their attitude about patient safety, and their perspective on quality of care, to name a few. I compile those results, and we discuss them in our leadership meetings. I'd be happy to show you those."

"Thanks, I'd like to see those data," I responded, trying to encourage Karin to continue to engage. "And do you ever sit down with staff members to ask them what's going on that's causing them to give your department such low marks."

"Oh, I have a few friends who I've known for years who work on the units. They tell me what's going on," Karin offered.

Alarm bells started going off in my head. "And what exactly do they tell you?"

"They tell me that things are really OK on the unit," Karin replied, seemingly oblivious to the fact that her friends' reports directly contradict the survey results. "It's just that the staff members get upset when the hospital does things like making them pay for parking. Then they blame our department's leadership team for that, but we have no control over those decisions."

"I'd be interested in hearing directly from your staff members what they believe are the problems," I told Carol and Karin.

"Perhaps it helps for me to explain how our evidence-based approach works," I offered. Heads nodded. "There's good research regarding how to accomplish change. We've learned that the most important factor—40 percent of what goes into being successful—involves what 'the person making the change believes is necessary to achieve the goal.' That's why I want to hear from the staff members."

"We can arrange for that," Carol committed. "And I'm curious about what else contributes to success."

"Well," I continued, "another 30 percent is based on relationships. People need to have social support to sustain their efforts. Good relationships refuel people because they provide encouragement to get going and enthusiasm to reinforce any progress that's made. And good relationships provide people with the opportunity to engage in a 'two heads are better than one' discussion about what to do when they get stuck."

"The third factor, which contributes 15 percent to a successful change initiative, is the ability to think optimistically. This is especially important when people have experienced a setback—which is inevitable, by the way, when trying to change an old pattern. Fortunately, optimistic thinking is a skill that can be taught and learned—and it prevents relapsing into feeling helpless and hopeless.

"Now here's the bad news," I said, looking Carol in the eye. "The final 15 percent of what it takes to be successful is derived from the leader, mentor, or coach. Consider how many change initiatives are top-down, and you'll understand why the majority of them fail."

Carol sat up like a shot of electricity had jolted her. "This explains a lot. We've been making people sit through classes where they're told what to do differently. We've tried telling staff members to follow a script when dealing with problems, and we've plastered the units with posters touting the slogans of our latest program. So much money. So much time. And none of it really changed anything."

"I can tell that you want to make a difference," I empathized. "I'd like to suggest that in addition to getting input from your nurse managers, we ask the staff members who they believe are the most positive problem-solvers on their unit. Then I'd like to convene a kickoff meeting that brings the two of you together with Jan and Maureen along with that select group of staff who express a positive outlook."

"I don't understand," Karin said with a quizzical look, "how are we supposed to address the problems by meeting with the positive people. Don't we need to hear from the staff members who express the most negative opinions about what's happening on their unit?"

"The focus groups will give those folks a chance to voice their concerns," I explained. "But studies show that when our brains become focused on the negative, we lock into fight–flight–freeze reactions. It's nearly impossible to think of creative solutions when we're in a negative frame of mind. That's why we want to hear from everyone initially. However, we want to create a PROPEL team made up of five to seven staff members whose positive mind-set enables them to offer some innovative ideas for resolving your long-standing issues."

"Yes, but we'll still have to deal with the unhappy staff members," Karin contended, "and they're the ones who have derided and derailed our previous efforts."

"Of course, your concerns are valid," I affirmed. "Consider how that happens. The actions of most negative people have discouraged and defeated the efforts of the rest of the staff members who are trying to have a good shift. We've all experienced that phenomenon."

They nodded in agreement. "It's about tipping points," I continued. "The Gallup employee engagement research has shown for years that 15–20 percent of staff members on a typical unit are actively voicing their unhappiness. About 30 percent are engaged in trying to do good work and make improvements. That leaves around 50 percent of the staff members in what Gallup labels the 'disengaged' group—the folks who come in, do the minimum to get by, and can't wait to leave when their shift is over. It's that 50 percent who tip in the direction of whichever side is winning—the most negative or the most positive people. Right now, it sounds like your most negative staff members are pulling everyone else down. Teaching a team of your most positive people to use the PROPEL Principles will empower them to win the hearts and minds of the majority."

"I like that you're bringing a fresh perspective to problems we haven't been able to solve," Carol interjected. Looking over to Karin, she continued, "And I've been reading about the positive psychology research. It started with Martin Seligman at Penn, and there's serious research being done at places like Stanford, Harvard, and UNC Chapel Hill. Our academic medical center may be the perfect place to test this approach in a healthcare setting. We're a major research institution, so let's make this a pilot study, with before and after measures that will show whether this PROPEL initiative produces any real results."

"That sounds great," I responded enthusiastically. "We'll start by conducting focus groups with the entire staff members on each unit, a part of which will involve asking them to recognize their most positively engaged coworkers. We'll ask you, Karin, Maureen, and Jan to participate in an initial meeting with six to eight of the most positively engaged people on each unit to identify what 'they' believe a positive outcome would look like.

"After that kickoff meeting we'll provide coaching to the managers and these newly formed PROPEL teams to teach them how to use the PROPEL Principles to achieve their positive outcome. After they've acquired this new set of skills, we'll help the PROPEL teams work together with their coworkers to help them experience a more positive work environment. The whole process will take 6 months to a year."

"I think we have a plan," Carol stated with conviction. "Karin will get the 'before' statistics complied, while you conduct the focus groups. I like your suggestions to bring employees from every level together to discuss our problems—that's a new approach for us. I'll arrange for an off-site retreat for our kickoff meeting." And with a firm handshake, our meeting concluded.

## My OMG Moment with Carol

I knocked on Carol's door after meeting with Jan and Maureen and their staff members. I could feel my anxiety causing my throat to tighten. Carol greeted me with her warm smile and offered me a seat next to her desk piled high with books, papers, journals, and file folders. "I was just sitting here thinking," she said, "about the problems our department is facing. Now that you've met Jan and Maureen and conducted the focus groups, I'm wondering what you think might help."

"I have some thoughts," I began. "But first I have to say how courageous I found Jan to be. She still has a strong desire to make L&D a good place to work. But she's been struggling to overcome some monumental challenges with her staff members. How much do you know about the problems that are occurring?"

"I review every one of the disciplinary actions Jan submits to HR," Carol said while shaking her head in disbelief. "I know that Jan has been doing everything she can do deal with her problem employees."

"Yes," I acknowledged, "but Jan's become locked into reactive mode, completely caught up in the negativity of her situation. We know from the neuropsychology research that fight–flight–freeze reactions keep people ruminating on what is wrong and how things could get worse. That's making it impossible for her brain to think of any possible innovative solutions for improving the situation. Jan is consumed with a mix of anxiety, anger, and despair, which is hurting her ability to maintain satisfying relationships."

"I know how she feels," Carol said, shaking her head.

"As I mentioned when we first met," I continued, "Jan needs to shift from fearing the worst to imagining the best. Having a positive vision of an outcome in which you're able to live by your deepest values is what generates the passion to work furiously to achieve that result."

"Our L&D focus groups revealed that the vast majority of staff members are disengaged," I recounted. "In addition, you have some senior nurses who feel entitled to do whatever they want and threaten anyone who dares to stand up to them. The bad behavior of a few nurses has been going on for so long the rest of the staff has become resigned to living with it or they have quit. The new nurse graduates are especially vulnerable, which is why they've all quit. L&D has become a unit that eats its young.

"But there were a few people we found in the focus groups who believe that things could get better. We'd like the leadership team to co-create a set of values and a vision with those few staff members who are still engaged," I continued. "It's crucial to harness their ideas and energy for tackling the challenges in L&D. We'll boost their ability by teaching them to use their strengths to be at their best so they can make a meaningful difference. I can see a path forward for Jan and her Team."

"And Maureen?" Carol inquired.

"Well, that's a different story. Maureen put off our meeting twice, and when we finally did get together, she was blunt about her feelings regarding consultants," I acknowledged. "She told me in no uncertain terms that she knew I was just another person who had been sent there to find fault with her. She made it clear that blaming her for the vacancy and retention issues on her unit was 'a load of crap.' The problem, she insisted, was that the young staff she hires today do not have a good work ethic and routinely fail to meet her expectations for providing excellent—in fact I'd say perfect—patient care. She's adamant that she has zero tolerance for mistakes and believes it's her job—no, duty—to admonish and punish people when there are problems."

"I've heard that philosophy from her myself," Carol confirmed. "What are your thoughts about working with her?"

"Maureen is very matter of fact," I observed. "So I'm going to try to give her a new set of facts. She's committed to evidence-based practices for her nurses; perhaps she'll benefit from learning about the evidence regarding what effective leaders do to achieve success."

"Tom, have you ever heard the old saying that the greatest obstacle to learning is believing that you already know?" Carol asked.

"Well, if you're telling me that's the case, then it's going to require some external source of motivation to have a chance of making a difference. Have you told Maureen what's at stake for her and for you? If not, are you prepared to tell her?" I wanted to know.

"Maureen has worked here even longer than I have, and she has a lot of friends. We've worked together for 15 years. I'll try talking to her again," Carol promised.

I did not feel reassured by Carol's somewhat evasive answer, but agreed to make good on my offer to show Maureen the studies illuminating effective management practices with modern-day knowledge workers.

"The staff members who attended the focus groups on Maureen's unit made it clear that they love taking care of GYN cancer patients and that they hate working for Maureen. Their chief complaint is that Maureen routinely accosts people in the hallway near patient rooms and other staff members to berate them for something they've done wrong. Frankly they're skeptical that Maureen will ever change."

"Let's hope this feedback will be another source of input that will influence Maureen," Carol commented as our meeting concluded.

## Jan's L&D Kickoff Meeting

As Carol opened the meeting, she shared a mix of emotions with the formal and informal leaders in the L&D unit. "I've seen our women's services department slide downhill over the past few years. Our patients are unhappy—and sometimes unsafe. Our staff members are unhappy, and I've heard that at times they feel unsafe as well. Obviously, all of this makes me unhappy, too.

"I've brought in a new nurse manager and a number of consultants over the past several years, but we haven't turned the situation around YET. I emphasize YET, because I will not stop working on these problems until they are fixed," Carol announced. "Today we're going to try another approach. Dr. Tom Muha is a positive psychologist, and he's going to work to help us learn how to be at our best as individuals and as a team. I believe that he offers us a new approach for how to transform the L&D unit."

"We're part of a great research institution," the clinical director continued, "so we're accustomed to trying promising new therapies. I believe it's time for us to try a new evidence-based strategy. You have been asked to be on a PROPEL team comprised of our best staff members to bring the rest of the staff members up to your level. Please join with me in welcoming Tom."

I began with what seemed like a straightforward question: "What would it look like if L&D was a great place for staff members and patients alike?" But it took an hour at the kickoff meeting for the three leaders and six staff members to arrive at picture of a positive outcome they could all agree on.

In the beginning, the group was focused on the toxic environment in which they worked, and their brains riveted on what was wrong with their unit. For example, people made statements such as "the bullies would not be intimidating the new nurses." "Stopping the bad behavior is a logical goal," I acknowledged, "but it's not a psychologically successful way of thinking. Continuing to dwell on what you do 'not' want keeps your brain focused on the problem," I explained, "causing you to feel threatened and activating your fight–flight–freeze reactions. Negative emotions such as anger, anxiety, and discouragement are aroused and block access to the higher level problem-solving parts of your brain."

The group didn't believe me. They were sure that "no bullying" was the outcome they were seeking.

"Do NOT think of a grizzly bear chasing you," I instructed, "because we don't want anyone in the group imagining what it would be like to be attacked by a grizzly bear. Please do 'not' think about having a bear tear you from limb to limb."

Everyone was now thinking about being attacked by a bear, of course. "Who senses their mind become mildly anxious and their body moderately tense?" Heads nodded. "The primal part of your brain is preparing your mind and body to defend yourself. Good reaction when you're dealing with a bear. Not so good when you're trying to create caring relationships.

"To achieve a positive outcome, you need to picture already having accomplished a good result. Those positive pictures stimulate the left prefrontal cortex, the uniquely human 'executive functioning' part of your brain. This is the portal to gain access to higher level functions such as creativity, faith, strengths, and optimism—all the resources you need to overcome a challenging situation."

"Okay," they said, "we get it." But the group continued to struggle by making vague, general statements such as "We want our new nurses to be happy."

"Happy is a positive feeling, but not a behavior. Your left prefrontal cortex needs to see the actions that would ultimately lead to that feeling. Be more specific," I requested. "If I were on your unit, what behaviors would I see occurring that would put a smile on a nurse's face?"

Those questions opened a lively discussion that pinpointed specific behaviors the group wanted to see. Here are some examples:

- An experienced nurse asking a new nurse how she could help
- RNs and techs coordinating how they would care for patients
- Staff members checking in on how their coworkers were doing that day

- Charge nurses establishing a no-passing zone for any staff member who walks by a room in which the call bell is ringing
- Staff members leaving the unit at the end of their shift expressing gratitude for the help they received

Once the group could picture the actual behaviors they wanted to see on the L&D unit, we discussed the intrinsic core values that drove the individuals in this group to perform in a highly functional manner, even in the face of coworkers' dysfunctional behavior. After some consideration, the group winnowed their core values down to "CTP—camaraderie, teamwork, and professionalism."

The PROPEL team could see the behaviors they wanted the rest of the staff members on their unit to use more consistently. They understood that it would be incredibly valuable for them to figure out how to bring the majority of disengaged staff members over to their side—becoming high performers whose behaviors exemplified CTP.

It was now time for the group to move into the final phase of the kickoff: figuring out the first steps to move from their current reality to their vision of working on a unit characterized by CTP. When they were reminded of the problems plaguing their unit, their old response pattern was reinvigorated. "The bullies will ridicule this idea. I can hear them now, 'Now ain't that sweet. This little girl got someone to help her 'cause she couldn't do her own work!' How do we respond to that?"

"What if you didn't?" I asked. "What if you started with the people in this room? You all were identified in the focus groups as the most positive, professional staff members on the unit. What if you ignored the bullies and savored the fact that you'd helped each other? You'd be following Gandhi's advice, 'Be the change you want to see in the world.' You could choose to leave your shift feeling good regardless of what anyone else might say."

"But how does that help change our unit, if there's just a few of us putting these ideas into action?" one of the nurses wanted to know.

"Consider what's happening on your unit now," I posed to the group. "How many bad apples are making it miserable for everyone?"

"Right, it's just a handful," another nurse exclaimed.

"This is how tipping points work in organizations," I explained. "We've all seen how a few negative people can pull everyone down, especially the newer, more vulnerable staff members who are easily swayed by whatever is going on around them. If that's true, then it's also possible that a few top performing people could be a positive influence on those staff members who bend in whatever direction the wind is blowing.

"The good news," I continued, "is that there are typically around 30 percent of engaged staff members who would welcome opportunities to offer help, express appreciation, check on a coworker who seems stressed, or catch someone doing something right. But they need to be encouraged to do so—and that's where PROPEL teams come into the picture."

"You're right," a nurse remarked. "There are plenty of times we could say something positive."

"You could do this," Jan encouraged.

"We have to do something," a tech asserted. The comments continued and the enthusiasm mounted.

Carol and Karin had been quiet during much of the meeting, making space for the staff members to develop the initiative from the bottom-up. Now Carol wanted to know what the senior leaders could do to help.

The room became quiet, for everyone was keenly aware that Karin was friends with some of the most negative nurses. Jan conjured up her courage and said, "'Staff members shouldn't have to deal with bullies; that should be the job of 'leadership'. We need a no tolerance policy for bad behavior. If I receive a complaint, I will validate it with witnesses who saw that person creating a hostile work environment. I want to be able to issue an immediate disciplinary action without anyone excusing the behavior. I don't want to have to keep debating with my bosses whether that nurse should get a pass for bad behavior."

Carol immediately agreed. "I'm going to pull the leadership team together to draw up some clear guidelines with consequences, and we're going to stop making exceptions," she said, shooting a look at Karin, who slumped in her chair with a look of resignation.

"That's great," I said enthusiastically. "Let's end the kickoff by going around the room and having everyone say what actions they'll take to be the positive change they want to see."

- "When we're gathering for report, I want to express appreciation to each person who helped me during my shift."
- "I want to buddy up with the nurse working next to me to make sure we each get a lunch break."
- "I'm going to monitor any new nurse who's working on my shift so I can offer another pair of hands when she is getting overloaded."
- "You can count on me to support those ideas by asking others what kind of progress they're making."
- "I'll start a group e-mail so we can share stories about our ups and downs."
- "I'm going to start checking in every day with whoever is working from the PROPEL team to find out what I can do to help," Jan offered.
- "Karin and I are going to walk through the unit much more frequently," Carol added, "and we're going to change our focus to catching people doing things right."

After years of struggling in their own silos, this group of dedicated professionals had been brought together to become the trailblazers whose collective wisdom could be harnessed to turn their L&D unit around. As the meeting came to a close, big hugs signified that CTP provided a unifying force that could help this PROPEL team to "be the change they want to see in the world."

# Maureen's Women's Services Department Kickoff

It was 8:15 a.m. in the morning, and the meeting scheduled for 8 o'clock had not yet started. Carol, Karin, and select members of Maureen's staff members had now been waiting 15 minutes and counting. All we needed was Maureen. Carol called her but got no answer.

At 8:30 a.m., Carol left another voice mail, this one clearly angry. "I don't know where you are or what you're doing, but I want you at this meeting...NOW!"

With that Carol looked at the group and said, "I'm sorry about this delay. I know it took a great effort to rearrange your schedules so we could meet this morning. I appreciate it because we have some important work to do. So, we're going to get started.

"As you know our Women's Services Department has been struggling. Our staff satisfaction is low, and our vacancy rate is high. We've brought in temporary help. But I know it's not easy to work with someone who doesn't know where the supplies are located, or how to use the computer system. Or even your name."

Carol continued: "The people in this room have hung in there with us as we've tried to remedy the situation, and I want you to know how deeply grateful I am. We will not give up. We will find a solution, and I want you to be a part of that process. I've been learning—admittedly the hard way—how important it is to involve the staff members. I've hired consultants, followed their recommendations, sent you all to classes, and tried mandating solutions. None of that has worked, so we're taking a different approach—we want you to be a part of finding a solution.

"I'd like to introduce Dr. Tom Muha, whom you may have met when he was conducting focus groups on our cancer unit. As you discovered, he asks a lot of questions—thought-provoking questions, hard-to-answer questions, and solution-oriented questions.

"He's shown me that sometimes I need to get out of my own way," Carol admitted. "I'm learning to stop reacting to problems and to redirect my thinking to more positive approaches. For me, that means talking to people I trust, who are supportive and optimistic that we can improve our situation. You are those people. Tom is going to help us put our heads and our hearts together so we can make your unit a great place to work and a wonderful place for women to recover from their cancer surgeries."

"Thank you, Carol," I said. "That was such a heartfelt way to get us started. I'm wondering how the rest of you felt hearing Carol's words?"

It was quiet for a few moments. Then one of the younger nurses opened up: "I'm so glad that Carol shared her feelings with us. Sometimes it feels that nobody cares about what's happening on our unit. The last few years have been hard on those of us who've stayed. We love taking care of our patients. I don't understand why we can't seem to find a way to take good care of each other."

"But let's be honest here," another nurse chimed in, "there's a good reason why we don't feel anyone cares about us. All we ever hear about is what we do wrong—never a word about the great work we do."

There was a chorus of consensus from others.

"And I'll bet you've spent a lot of time talking about what's wrong with your unit," I speculated.

"Every day," someone shouted out as everyone else chuckled.

"I'd like you to consider a different approach. I'd like you to move beyond what is and tell me what you would like it to be. Specifically, what would it look like if I came onto your unit a year from now and saw you behaving in ways that demonstrated you were happy in your work?"

Silence.

More silence.

Uncomfortable silence.

"What is the silence telling me?" I wondered aloud.

"It's been so long, I don't even know any more," one of them said. "And it's not up to us, anyway. We don't have any control over what's going on."

"I'm a guy who likes research," I responded, "so I'm going to tell you about a study I think you'll find relevant. Many years ago, a psychologist set up an experiment with two groups of dogs. The dogs were placed in a cage that had a lever the dog could push with his paw. In half of the cages, the lever worked to turn off a mild electric shock; but in the other half of the cages, the lever did nothing to alleviate the annoying stimulus. After multiple trials, the first group was quick to push the lever, while the second group laid in their cage resigned to their fate. Then the experimenter activated the lever for the second group of dogs who were receiving the mild shocks, but the dogs remained passive. He even removed the top of the cage so the dogs could jump out—but they didn't move. Researchers call this 'learned helplessness,' a phenomenon that's been observed in humans as well.

"Now I'd like to ask you again," I continued, "to imagine what it would it look like if your unit was a wonderful place to work?"

"We'd be appreciated for our dedication to taking care of our patients. And when problems occurred, we'd all learn from them rather than receiving a 'shocking' reprimand," a staff member asserted.

I explained the brain's need to create positive pictures of actual behaviors to stimulate its ability to figure out how to accomplish a goal. "So help me see it. What activities would be occurring if you were receiving appreciation? And what would I observe if the staff was engaged in learning from a mistake?"

"We could start praising each other," a nurse offered. "We don't have to wait for our nurse manager to give us that."

"We need to start asking each other what kind of shift we're having," another nurse suggested. "Then we'll know what was going on with one another's patients. I love hearing the stories about one of us being able to help a woman who was coming unglued after her cancer surgery. It's great to be able to give hope to someone who is struggling."

"And when things don't go so well we could huddle up," stated another nurse. "This group can figure out what went wrong and develop an understanding about what we could do differently next time."

The group had broken out of their helpless stupor and were able to create several strategies for how they could start improving their unit immediately.

Then Maureen showed up. The meeting was half over. Carol made a beeline in her direction. "Where have you been? Why didn't you answer my calls?"

"We had an emergency with a patient that I had to attend to. There was nothing I could do," Maureen said defensively.

Carol was momentarily stymied. "We'll talk about this later," she finally blurted out.

Maureen walked away without saying another word, got herself a cup of coffee and a pastry, sat down, and proceeded to enjoy her snack.

The rest of her group sat in stunned silence. "Let's take a 10-minute break." I suggested. The group dispersed, and Karin went to sit with her friend Maureen.

I had a sense that battle lines were being drawn, and suggested as much to Carol. "No," she tried to reassure me, "I will talk to Maureen and get her on board with this initiative. I've told her before and I'll tell her again that what's happening on her unit is unacceptable and has to change."

It sounded like she was going to be doing more of the same. But the group had reassembled, and I decided not to point out the low probability of her approach being effective in front of her staff members. We were just starting to work together, I reasoned, and didn't want to jeopardize our budding relationship.

Instead, I opted to ask Carol to summarize the group's work up to that point in order to bring Maureen up to speed. "We've been discussing the staff members' feeling that their hard work with patients is underappreciated. They get a lot of gratitude from their patients but not much from coworkers or leaders. The staff members shared some ideas about how they could support one another. They also discussed how they could huddle up when problems occurred to determine what lessons could be learned."

Maureen had a surprisingly supportive response: "Sounds good. I like these ideas. What can we do to make it happen?"

"Excellent question," I responded with some enthusiasm to reinforce Maureen's cooperative attitude. "Deciding on specific steps is, obviously, important. And having a clear picture of what the positive outcome would look like activates your brain's executive functioning resources. So, I'd like to sharpen the vision and make sure everyone's willing to work together to achieve it."

A constructive conversation ensued among the staff members, with Carol making supportive comments that greatly encouraged the staff members. Ultimately, they chose their vision statement:

> We will start our shift with a quick huddle to remind us that we're here to make a difference in the lives of our patients. We will regularly check in with one another to ask "how are you doing?" and "how can I help?" And at the end of our shift our manager will join us in appreciating the good work we've done to help our patients and coworkers. We will have weekly meetings in the conference room with our manager to

respectfully discuss any problems that occur. We'll work together to develop a plan to prevent that issue from occurring in the future.

It was time to wrap up the meeting by identifying first steps each person could take. "Back to the question Maureen posed a little while ago. What will each of you commit to doing between now and our next meeting to start moving toward your vision?"

"I'll initiate the huddles to start a shift I'm working," someone offered.

"I'll do it if she's not here," another nurse said.

"I will schedule times every week to meet with staff members to discuss problems," a senior nurse vowed.

"I'll gather the staff members at the end of the shift so we can have a minute to express our appreciation to the people who helped us," one of the techs declared.

"You'll see me walking through your unit more often to let you know how grateful we are for your excellent patient care," Carol added.

Everyone but Maureen and Karin volunteered their action plan. "So, we still need to hear from two more people," I pointed out.

"I'll drop by the unit more often as well," Karin stated.

"And what will you do while you're there," I ask.

"I'll check in with staff members to see how it's going" was her tepid reply.

"And Maureen, what will you do?" I asked as all eyes riveted to see her response.

Pause.

Sigh.

"I'll support everyone's efforts" was her half-hearted response.

I pressed for more details: "What exactly will we see you doing?"

"I'll check to make sure that people are doing what they say they'll do" was Maureen's ominous reply.

I continued to push for a more positive approach: "And what will you say if they're following through on their commitments?"

"I know what you want me to say, Tom. So here it is… I'll tell them they're doing a good job," Maureen stated with the tone of a teenager who was being forced to apologize for a misdeed.

I redirected my attention to the rest of the group: "Remember, you have the ability to take action to make your unit better. We'll be meeting every week to discuss progress toward your vision. And we'll provide some evidence-based positive psychology tools that can help this PROPEL team to succeed. I'll leave you with my favorite Gandhi quote: 'Be the change you want to see in the world'."

## Next Steps

After the kickoff meetings, my team and I began to meet with Jan and Maureen, as well as the people on each of their PROPEL teams. We met with Carol monthly to give her progress reports. Chapters 5 and 6 elaborate the stories of what happened next.

## Chapter 5

---

# The Transformation: How to PROPEL a Staff to Success

---

## A Nurse Manager Overloaded with Problems

Jan, the nurse manager of the labor and delivery (L&D) unit, came to work a little before 7 o'clock one morning to speak to a few of the nurses coming off the night shift. She expected employees would comply with the hospital's flu shot requirement, but she found herself needing to warn staff members they would be suspended if they didn't meet the vaccination deadline. "Why does getting staff members to do what's expected always meet with such resistance?" she wondered.

As Jan opened her office door, Susy, one of the new nurse graduates she had recently hired, rushed up to her with a panic-stricken look on her face. "I'm afraid to walk out alone to my car. Joselyn just told me she'll be waiting for me because I reported that she'd come to work drunk last night and fell asleep for a couple of hours during the shift."

"What exactly did Joselyn say to you?" Jan asked.

She told me "When you turn me in, you threaten my job, which threatens my kids—and I don't let anyone threaten my kids. I'll see you in the parking garage. You're gonna end up in a world of hurt."

"That's totally unacceptable," Jan told Susy. "I'm going to walk you down to the assistant director's office and we'll let her deal with this."

Susy repeated her story to Karin, to which Jan added, "This is the kind of crazy stuff I've been telling you has been happening. We've got to put a stop to it!"

"Well, let's not rush to judgment," Karin responded. "Joselyn has already spoken to me and explained that she'd taken some Nyquil before coming to work. I've known Joselyn for years, and she was upset at being falsely accused."

"But she wasn't falsely accused," Susy insisted. "She was slurring her words and asking her friends for help reading the labels on her patient's medications. They finally told her to go lie down and sleep it off."

"I'll look into it," Karin offered in a half-hearted voice. "But we really don't have enough evidence to prove what you're saying is true. I'm afraid this will likely end up one person's word against her friends and hers."

## Jan's First Coaching Session

Later that week I met with Jan. "Hi, I'm Jan. Nice to see you," Jan said in a cheery voice that didn't match the beleaguered look on her face.

"How have you been doing since the kickoff meeting?"

"I'm miserable working in this lunatic asylum," Jan blurted out. "I've never seen anything like what's happening here, and nothing I do makes a bit of difference."

"Wow. Sounds bad. What's going on?" I wanted to know.

Jan recounted the story of the new nurse who had been threatened. "I have her resignation letter right here on my desk. The bullies on the unit won again," Jan said angrily. "And this is the tip of the iceberg. I've lost every single new nurse I've hired since I took this job 18 months ago. I'm not sure why I'm staying. My husband and friends all tell me to quit, but I've never given up on anything in my life."

"Sounds like there's a lot more to the story than this latest incident," I suggested.

"My first week on the job I was handed an employee file by the person who keeps track of time and attendance. She told me 'You need to suspend this employee today because she's been late too many times'. I didn't have a clue how to do that then, but I'm damn good at it now.

"It's been one battle after another trying to clean up this mess," Jan told me as she began to spill her heart. "A few days ago I was called into a meeting with a unit clerk and her union representative because the clerk was refusing to file any of the paperwork. 'It's not my job', she was insisting, because her job description didn't specifically mention filing duties. 'Not my job' is standing operating procedure on the unit."

Jan was on a roll now, "In fact, I had to have HR change the job description for the housekeeping staff. They were refusing to strip the beds when the sheets needed changing. The housekeepers demanded that the RNs do it because they said that their job description stated they were only required to 'make the bed'. These people are crazy. The inmates are running the asylum!

"Those are a few examples of the 'just say no' culture," Jan continued. "Not long ago the techs refused to clean any equipment the physicians used because they thought the doctors should clean up after themselves.

"The issues with staff members never end. Last week I got called in the middle of the night because there was an argument with a patient's family member," Jan told me. "A husband had put a tray of food out in the hallway because it was making his wife, who was in labor, nauseous. Her nurse stormed into the room and demanded to know who had placed the food in the hallway. The man tried to explain why he'd done it, but the nurse made him go pick up the tray and take it down the hall to the place it was supposed to go.

"When the couple complained, I was told by HR to fire the nurse. But I was the one who took heat from the rest of the nurses for not defending their friend," Jan raved on. "I tried to talk to the nurses about the importance of patient satisfaction, but they tell me, 'The patients should count themselves lucky we're here, otherwise nobody would be taking care of them'. A group of them even went to HR to file a complaint against me for being unfair and firing that nurse for no good reason. Thankfully HR already knew the real story.

"And the craziness has spilled over to the doctors as well," Jan fumed. "When we were preparing for the Joint Commission inspection, I took the patients names off the doors to their rooms to comply with HIPAA requirements. One of the gynecologists stormed into my office and screamed that I was creating an unsafe patient environment because she couldn't tell who was in which room without checking at the nurse's station first."

Jan's face was beet red. "I can't take this much longer. My heart races. My temper flares. I'm working as many as 80 hours some weeks, bringing in food, even picking up staff members in my four-wheel drive during snowstorms. But all I get in return are complaints and criticism. I've tried going to Karin, but she won't back me up. She's been friends with a lot of the senior staff members for years and has been letting them get away with this crap. Now I understand why the nurse manager who was here for 5 years before me gave up and let staff members do whatever they wanted.

"I have to say I'm confused about how being positive could possibly change the outrageously negative people on my staff," Jan asserted. "In the beginning, I tried to be positive with them; but they literally laughed in my face and continued to do whatever they want. I can't tolerate what they're doing."

"Of course not," I agreed. "And I'm curious how much of your time and energy these problem people are absorbing?"

"Ooohhh… almost all of it," Jan sighed. "I spend 80–90 percent of my day dealing with this crap. But what's worse is that I spend the same percentage of my personal time worrying about what else will go wrong and how I'll be blamed for it. That's mostly what my husband and I talk about. It's what I dream about while I'm tossing and turning at night."

"That doesn't leave much time or energy for the positive people on your staff," I pointed out. "You do have some of those, right?"

"A few, but a lot of the good nurses have left because they don't want to work in this kind of toxic environment," Jan said ruefully.

"But there are some good nurses remaining who have a positive attitude with their patients and coworkers?" I inquired.

"Yes, but I still don't get how this positive approach will make any difference in dealing with the serious problems this unit is facing," Jan professed.

"Change is possible. I spent a year studying a hospital that was able to go from struggling to successful," I explained. "In fact, they became one of the top 100 hospitals in the country. One of the first things I learned was how important it is to have a vision of the future that you're passionate about achieving. Would you be willing to think about what a positive outcome would look like if our working together was wildly successful?"

"Sure," Jan said doubtfully.

"Thanks. That will be your homework for this week. My homework will be to prepare an explanation of how this PROPEL positive psychology initiative might help you create a high-functioning unit." And with that, our first coaching session came to a close.

## Jan's Second Coaching Session

"I'm embarrassed by the numbers you're going to see," Jan blurted out as we began talking. "I've been trying to improve the unit, really I have; but the patient and staff satisfaction numbers keep going down. What's wrong? Why are things getting worse?"

"I believe you've been working hard," I acknowledged. "You're like the new sheriff in town who has to clean out the bad guys. And after what I heard last week, you've had some seriously poor performing employees. But I have little to offer beyond what the other experts have told you to do regarding the disciplinary process. What I suggest is that you make those meetings as short as possible. You're spending almost all your time dealing with employees who have a low potential for improving your unit. Can you picture yourself abbreviating your approach?"

"You betcha, I can. I hate sitting in my office listening to staff members try to justify their bad behavior. And when I try to tell them why what they did was wrong, it ends up in an ugly confrontation. Are you telling me that I should just give them the paperwork to sign, explain their infraction and the consequence, and be done with it?" Jan ask.

"Has the other approach worked?" I queried.

"No, in fact it makes it worse because both the employee and I end up getting upset," Jan admitted.

"Then find the shortest possible method for dealing with disciplinary issues that HR will allow. Now, let's move on to our agenda," I suggested. "Did you do your homework about what it would look like around here if this PROPEL initiative worked wonders?"

"I've been thinking about it. I remember when I was a new nurse in another hospital and how much I loved working with those people. I had a wonderful preceptor who took me under her wing and taught me how to be great nurse. She taught me that the patient always comes first, not the computer or the supplies or the other staff members. Pay attention to what the patients tell you so you'll know what they need to get better, she told me. I learned to recognize when a patient started to deteriorate.

"Once I knew what I was doing," she added, "I was able to help other nurses working in rooms next to mine when they got overwhelmed. It was amazing how good it felt when we helped each other out. In fact, at the end of our shift we'd all walk out together because we made sure everyone's patients were taken care of before anyone left. That was the best time of the day. We told one another how much we appreciated getting help with Mr. Jones or Mrs. Smith."

"Can you picture your staff members learning to do those things?" I ask.

"No!" Jan quickly retorted.

"Take a deep breath…and now another…and now close your eyes," I suggested. "Use your imagination to create a mental picture. Let your mind's eye see the look on the faces of the best nurses you have working here if, somehow, they were able to experience that feeling that comes from expressing gratitude while walking out together. Just imagine it."

Jan relaxed for a moment, then fired off. "Okay, I guess I can do that. But what's the point? It'll never happen with these people!"

"This exercise is for you, not your staff members. Picturing a positive outcome will shift your brain away from fight–flight–freeze reactions. And that opens the door to creativity, positive emotions, planning capabilities, faith, and much more," I explained.

"Will this help me manage my stress?" Jan wanted to know. "It's exhausting me. I throw up before every staff meeting because I know I'll hear a barrage of complaints. My heart feels like it's going to pound out of my chest whenever I have to discipline someone. I dread having to listen to how unfair I'm being."

"When you picture those negative outcomes, your brain fires off stress chemicals such as adrenalin and cortisol," I explained, "which ramps you up for a fight and keeps you on edge for hours as you ruminate over an issue. Your vagus nerve extends down from your brain to your heart, stomach, and gut, which is why your body reacts as well. When you picture a positive outcome, your brain says 'everything looks like it'll be okay, so no need to keep producing stress chemicals'. Besides, when you imagine what might happen in the future, you're making it up. So, you might as well make it up with a happy ending. If nothing else, it'll make you feel better."

"But just thinking about a positive outcome won't make it so," Jan fretted. "There's only one of me and 150 of them."

"Correct," I concurred. "That's why you need an alliance with your PROPEL team."

"So, I'm supposed to start working with my most positive people to change the staff's behavior? The bullies have sabotaged everything I've tried to do, so why would this be any different?" Jan wondered aloud.

"Think about how the bullies have remained in control," I said. "Their hostility brings everybody on the unit down. Your top people have been tucking their tails between their legs, and you've been ignoring your best staff members. What would happen if you spent most of your time working with a PROPEL team—a small group of staff members who are dedicated to changing L&D? If a handful of your most negative staff members can tip the majority into a downward spiral, isn't it possible that a group of highly engaged staff members could spark a positive upward spiral?"

## Focus Group Feedback

The following week Jan received the focus group results. The staff members had relayed many of the same horror stories that Jan had shared and had come to a disturbing conclusion: "The staff is extremely dissatisfied with the disrespect among coworkers and disregard for patient needs. And they blame you, Jan."

"But I'm the one who's been working 60–80 hours a week to deal with the problems! How can they blame me? I'm trying to put an end to what's been going on for years—starting long before I got here." Jan was in disbelief.

I empathized with Jan's predicament and suggested that PROPEL offered a radical new approach to what she had been doing. But Jan was in a state of shock and muttered something about getting out of there and going home.

"Here's my cell number," I said, handing Jan my business card. "Please call me so I can help you with your reaction to this news."

## Jan's Moment of Truth

The next day Jan called me: "Tom, I'm not coming into work today, and I'm not sure that I'll be coming back at all." I could hear the despair in Jan's voice. The news had been devastating; after working for nearly 2 years to turn around the performance on the L&D unit that she managed, nearly everyone on her staff was unhappy with her and the workplace.

Jan was painfully aware that she, too, had become increasingly unhappy in her job. She had tried hard to straighten out the serious problems she had inherited. Now she was discovering that despite giving it everything she had, even the "good" nurses were profoundly dissatisfied and many had disengaged from trying to make their unit work well.

This was the moment of truth for Jan. She was sorely tempted to give up and allow her negative emotions to prevail. Fear had stricken her heart as she faced the most serious challenge of her career. The fight–flight–freeze reactions hardwired in her brain were in overdrive, churning up her most negative emotions—anger, anxiety, and even depression.

As our conversation continued, she lamented, "I had no choice but to take on the role of the tough new sheriff in town over the last couple of years. It was the only way to get some semblance of control over the situation. I couldn't put patients at risk by allowing the outrageous behavior of certain staff members to continue." She was right, of course.

"Jan, I've seen how other healthcare leaders used PROPEL strategies to achieve incredible improvements," I assured her. "The only guaranteed way for us to fail is to quit now. What would the preceptor in your first job tell you to do at this moment?"

"She'd tell me to try another approach," Jan replied.

"And if you succeed, it will be the defining moment of your career," I offered.

"I don't know...," Jan said uncertainly.

"Of course you don't. But you have a vision that you're passionate about and you're a persistent person. That combination of passion and perseverance is called 'grit' by positive psychologists, and it's the best predictor of who will succeed," I suggested.

After a long silence, Jan responded, "I'll try."

"And you won't be feeling you're in this alone anymore," I assured her. "The kickoff meeting allowed your biggest and best supporters to come together to create a shared vision of the outcome you are all passionate about achieving. This select group of your most positive people is ready to work with you to figure out how to turn things around on your unit using the PROPEL Principles. And Carol pledged to put an end to giving people a pass if they break the rules."

## The PROPEL Initiative

Over the next few months, I met with Jan and the staff members who had volunteered to be on the PROPEL team. Team members would choose someone to be their "buddy" for the shift. By infusing a high number of positive interactions, the team was able to win over one coworker at a time. They would help someone out with patients and provide positive reinforcement to that individual when they reciprocated.

After several months, there were many staff members who had joined forces with the PROPEL team. They asked Jan to put up white boards they could use to publicly share their "kudos" for the assistance they received during their shift. And when the next shift arrived, rather than hearing how horrible it had been on the unit, they saw how terrific the staff members had been at living their values of CTP (camaraderie, teamwork, and professionalism).

The PROPEL team continued to create a culture of high performance in weekly meetings as they discussed progress and setbacks. They learned from both positive and negative experiences, and continued to collaborate to find a way for their unit to implement each of the PROPEL Principles:

- Each member of the PROPEL team spoke to one or two of the most positive coworkers about CTP. They shared their vision of how staff members could work together to generate enough positivity to overcome the negative voices on the unit. They recruited their most engaged colleagues, eliciting their ideas and support to build and broaden the *Passion* necessary to ultimately prevail.
- The PROPEL team made specific requests to their hesitant (read disengaged) coworkers to increase the amount of positive interactions over the number of negative exchanges to improve *Relationships*.

■ As the number of people committed to creating positive relationships grew, small groups gathered to discuss problems that popped up during a shift. The PROPEL team had learned how to instill *Optimistic* thinking into these conversations, directing colleagues away from blaming coworkers and focusing on what to do to change the situation.

■ The PROPEL team became big fans of using their strengths. They clung to their chart showing the results of the strengths test they had all taken. The group loved knowing their own best qualities, as well as those of the teammates. When the problem-solving discussions determined a solution to a problem, they pulled out their strengths chart to see who might be best suited to *Proactively* take the lead in making things better.

■ The PROPEL team established a routine for lunch breaks so staff members could maintain the *Energy* all the way to the end a 12-hour shift (precisely when most mistakes and negative outbursts had been occurring).

■ Jan began "staff satisfaction rounds" to catch people doing things right. She would emphasize how people were creating their *Legacy* by practicing CTP behaviors. She expressed gratitude to staff members for the meaningful difference they had made by helping a coworker. And she was especially appreciative when a staff member improved a patient's experience.

## The Results

Eighteen months later, Carol and I attended the hospital's annual award ceremony. Jan was accepting an award for the most improvement of any unit in the hospital. Since beginning to use the six PROPEL positive psychology principles to improve performance, the L&D unit had achieved a total transformation in its workplace culture. It was with great pride that I sat in that huge auditorium listening to the CNO describing the terrific turnaround in L&D that was being recognized in the hospital's annual award ceremony.

Jan had become a highly regarded leader in this prestigious medical center. As she walked up to the podium to receive the glass trophy for the vast improvements her units had been able to attain, she exuded confidence. What a change from that day when she almost gave up because she felt completely inadequate to take on the challenges she was facing. When she turned to face the audience, her staff members stood and cheered wildly. It was the first of many triumphant moments that Jan would experience over the next few years.

After the applause died down, Jan credited her staff members as the people responsible for achieving the remarkable results. She told the audience, "While the numbers are impressive on the various measures that indicate how well our unit is doing when it comes to taking care of patients, the most notable change is how well we've learned to take care of one another."

Jan reflected back 2 years to a time when she had trouble getting the nurses to post their pictures on the board at the entrance to the unit because they did not even want to be identified as working with a group that had such a bad reputation. "Now my problem is that every time a nurse gets her hairstyle changed she wants a new picture to replace the old one!" The audience laughed, and Jan went on to say, "This was but one indicator of the tremendous amount of CTP that is displayed on our unit these days.

"My life has changed tremendously as well," Jan shared. "A couple of years ago, I was spending 80–90 percent of my time in disciplinary discussions with poor performing staff members. Today, my job is better because I'm able to spend 80–90 percent of my time catching people doing things right and giving them the recognition and rewards they deserve. I leave most days feeling terrific about my job, which makes my husband and kids much happier to see me when I get home.

"It was learning to use PROPEL—six positive psychology principles—that enabled my unit to make this massive transformation," Jan told the audience. "I worked with a PROPEL coach to overcome the devastating impact the negative people had been inflicting."

Jan spoke of how her professional life was transformed through the coaching conversations. "Those discussions helped me personally; I discovered how I could stop the downward spiral of negative reactions that overwhelmed me at times. I found it's possible to stay focused on the important positive outcomes I'm passionate about achieving." Her voice cracked a bit as she said, "Being clear and committed to living my values was a crucial first step that led me to this stage today. I no longer let anyone pull me into their downward spirals.

"I learned how to work with the most positive people on my staff to combine our efforts to gain control of the culture on our unit. That strategy works incredibly well," she said as she illuminated her PowerPoint presentation.

Jan ran through a sampling of results she and her staff members had achieved, starting with an overview of the improvements (as shown in Figure 5.1). "As you can see, we've made some impressive gains."

| SURVEY RESULTS | COST CONTAINMENT |
|---|---|
| • Employee Satisfaction Scores | • Agency Staff Expenses |
| • Employee Engagement Scores | • Sick Leave/Call Out/FMLA |
| • Patient Satisfaction Scores | • Call in of Staff on Standby |
| • Quality of Patient Care Scores | • Turn Over/New Staff Orientation |
| • Teamwork Scores (RN-RN and RN-MD) | • Patient Safety Problems |

**Figure 5.1   Overview of PROPEL study results.**

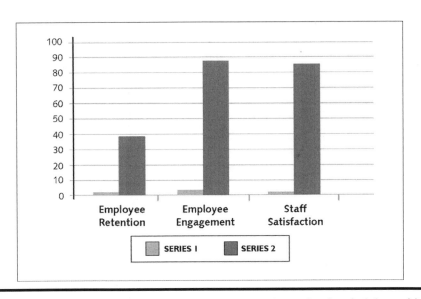

**Figure 5.2   Organizational climate assessment. (Independently administered by the Jackson Organization/HealthStream Research.)**

"Our Staff Satisfaction Scores," Jan's next slide (shown in Figure 5.2) revealed, "have risen 84 percentile points in an independently administered pre- and postsurvey. When my staff members were first surveyed, they were at the lowest possible level," Jan confessed. "They were flatlined at 1 percentile compared to units in the national database of hospitals. One year later," Jan told the crowd, "you can see that the scores on our unit have risen to the 85th percentile."

"What is especially gratifying," Jan disclosed, "goes beyond getting good numbers. It's seeing the smiles on the faces of my staff members when I walk through the unit. There's a palpable difference that I can feel in my heart," she said as she looked directly at the staff members in the audience. They jumped to their feet and broke into applause, demonstrating the degree to which they shared Jan's feelings.

"Employee Engagement Scores," Jan's pre- and post-test slide demonstrated, "have also risen, jumping from the 3rd percentile to the 87th. The PROPEL coaches had predicted this was likely to happen based on prior studies showing that increases in staff satisfaction are a prerequisite for improved employee engagement—but I never thought this level of improvement was possible."

Jan said what had surprised her most about staff engagement was that it was not a result of an agenda she was driving. Instead, the coaches had helped the staff members discover how to tap into their own intrinsic motivation to make the units work well.

"Staff Retention Rates soared as well," she said. "As you can see in the pre- to post-test results, the needle moved from the 1st percentile to the 49th. I must confess, it's embarrassing to show that initially nearly everyone wanted to transfer off my unit. It was particularly heartbreaking to lose 100 percent of the new graduates who spent their first year on my unit. I'm proud to tell you that our PROPEL team has improved our retention rate for new nurse grads from 0 to 80 percent.

"I used to dread getting the results of my Staff Satisfaction and Engagement Survey," Jan confessed. "But this year," she said as she put up the next graphic (shown in Figure 5.3), "you can see that our L&D unit has achieved scores significantly above units in the rest of the hospital on the Gallup Q12.

"Our Patient Satisfaction Scores," Jan continued, "have taken an upswing as the culture on our unit has become more positive." Her next slide (shown in Figure 5.4)

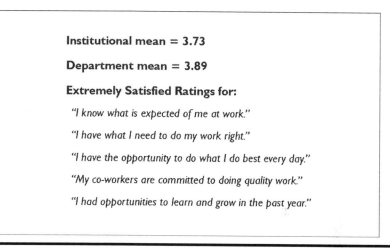

**Institutional mean = 3.73**

**Department mean = 3.89**

**Extremely Satisfied Ratings for:**

*"I know what is expected of me at work."*

*"I have what I need to do my work right."*

*"I have the opportunity to do what I do best every day."*

*"My co-workers are committed to doing quality work."*

*"I had opportunities to learn and grow in the past year."*

**Figure 5.3    Gallup Q12 results.**

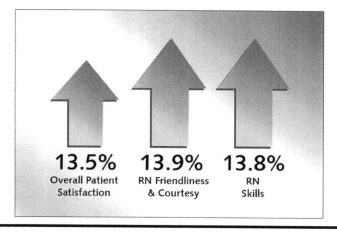

**13.5%**
Overall Patient
Satisfaction

**13.9%**
RN Friendliness
& Courtesy

**13.8%**
RN
Skills

**Figure 5.4    Patient satisfaction scores.**

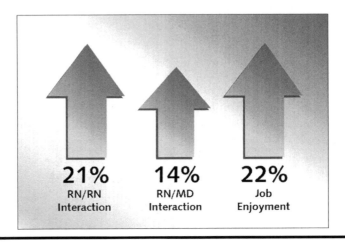

**Figure 5.5   NDNQI scores.**

provided the evidence. "At the end of the 1-year PROPEL engagement, our Press Ganey surveys showed patient satisfaction up 13–14 percent on average."

"Amazingly, the patient satisfaction on our unit has continued to rise almost every month even after the PROPEL coaches left and the study ended. We're approaching a 50 percent improvement in our patient satisfaction scores since we first started using the PROPEL Principles.

"Nursing Quality Indicators have also taken a significant uptick," Jan pointed out in her next slide (shown in Figure 5.5). "I'm particularly pleased that our National Database of Nursing Quality Indicators® (NDNQI) scores involving teamwork among our nurses and with the physicians have shown significant improvement.

"Increasing Camaraderie, Teamwork, and Professionalism," Jan explained, "was the outcome the leaders and the top performing staff wanted to achieve at the start of the PROPEL study. The metrics I've shown you are proof that learning to use the PROPEL Principles enabled us to work as a team to realize the vision we created at the outset. It is one thing to sit in a training session to learn about teamwork," Jan asserted, "and quite a different experience to have a coach at your side helping you implement the lessons."

"Our Patient Safety Metrics improved, as would be predicted by the upward shift in the quality of care indicators," Jan explained. She flashed another slide (shown in Figure 5.6) showing the results of the most recent Patient Safety Survey. "Job satisfaction once again was the leading indicator of change, followed by improved relationships among staff members." Jan added, "One of the biggest lessons I've learned is the importance of getting those pieces in place to improve the safety climate, which enabled our unit to achieve success in an area we'd been struggling with for years.

"The result," Jan proudly reported, "was that preventable complications following surgery dropped by almost 60 percent. Our staff members' attitude about adhering to the safety protocols is dramatically different, and that's led

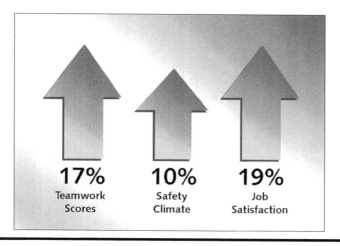

**17%**
Teamwork
Scores

**10%**
Safety
Climate

**19%**
Job
Satisfaction

**Figure 5.6   Patient safety survey scores.**

to significant improvements in patient safety." Jan described how PROPEL had changed her focus, "Rather than trying to hold the staff members accountable for following the patient safety guidelines, I've learned how to help them become 'countable'. Their new attitude has become 'you can count on me to do my part'. It's much more effective, I've discovered, to cultivate inner motivation. That's what drives staff members to want to see improvements in the patient safety statistics every month.

"Cost Containment is always a challenge," Jan told the assembly. "But all the improvements our unit made helped me stay within my budget for the first time," Jan proudly announced as she showed her last slide (shown in Figure 5.7) illustrating how many expenses she had been able to control on a yearly basis.

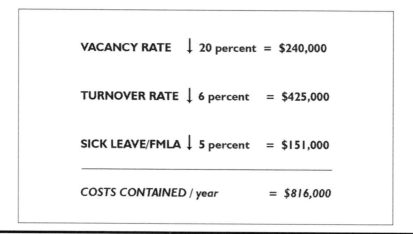

VACANCY RATE   ↓ 20 percent  = $240,000

TURNOVER RATE ↓ 6 percent   = $425,000

SICK LEAVE/FMLA ↓ 5 percent   = $151,000

COSTS CONTAINED / year      = $816,000

**Figure 5.7   Cost containment.**

Jan told the audience, "I've nearly eliminated the use of agency nurses, saving me $20,000 every month. By retaining almost all of the new nurse graduates, I'm no longer incurring the $58,000 in turnover expenses that the *Journal of Nursing Administration* calculates it costs to replace one nurse. The most surprising number, I must tell you, is the dramatic reduction in the use of sick leave and family leave. Because I have far less need to call other staff members into work when their colleagues call out, I not only save money but also avoid the hassle of having to call in someone from a day off. That's contributed to a substantial increase in the well-being of my staff members."

Jan concluded her comments that day by saying, "I don't know how to calculate what having a healthier staff is worth in financial terms, but my personal payoff for seeing my staff's well-being skyrocket is a heart filled with joy."

After the ceremony, a long line of leaders were eager to learn more about the PROPEL Principles. Jan had copies of the one-page overview (shown in Figure 5.8) that she had pinned up near the computer in her office. "This is what I refer to when I ask myself what to do when a challenge flares up on the unit."

To increase **Passion** for creating positive results, ask questions designed to create both a long-term vision and short term solutions:

> "*What would make working here a great experience for you?*"
> "*What would a positive outcome to this immediate problem look like?*"

To create **Relationships** that are collaborative, ask:

> "*What ideas do you have for making teamwork really terrific?*"
> "*Who could you turn to for support to help you deal with this problem?*"

To improve **Optimism**, ask:

> "*How can our unit more consistently perform at its best?*"
> "*What's made us good at solving this kind of problem in the past?*"

To teach people to be **Proactive** rather than reactive, ask:

> "*What's the most important action we could take to improve your unit?*"
> "*What's the first step to take to move toward a positive outcome?*"

To generate **Energy** among the staff, ask:

> "*What could we do to take better care of each other?*"
> "*What helps you rejuvenate yourself when you're at home?*"

To understand the **Legacy** each individual wants to leave, ask:

> "*What would make a meaningful difference in how we treat patients?*"
> "*What would you like to do to make your job more fulfilling?*"

**Figure 5.8 The PROPEL Principles. (Courtesy of Dr. Tom Muha, The PROPEL Institute, www.PROPELinstitute.com.)**

# Chapter 6

## Devolving before Evolving: How to Command-and-Control Staff into Anger and Apathy

### A Nurse Manager at War with Her Staff

She was late, but at least she showed up. Maureen, the nurse manager of the Women's Services inpatient unit, had missed several of our scheduled meetings since the kick-off meeting. "I sit on a lot of important committees," she explained, "so I'm always running at full speed trying to stay on top of the responsibilities I have. And now my boss wants me to meet with you." The disdain was palpable.

Maureen moved a pile of papers from the chair next to her desk so I'd have a place to sit. There were so many stacks of documents crowding her small office that it felt a bit claustrophobic. She logged onto her computer and continued her rant.

"I've worked here for over 20 years and have seen a lot of consultants come and go. Nothing they've suggested has ever worked," she informed me while perusing e-mails.

I sat quietly, praying my calm presence would be contagious.

Maureen leaned back in her chair to take a hard look at me, arms crossed. "I don't believe in coddling staff members," she continued. "They get a paycheck. That should be plenty of 'positive reinforcement'." She stretched out those last two words, making little quotation signs with her fingers. "Don't you think?" She tipped back farther in her chair.

I glanced at the coffee mug on Maureen's desk; white with bold black letters that read, "Tough times never last, but tough people do." Her gruff voice pulled my gaze back to her face.

"I know why you're here," she tapped her desk. "I know I've got a lot of travel nurses on this floor, and I know they cost the hospital more money. But I'm not the reason people keep leaving. We're dealing with 'cancer patients' here!" She was close to shouting now. "Some nurses can't cut it!"

Maureen was sidestepping the larger issues. Carol, her director, had explained to me that the travel nurses on Maureen's unit (hired via a staffing agency on a temporary basis) were costing the hospital 20 percent more in payroll. "But the bigger problem," Carol said, "was that it was costing the hospital $58,000 to replace each nurse—and nearly half of the RNs on Maureen's unit had quit." Carol was also concerned that with travelers comprising half of the staff members, there was bound to be a negative clinical impact. "As talented as any travel nurse may be," Carol had explained, "he or she will never be as invested in the organization as a full-time permanent staff nurse. Assignments are usually short (13 weeks is the norm), and then its home (which can be the other side of the country) or off to another assignment."

Because she had so many vacancies, Maureen had only a thin core of regular staff members who had a rapport with the physicians and pharmacists (essential to patient care), familiarity with the floor's computer software system (essential to patient safety), any depth of knowledge about the organization as a whole (essential to efficiency), and any sense of long-term dedication to their jobs (essential to a strong bottom line).

In talking to the remaining full-time staff members, I found they were fatigued by the steady stream of new faces and personalities coming and going on the unit. They were expected to orient the temporary staffers, cutting into the time they had to care for patients–which further increased their stress. In addition, they were demoralized by Maureen's command-and-control style of management, which was the *real* reason the unit had trouble recruiting and keeping nurses.

"Before you arrived for the end of the kickoff meeting, your staff members had spent a lot of time discussing what your unit would look like if they were able to function at their best," I responded, trying to refocus the conversation to a more positive topic. "The staff's description of what they believe it will take to remedy the situation provides some important insights. Let's review it:"

> We will start our shift with a quick huddle to remind ourselves that we're here to make a difference in the lives of our cancer patients. We will regularly check in with one another to ask "how are you doing?" and "how can I help?" And at the end of our shift our manager will join us in

appreciating the good work we've done to help our patients and coworkers. We will have weekly meetings in the conference room with our manager to respectfully discuss problems that occur and we'll work together to develop a plan to prevent those problems from occurring in the future.

"Yeah, yeah, yeah. Do you know how many 'vision statements' I've heard? This is part of this game you consultants play: 'think positive and it will happen'," Maureen chortled. "But nothing ever happens!"

"You sound amused 'and' angry," I ventured.

"Damn right. This is a waste of my time. I'm already working 70 hours a week. Frankly, I don't have time for this power of positive thinking BS," she stated emphatically.

"You're obviously working hard, and you're clearly frustrated with the other programs that Carol has tried. I get that." I paused to see Maureen's reaction. She looked at her phone to see her latest message.

I tried offering a new perspective: "That's why we're going to be doing something fundamentally different than what you've experienced. PROPEL involves staff members as partners in helping to figure out how to accomplish the goals that Carol has established."

Maureen looked up, her face twisted in anger. "The day I need staff members to tell me what to do is the day I resign."

Her aggressive reaction felt like a slap across the face. I was stunned.

"I have a committee meeting in 5 minutes, Doctor; so I need to be on my way," Maureen said as she stood and opened the door.

"I'll see you next week," I said while trying to muster as much of a positive tone as I could.

## Circling Back to Carol

I worked my way through the maze of hallways leading to Carol's office. I was still wrestling with my first exchange with Maureen. But I now understood the feedback I'd heard from the focus groups with her staff members. They told story after story about exchanges with Maureen that left them feeling humiliated, dismissed, and utterly disrespected.

"Carol, you've mentioned several times that you've been talking to Maureen about participating in PROPEL. How's that going?" I inquired.

"I've spoken with her twice since we last met. I told her in no uncertain terms exactly what I expect her to do," Carol told me. "Why do you ask?"

"Because I ran into a 'buzz saw' when we met. As you know, Maureen arrived so late at the kickoff meeting that she missed the opportunity to understand the staff's perspective on how to solve their unit's vacancy problem. And when I tried to discuss the possibility of aligning Maureen's thoughts for rectifying the situation with her staff's vision, she made it perfectly clear she distrusts consultants, particularly those who want to encourage staff members to participate in finding ways to help make changes on their unit," I lamented.

"Maureen has not always been this way," Carol explained. "When we were staff nurses starting out together, she was one of the most compassionate people I knew. And I know she still cares deeply about patient care; that's why she gets so upset with staff members when patients complain. I'm really hoping you'll be able to help her; she needs to reclaim her positive attitude."

"It sounds like you care about Maureen; you've been colleagues and friends for a long time," I empathized. "Maureen cares about the patient's well-being. But she also needs to care as much about her staff's well-being—and her own for that matter. That is going to be essential to retaining the staff members she's got left, much less recruiting new nurses," I maintained.

"Yes, that's true," Carol acknowledged. "That's what makes this so difficult. I'm trying to help Maureen get back to being that caring person she used to be. I've tried everything I know to get her unit's problems under control. I'm losing sleep over it."

Carol shook her head. "I think Maureen has 'compassion fatigue'. She's putting in long days, sitting on too many committees, and rushing all over the hospital. She isn't herself these days. I've worked with her for a long time and I know she can do better. I've tried to get her to slow down, cut back, and get more rest so she can take a positive approach with her staff members."

"You're a very loyal friend, and loyalty is a good value to have," I empathized. "And you have other loyalties—to the hospital, to the staff members on the cancer unit, and to the patients. The situation with Maureen involves competing values, creating conflicts for you with the C-Suite, the staff, and Maureen. You're trying to exert as much influence as you can to correct the situation, but it's hard to control other people. They need to be willing to change. People need to have intrinsic motivation as well as external incentives."

"Going forward," I continued, "how could you try to help Maureen find a reason within herself to be willing to learn to take better care of herself and her staff members? On the flip side of the coin, how could you help her staff members be willing to work on changing the culture on their unit rather than resigning—literally as well as figuratively?"

"I know what you're saying is true," Carol affirmed. "I need to take less responsibility for trying to encourage Maureen to change her life and her leadership style. I've got to make it clear that it's her choice, her responsibility to maintain a work–life balance. Either she wants to learn what it's going to take to stay in her role or we're going to have to find another position that suits her."

## Maureen's Second Coaching Session

"Tell me more about your busy schedule," I asked as soon as Maureen invited me to her crowded office.

She was quiet as she moved the ever-present pile of papers off the chair beside her desk. Seemingly exhausted by the task, she plopped down into her chair with a heavy sigh. "I'm usually here for the change of shift at 7:00 a.m. and stay through report at 7:00 p.m. In between, I have meetings scheduled nearly every hour. Then I go home and answer the e-mails I wasn't able to respond to during the day."

"How many days a week do you do that?" I asked sympathetically.

"That's my Monday-to-Friday schedule. Saturdays and sometimes Sundays I come in to catch up with payroll, scheduling, committee reports, and all of the other work Carol asks me to do," Maureen said proudly.

"So, that means you're working at least 70 hours a week?" I inquired.

"Yes," she said, "I'm one of the senior nurse managers and I have to set an example for other nurses who are coming up through the ranks. Besides, all that running around keeps me energized. You're asking my staff members what enables them to be at their best. Well, for me it's helping this place run as close to perfect as possible."

"Don't you get exhausted working that much?" I wanted to know.

"I don't believe that you can be successful without having stress," Maureen shot back. "Hospitals are fast-paced places, and you have to put yourself into overdrive to stay ahead of the game. People recognize me as an expert, which is why they want me in so many committees. They know I have the answers. Besides, I don't require as much sleep as other people; 5 hours a night is fine for me."

"Sounds like you're really dedicated," I reflected. "Do you have any time to enjoy your personal life?"

"I'm married to my job," she quipped while checking messages on her phone.

"Any good marriage requires having some fun so you can enjoy the relationship and be able to work well as partners. What do you do to rejuvenate yourself?" I probed.

"I don't have time to 'rejuvenate'," she fired back. "It's all I can do to stay on top of things now. If I slack off, imagine what would happen. The staff screws up far too often as it is. I have to keep a close eye on them for the sake of the patients. I'm tough," she asserted holding up her coffee mug emblazoned with her mantra: "Tough times never last, but tough people do."

"Have you always been this tough?" I questioned.

"No. I had to learn the hard way what happens if you're not tough. Mistakes happen. It's my job to make sure that they don't," she stated emphatically, her eyes blazing now.

"Has the number of mistakes gone down the tougher you've become?" I tested.

Maureen looked stricken. "They've been going up. But you can't blame that on me. I work harder than any other nurse manager here. It's this millennial generation. They don't care as much about their work as people from my generation."

"I believe that you do care deeply about the patients' welfare, and I'm convinced you have to be the hardest working nurse manager in the hospital," I offered.

As calmly as I could, I told Maureen, "One finding on effective leaders is that they take care of themselves so they have good energy for taking care of their staff members. Imagine what might happen if you took more time to take care of yourself. Would you be able to relate better with the staff members? Would they, in turn, be better able to take care of the patients?"

"They don't pay me to take care of myself. They pay me to take care of patients," Maureen retorted.

I made a request: "Notice what happens as your week wears on and the number of hours you've worked accumulates. Monitor your energy level and how that correlates with the number of negative interactions you have with staff members. Would you agree to keep track of that?"

"Whatever. Carol keeps telling me I have to do this, so that's what I'll do," Maureen managed to say without the slightest hint of sincerity.

"Being able to engage in positive conversations with staff members could have real benefits. For example, there's some recent research on how creating a culture of psychological safety has been shown to improve patient safety?"

"I knew you'd be like the other consultants. You're going to pin the patient safety problems on me because I haven't created a safe culture!" she shouted.

"This isn't about blaming anyone. It's about changing the behaviors of everyone involved in the situation so that the problems are resolved. Doing more of the same and expecting a different result is making everyone crazy," I responded firmly. "Do you agree that developing some new teamwork behaviors that would allow everyone on your unit—including you—to work more collaboratively could help to achieve a positive outcome?"

Maureen sat silently, arms crossed, staring me down.

"This is who I am, DOCTOR Muha," Maureen sneered. "I will always try my hardest to protect the patients. And if that means I have to work 75 hours a week to keep an eye on the staff members, then so be it. I've had to be tough, and I'm not about to change now."

"And yet the world around you is changing," I pointed out. "As you mentioned earlier, younger staff members are somewhat different than older workers. Millennials need a different kind of manager than the traditional generation."

Maureen had returned to silent mode.

"And it's possible for anyone to change," I continued. "In fact, look back at your career and remember the vast number of changes in technical skills that have occurred as a result of evidence-based nursing. You and your staff members have adopted those changes. The same principle applies to work relationships—there is a lot to be learned from the research regarding best practices for creating high-functioning teams."

"You can't teach an old dog new tricks. I have to get to my next meeting" was Maureen's curt reply.

## Meeting with Maureen's PROPEL Team

"What progress have you made toward the 'at your best' vision you developed at the kickoff meeting?" was the first question posed to the PROPEL team.

"We started having huddles in the morning, and we're trying to check in with one another. But it's tough when you're working with a bunch of travelers. They want to do their shift and get out of here so they can party," reported one of the younger nurses.

"And the part about leaving your shift expressing gratitude isn't working at all. Maureen shows up every afternoon to check on us and always, always, 'always' finds something wrong. And she thinks that berating someone at the nurses' station will make an example out of them, but all it does is make an ass out of her," another nurse bemoaned.

"It's demoralizing," one of the new nurse graduates said. "As soon as my 1 year commitment is up, I'm outta here."

"It sounds like it's really hard to sustain your energy for working on the unit when Maureen is constantly finding fault with your efforts," I empathized. "Each of you has said that your passion is taking care of women struggling with cancer. I wonder whether you could appreciate each other even though Maureen is so critical."

"It makes me so mad," a tech admitted. "She's so unfair, picking on anyone who's not one of her friends. Her buddies are the ones ratting us out to her. I got into a screaming match with one of them yesterday."

"As if taking care of cancer patients wasn't hard enough, having to work in this environment must make your jobs exceedingly difficult," I reflected. "What you're describing are the fight or flight reactions we all have in stressful situations. In fact, these reactions are hardwired into your brain. And along with them come negative emotions such as anger, anxiety, and despair."

"You're describing what it feels like around here when we're leaving at the end of our shift," a nurse remarked. The team laughed in recognition of their shared feelings.

"It doesn't have to stay that way," I suggested. "You don't have to stay stuck in your negative reactions."

"Maureen will never change," the tech stated flatly.

"Even if she doesn't, you can change," I explained. "You do 'not' have to remain stuck in your negative reactions." Positive psychology research tells us that generating many more positive statements to offset critical comments enables people to counterbalance their emotions in order to maintain a sense of well-being.

"Be aware that this approach won't work with the most negative people," I advised, "at least not right away. But think of the people—at home or at work—where you could explore what happens when you generate many more positive than negative interactions."

"But it's hard to do when you're being put down every day," confessed a senior nurse.

"You have to decide whether to let someone else determine your emotional state," I explained. "You can take this opportunity to define for yourselves what kind of relationships you want to have."

"But the staff on this unit does make mistakes. How will becoming more positive help with that problem?" asked the experienced nurse.

"Positivity is a prerequisite for creating solutions to problems, studies have shown. It provides the fuel necessary to keep working toward goals when you experience setbacks. Your experience working on this unit tells you that the opposite is true. Negativity has kept you stuck for years in a downward spiral," I observed.

"Maureen will detest this. She hates what she calls touchy-feely mumbo jumbo," one of the techs told me.

"You will need to shift from pessimistic thinking—'she will never change'—to optimistic explanations—'I can improve my situation'. Focus your mind on seeing possibilities rather than giving into feeling helpless and hopeless. And when you become proactive by doing something to move toward the solution you're envisioning, you'll feel empowered," I explained.

"Remember Gandhi's advice about how to effect change when facing a powerful force: 'Be the change you want to see in the world.' Are you committed to creating more positive relationships?" I asked.

"Yes," everyone on the PROPEL team agreed.

"Have we agreed that your homework between now and our next meeting will be to pick one or two people to concentrate on creating more positive than negative interactions?" I inquired.

"Yes" was the unanimous response.

## Maureen's Next Coaching Session

"Tell me about any progress you may have made by paying attention to your energy level," I requested.

"None" was her hasty reply. "I'm so busy rushing to back-to-back meetings and trying to get up to the unit that I don't have any time for 'awareness'," Maureen elongated the word. She was at her overcrowded desk checking e-mails as she spoke.

Trying again, I inquired, "Did you notice when confrontations with the staff members occurred during the last week?"

"Whenever they need it," she said harshly, pivoting in her chair. "This is an intense environment, and I'm an intense person. A perfect match, wouldn't you say?"

"You certainly seem to be tense, and your staff says they feel tense as well," I observed. "Do you think having this much tension is working for you or for them?" I probed.

Unaccustomed to this forthright approach, Maureen simply stared at me. Figuring I wasn't getting anywhere by tiptoeing around the issues, I continued: "You seem frustrated much of the time—and frequently angry. Your staff feels the same way. How is this negativity helping anyone? You? Staff? Patients? Your turnover rate has been increasing for years. What do you have to lose by trying to generate some positive energy with your staff members?"

"Tom," she said in the softest tone I'd ever heard her use, "you can't teach an old dog new tricks."

"There's another old saying that the research has proven to be more accurate: 'Whether you think you can, or you think you can't, you're right'," I countered. "People can develop new cognitive and behavioral capabilities that allow them to adapt to changing situations. Recent neuroscience research has shown it is possible to build new pathways in our brain at any age. The only thing that stops a person from learning something new is believing she can't."

"So, I'm supposed to let staff members get away with poor performance?" Maureen was becoming agitated again.

"Your approach is making matters 'worse'," I continued. "You're intensifying your efforts to control the situation by ramping up your negative reactions and expecting a different result. Working harder, feeling frustrated, and having angry outbursts is leaving you exhausted. When problems arise, you're too tired and mentally drained to respond well. Positive leadership practices, on the other hand, would have you replenishing your energy and engaging in collaborative problem solving. PROPEL is your opportunity to learn how to do that."

"I'm not the type of leader that will ever let the tail wag the dog," she insisted.

"Working with staff members is not abdicating your responsibilities. It's changing how you go about attaining the results. The only thing that's holding you back from learning new leadership skills is your belief that you can't," I protested.

"Well, this isn't some new age tech company where we can let employees do their jobs whenever they get around to it," Maureen insisted. "This is a hospital, and we need to control what our employees do to protect patients."

"Isn't it possible that both of our positions are true?" I suggested. "Of course, the hospital must meet the standards for providing patient care, so some controls must be in place. That doesn't preclude learning to use a positive leadership style to engage staff members in finding ways to achieve those outcomes."

"You've been working in this hospital for 2 months and I've been working here for over 25 years," Maureen retorted. "I know what I'm doing."

"Would you at least be willing to meet and listen to your staff's suggestions for improving the unit at their next meeting?" I asked.

"Carol tells me I have to."

Maureen never showed up for the meeting.

## The Moment of Truth

After several months of PROPEL team meetings, the staff members finally asked Carol to meet with them. My meetings with Carol had prepared her to face the possibility that her colleague of more than 25 years might be unwilling (although Maureen would say "unable") to change.

The PROPEL team had prepared well, and each person took a turn explaining their perspective to Carol:

> "We've been meeting regularly since the kickoff. Thanks for setting that up. Since then we've made real progress toward our vision."

> "We've learned that we can make our lives better. By creating many more positive exchanges for every negative encounter, our relationships are much happier—here as well as at home."

> "We've been having huddles at the start of our shifts to talk about what we can do to work more collaboratively."

> "We're helping each other much more than we did in the past when we all were doing our jobs on our own."

> "While we express appreciation to one another for the help we're receiving, the frequent criticism we receive from Maureen continues to make our unit a terrible place to work."

> "We live in fear of Maureen's angry reprimands, which she delivers in front of patients and the rest of the staff members."

> "We're continuing to lose good nurses because of Maureen's behavior, which means we have to spend a lot of our time orienting new people."

> "Precepting takes away time we could be spending with our patients."

> "We're not going to take it anymore. We know it doesn't have to be this way. We need your help."

Carol asked the staff members for more details. Two people reported incidents:

> "I had just finished hanging an IV bag for a patient when Maureen stopped me outside of a patient's room whose call bell was ringing. She started yelling at me in front of the other staff members and the patient. 'Are you deaf or just incompetent? How many times do I have to tell you to answer call bells IMMEDIATELY!' I started to cry; I was so humiliated. But that made Maureen even angrier. As she stormed off, she told me I wasn't cut out to work with cancer patients."

> "As a new nurse on the unit, I was assigned Susan as my preceptor. But Susan didn't teach me nursing skills for working with patients; instead she had me changing linen and doing paperwork. When I complained to Maureen, she told me that Susan was the best nurse on the unit, and insisted I was lucky to have been assigned to her. After that, whenever Maureen walked by Susan, she asked if I was 'cutting it'. I felt like I

had a target on my back. One of the other nurses had warned me not to complain because Maureen and Susan are best friends – they go on vacations together. I should have listened to her."

## Carol Confronts Maureen

"I met with your staff members and was disappointed to learn that they've seen little improvement in your behavior," Carol told Maureen. "I was particularly troubled to hear that you've continued to reprimand staff members in front of their coworkers. I've told you that is not acceptable."

"I don't know what you want from me," Maureen replied defensively. "I'm doing my best to deal with a staff that really doesn't want to work hard to provide good patient care."

"I've make it perfectly clear what I expect from you, as you saw many months ago when I put you on a formal performance improvement plan and provided a coach to help you achieve it. Since then you and I have had some heart to heart talks about whether you really are motivated to stay in the nurse manager role. Your behavior tells me that you need to move on to another position that doesn't involve managing staff members."

"I can't believe this," Maureen stammered, "after all these years…"

"I can't believe it's come to this either," responded Carol. "That's why I have gone to great lengths to secure another position for you in our research department. I do believe that this is in everyone's best interests, Maureen, including yours."

## The End of the Command and Control Era

Fast-forward to a happy ending for the staff members: Maureen's "my way or the highway" style landed *her* on the highway. Carol moved her into a nonmanagerial role and replaced her with a new nurse manager who had been a leader on the labor and delivery PROPEL team.

Using the same PROPEL plan that she'd seen work so well on Jan's unit, the newly minted manager worked collaboratively with the nursing staff. Along with the PROPEL team, they resolved the staffing issue and transformed the quality of patient care in a matter of months.

Maureen also was transformed. After about 6 months of working in the research department, she came to talk to Carol. The intensity and anger had disappeared. She admitted that having a nine-to-five job with less stress had been just what she needed. And she thanked Carol for helping her get into a position that enabled her to enjoy life again.

Maureen's story is a tragic example of how a good nurse can burn out after moving into an extraordinarily demanding leadership role. The research on how good people burn out—and what can be done to prevent it—is provided in the detailed descriptions of each PROPEL Principle found in Chapters 7 through 12.

# HOW TO PROPEL HIGH PERFORMANCE IN HOSPITALS

In Chapter 2, you learned about positive psychology—the science of optimal functioning. Now it's time to learn about how that research forms the foundation for each of the six PROPEL Principles. Each chapter also includes a story that illustrates actual challenges faced by leaders and their PROPEL teams. Although significant aspects have been modified to maintain confidentiality, the strategies used and the remarkable results are authentic.

Chapters 7 through 12 provide practical implementation instructions that will ensure you to:

- Rekindle *passion* for being your best as an individual, a team, and an organization.
- Develop *relationships* among top performers to positively influence your staff members.
- Think *optimistically* to remain resilient in the face of conflicts and setbacks.
- Become *proactive* to turn innovative ideas into action using your top strength traits.
- Sustain *energy* over the course of your day and your career.
- Leave a *legacy* by empowering others to make a meaningful difference.

The following figure provides an overview of the PROPEL skill sets.

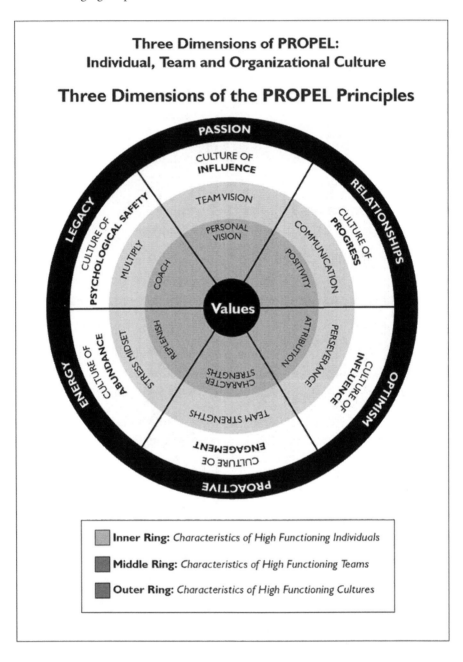

# Chapter 7

## Passion: Developing the Drive to Create Positive Outcomes

With this chapter we begin an in-depth examination of the first of the six principles of PROPEL—"passion." Here, you'll find a story illustrating how destructive passion hampered people's ability to solve complex problems and the research on how to increase productive passion in order to be more effective. The chapter concludes with the action steps that a group of professionals took to generate the harmonious passion they needed to work together to overcome obstacles and accomplish an outstanding outcome.

### Curtis's Story: The Problem

Curtis, nurse manager of radiology at an academic medical center, has many responsibilities, none more important than getting children magnetic resonance imaging (MRI) services when their physicians suspect a problem. Doctors use MRI in pediatric patients to diagnose cancer and diseases of the spine, bones, and brain. Kids who need an MRI for any of these reasons are ill—usually seriously ill. And their parents are scared.

At Curtis's hospital, conflicts between the MRI schedulers and the clinical staff members resulted in long waiting periods for appointments. Really long. Before Curtis learned to use the PROPEL Principles, these young patients were waiting 14–16 weeks to be seen. The doctors ordering the tests were frustrated about the delay, the parents were furious, and the children were being kept waiting. No one was happy, and no one was being well served.

This was Curtis's first job as a nurse manager. When he first joined the leadership team, he was filled with enthusiasm. He was sure that he would be able to fix some of the long-standing problems he had observed as a staff member in the radiology department. The combination of poor patient satisfaction, safety and service issues, high cancellation rates, interdisciplinary squabbling, low-volume, and highly paid staff members meant that expensive equipment was underutilized.

As changes in healthcare reimbursement took hold, the hospital administrators exerted enormous pressure on the radiology department to stop the hemorrhaging of money. Curtis dutifully explained the problem to his nursing staff, who told him the fault lay with the schedulers, who explained to him that the physicians were the ones to blame. The doctors indignantly asserted that the problems were due to the impossibly slow pace of the technicians operating the equipment. When approached, the clinical technicians (techs) pointed their fingers at the nurses, claiming they were slow prepping the patients.

Curtis was initially undaunted. He proposed some feasible ideas about what could be done. To address the low-volume and high cancellation problems, he wanted to extend the hours of operation so that patients could come after work or bring their children in after school. He sent e-mails to the scheduling committee as well as the rest of the staff members asking them to start working together to figure out how to move beyond the outdated nine-to-five model.

Curtis believed that his radiology nurses would willingly support an initiative to improve patient wait times and satisfaction ratings. He met with the scheduling committee. He sent e-mails to the staff members explaining the problem and asking for cooperation. It did not take long to discover that the vast majority of the deeply entrenched staff members (who had been working the same schedule for years) were highly resistant to changes.

Curtis's boss had served in the military for many years. He advised Curtis to take more of a command-and-control approach—tell the staff members what they were going to have to do to fix the problem and when they would have to do it. So, Curtis tried telling staff members what to do. But he discovered that setting expectations was insufficient, as staff members had no motivation to make his plan work and a strong incentive to sabotage it. After several months, Curtis was extremely discouraged. He had heard every excuse in the book:

■ "The techs refuse to take on more work."
■ "The schedule doesn't work because the staff members are calling out."
■ "There's nothing more we can do because the doctors won't cooperate."
■ "We can't make patient flow work now; we'll never be able to speed it up."
■ "The schedulers don't have the right software to make the changes."
■ "Why should we do more for the hospital after they put a freeze on our pay last year?"

Curtis's memo mandates didn't work, his boss expressing frustration with staff members didn't help, and the daily onslaught of problems eventually wore Curtis down. "This department is hopelessly dysfunctional," he began to mutter every time his pager went off.

Curtis's story serves as a good example of the importance of igniting people's passion for achieving a positive outcome before trying to implement changes. Without creating unifying passion, most people remain stuck in their old patterns. They lack the motivation to make changes. Trying to overpower people works only briefly; the staff members will figure out how to sabotage the change initiative.

If you want to improve people's performance—your own or your team's—the first step is to generate sufficient passion to overcome the built-in resistance all human beings have to change. After learning about the research on generating positive passion, Curtis *was* able to turn his team around. You'll discover how when you read the rest of his story at the end of this chapter.

# The Research on Creating and Sustaining Passion

## *Passion Defined*

Passion is the source of your inspiration and motivation. Enhancing passion for doing excellent work empowers you to perform at the highest level. Maintaining passion enables you to invest significant amounts of time and energy engaging in a job that you love to do because you believe it's important. Passion converts a profession into a calling.

Positive passion drives you to become invested in mastering the skills required to be a high performer; destructive passion leads to conflict and burnout. Sometimes healthcare professionals find their passion eroding. Sustaining a healthy passion for your work, studies show, is a crucial factor affecting the trajectory of your career. Your professional identity becomes a defining aspect of your personality, which— for better or for worse—determines whether you end up loving other aspects of your life or languishing in disillusionment.[1]

If you've completely lost your passion and feel burned out, then you need to replenish your energy. Read Chapter 11 to learn how to take care of yourself, and when you're rejuvenated, come back to this chapter to learn how to direct your energy effectively.

## *Two Types of Passion*

Passion falls on a continuum between harmonious or obsessive.[2] *Harmonious passion* occurs mainly because you choose to engage in the activity of your own accord. When the foundation of your career is based on this positive form of passion, it "occupies a significant but not overpowering space and is in harmony with other aspects of life."[3] As a positive force, passion motivates you to be at your best at work, in your marriage, with your family, and while enjoying leisure activities.

What does harmonious passion in daily activities look like? It's the ability to fully concentrate on the task at hand *and* create a positive experience. Think: generating positive emotions, feeling immersed in the activity, and leaving work with a sense of satisfaction. You're more able to adapt to changing situations and to deal with disruptions and obstacles.

Harmonious passion is developed by building skills that enable you to effectively manage problems by focusing your attention and energy on an outcome you believe has real value. People who maintain this positive form of passion are able to inspire others to help them; they are also able to remain resilient when facing setbacks.[4]

*Obsessive passion*, however, occurs when activities are undertaken to receive some external reward or recognition. Over time, a reliance on extrinsic motivators causes them lose effectiveness. People no longer find inner joy when engaged in their job. However, they feel compelled to complete tasks to avoid experiencing guilt, shame, or punishment.[5]

Obsessed individuals feel enormous pressure to perform well in their position, and failures cause their self-esteem to plummet. Hence, they develop an intense focus on getting all their tasks completed, making it difficult to disengage or shift their attention. Their obsessive pursuit of external goals often interferes with other aspects of life, especially family life.

The experience of obsessive passion is one of rumination about how to achieve the desired results, accompanied by the worry that their (or their team's) performance will be less than perfect. These thoughts create an uncontrollable urge within the individual to rigidly persist despite the risk of conflicts, negative emotions, or consequences. Their obsession with attaining their goal leads them to overcontrol their own and other people's behavior. They become extraordinarily defensive if challenged about their controlling methods and experience great frustration when their progress is impeded.[6]

## The Benefits of Harmonious Passion

A high level of harmonious passion predicts positive outcomes and high satisfaction in your career.[7] Studies show that harmonious passion leads to higher performance in your daily functioning.[8] For leaders, there is a significant positive correlation between harmonious passion and the expansion of emotional intelligence skills.[9]

There are numerous benefits associated with having a high level of harmonious passion:

■ More high-quality emotional experiences increase your level of psychological well-being, which is characterized by self-acceptance, positive relationships, autonomy, purpose, a growth mind-set, and an ability to manage complex environments.[10]

■ Better quality relationships develop with bosses, coworkers, and subordinates as well as with people outside of work as a result of more frequent smiles, openness to others' ideas, sharing positive activities, and mindfulness of what's happening in your environment.[11]

## The Downside of Obsessive Passion

Obsessive passion, however, has been linked to emotional exhaustion and burnout over time.[12] People who become obsessed with job performance are often able to maintain a high level of functioning at work for a time, but their personal life deteriorates because they devote insufficient time and attention to their work–life balance. Without the replenishing benefits derived from sources outside of the work environment, poor performance and burnout eventually prevail.[13]

Several studies of nurses have conclusively demonstrated the devastating effects of obsessive passion leading to psychological ill-being. Even controlling for the number of hours worked, researchers found that the conflicts created by perfectionistic thinking, ruminations, and controlling behaviors led to decreased life satisfaction and burnout. Conversely, the study established that harmonious passion protected nurses from the ill effects of burnout such as chronic fatigue, forgetfulness, loss of appetite, physical symptoms, insomnia, irritability, cynicism, detachment, anxiety, and depression.[14]

## How Burnout Affects the Quality of Healthcare Delivery

Psychologist Herbert Freudenberger first used the term "burnout" in the 1970s to describe the symptoms experienced by people working in "helping" occupations whose jobs entail unyielding stress and high standards. "Nurses experiencing emotional exhaustion feel depleted, overworked, and lethargic. Alienation from job-related activities has included emotional separation from work responsibilities, dissociation from coworkers, and pessimistic attitudes toward the work environment. Burnout can affect daily tasks at work, home, and when caring for family. Nurses with burnout syndrome view responsibilities negatively, find it difficult to work, and have an absence of innovation, causing an overall reduced performance with all daily responsibilities."[15]

The consequences associated with obsessive passion are profound. One study reported that more than a third of Pennsylvania RNs reported high levels of emotional exhaustion, a key component of burnout syndrome. The researchers suggest that if nurse burnout rates could be reduced to 10 percent from an average of 30 percent, Pennsylvania hospitals could prevent approximately 4,160 hospital-acquired infections annually with an associated savings of $41 million.[16]

These levels of dissatisfaction and burnout are not isolated to Pennsylvania but are reflected in a national study published in 2011, as shown in Figure 7.1. The percentage of nurses providing direct patient care who were classified as burned out ranged from 22 percent to 37 percent, depending on their work setting.[17]

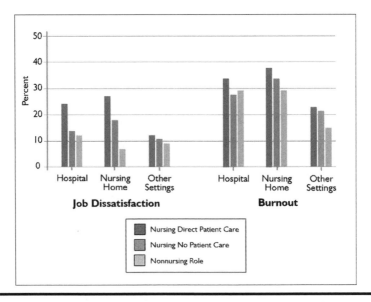

**Figure 7.1 Percentage of nurses dissatisfied and burned out, by setting and role, 2006–2007. (From McHugh, M.D. et al., *Health Aff.*, 30, 202–210, 2011.)**

Behaviors associated with obsessive passion and the resulting burnout are prevalent among physicians as well. In 2016, the Medscape Physician Lifestyle Report found that 46 percent of all physicians responded that they experienced burnout. This was a substantial increase from the 2013 Medscape Report in which burnout was reported in slightly below 40 percent.[18]

The symptoms of burnout that doctors reported included the following:

- Significant loss of enthusiasm for work
- Feelings of cynicism
- Low sense of personal accomplishment

A national survey published in the *Archives of Internal Medicine* in 2012 reported that U.S. physicians suffer more burnout than any other group of American workers.[19]

## How Do People Develop Obsessive Passion?

Becoming overly focused on external feedback diminishes decision-making capabilities due to the individual's lack of awareness of their inner values. Obsession with achieving external goals to gain approval from others can become such a powerful force that people lose touch with their intrinsic motivators. As their harmonious passion declines, so does their performance. Maureen's story in Chapter 5 illustrates obsessive passion in action and demonstrates how it led to tragic consequences for everyone involved.

Obsessive passion arises when a person overplays his or her best qualities to prove themselves. Many people are driven by a need to overcome an underlying sense of vulnerability that developed due to childhood deprivations, disruptions in relationships, parental divorce, or early failures in school. When things go wrong in the lives of young people, they often blame themselves, even when they had little or no control over the situation.

All young people make mistakes, but some are subjected to overly harsh criticism by authoritarian adults and/or ridiculed by bullying peers. These interactions can leave the young person feeling vulnerable and reacting defensively, a pattern that continues into adulthood.

For many people these experiences leave a lasting impact, creating an unconscious mind-set of uncertainty and insecurity in relationships with other people. A sense of helplessness in childhood often undermines one's confidence to handle challenges as an adult, resulting in a reluctance to fully engage, or overcompensation to prove oneself.[20]

For example, studies show that it's commonplace for leaders who experienced early struggles academically to overcompensate, hoping to prove their worth to themselves and others but resulting in the recurring deployment of their worst traits.[21] Their inner script might sound something like this: "I'm painfully aware that I didn't do well in school. I fear that people may have been right when they told me I was stupid. I've been lucky to get this far in my career so I must constantly show people how smart I am before they have a chance to see my lack of intelligence."

This negative narrative generates a subconscious fear that produces a need to create impressive strategies, but also to obsessively use overwhelming intellect to prove even minor points. Other people in their workgroup frequently become scarred when this type of leader is unable to let go of small issues, overlook minor mistakes, or be forgiving to colleagues who are unable to match their keen analytic ability. This pattern is particularly common in self-made leaders who, long after having proven their capability to succeed, continue to be haunted by a sense of inadequacy and self-doubt.[22]

When it comes to receiving and assimilating positive feedback, three dynamics work against individuals who have a compelling need to prove themselves. First, their style frequently alienates and even antagonizes people who could mentor them. Second, coworkers don't offer affirmations because they assume that talented individuals already know how good they are in certain areas. Third, even when a person with this background does receive positive feedback, they discount it because they underestimate their unowned strengths.

People who suffered childhood wounds are typically hypersensitive to criticism as it stirs deep-seated hurts from past rejection, humiliation, ridicule, and failure.

The impact of a vulnerable mind-set creates a constellation of effects that can deal a devastating blow to talented people because it creates inaccurate self-perceptions[23]:

- Underrating themselves
- Unfavorable comparisons to others
- Lack of awareness of their strengths
- Oblivious to their fatal flaws
- Critical of others' shortcomings
- Defensive when receiving critical feedback
- Discounting positive feedback

These misperceptions perpetuate a pattern in which people must constantly prove themselves but, ultimately, are handicapped by overplaying strengths to the point that they become fatal flaws. These individuals compound their problems by being puzzled and disheartened when others don't live up to their expectations. And their difficulty in receiving constructive feedback prevents them from learning how to break free from their dysfunctional pattern.

## Strategies for Overcoming Obsessive Passion

Many of us had struggles in the past that wounded us to some extent. Most people have developed some degree of vulnerability and display some symptoms of obsessive passion. Remember that passion falls on a continuum, and the majority of us are somewhere in the middle. PROPEL is about helping us develop more harmonious passion in our lives. Two approaches have proven effective in helping individuals who are stuck in a struggle with themselves and others: corrective mirroring and self-compassion.

### Corrective Mirroring

This self-directed approach involves correcting perceptions from the past and present. If you grew up believing you were deficient in some way, you'll need to increase your awareness of positive feedback and develop a receptive attitude to improve your self-image. Being in an affirming relationship with someone you trust to consistently offer this feedback is crucial, as is your willingness to accept their input. Setting aside time for several months for regular self-reflection on the occasions in which you appropriately used your strengths will enrich your self-image. In addition, visualizing how you will most effectively use your strengths to flourish in the future will be empowering.[24]

### Self-Compassion

Kristen Neff's research focuses on how to limit self-criticism and its debilitating effects. Her studies show that people *can* "stop beating themselves up and leave insecurity behind" by following the self-compassion ritual she's developed.[25]

She offers a free Self-Compassion Assessment on her website: self-compassion.org/test-how-self-compassionate-you-are/.

Neff points out that we're often overly harsh with ourselves, saying mean things to ourselves that we'd never say to a friend. She suggests reviewing how you treated a friend who was suffering some misfortune or failure and was feeling inadequate. "How did you respond? What did you say to offer comfort?"

Then she asks, "Recall a time you were suffering from a setback, adversity, or situation in which you felt inadequate. What was different about the way you responded to your friend versus how you reacted to your own negative situation?" Most people immediately recognize major differences, which can be broken down into three core components:

1. *Kindness vs. judgment*: How did you soothe your friend? How would you do that for yourself in troubling moments?
   "This is a moment of suffering. Suffering is part of life. May I be kind to myself in this moment. May I give myself the compassion I need."
2. *Common humanity vs. isolation*: What tone would you take with yourself if you changed your inner dialog from "this shouldn't be happening to me" to "these situations happen to everyone?"
   "I'm not alone. Others struggle just like me. We all experience pain in our lives, it's a part of being human. This is part of the shared human experience."
3. *Mindfulness vs. overidentification*: Where do you feel the painful emotion in your body? What label would you give it? How can you soften the sensation in your body?
   "If I name it, I can tame it. If I feel it, I can heal it."

Neff recommends daily practice to achieve the goal of self-compassion so that you can respond with kindness and support when you are struggling. In these moments ask yourself, "Where's a safe spot for me to go right now to take care of myself?"

## Applying the PASSION Research—Developing Personal Mastery

### *Values Clarification: The First Step for Increasing Harmonious Passion*

We can sustain harmonious passion when we're consciously aware of what is most valuable to us, and we take action to lead a life consistent with our values. Values are the principles, beliefs, and standards upon which we base our decisions about how we want to live our lives—now and in the future. Our choices, whether we are aware of it or not, reflect our values. If the outcomes in your personal life, love life, or work life are not as satisfying or successful as you want them to be, stop looking at external causes. Those may well be valid concerns, but you often have little or no control over them. What is important is to look at how you're contributing to creating suboptimal outcomes as well.

Most people are not consciously aware of their values. Although they frequently lie below the surface of awareness, values exert a profound effect on how we choose to live our lives. All of our thoughts are filtered through the values that we develop during the significant ups and downs we experience in life. Everything we do or say reflects the values we've developed as a result of those experiences. All that we hope for is based upon what we've learned about how we want our life to work, and our fears about how badly we'll feel if the worst were to happen to us again.

With so many influences from our past, we can easily be unclear or confused about our values. We learn one set of standards from our parents. The church provides another source. Friends and peers offer other values. Then there are the value conflicts we're exposed to by opposing political groups, television networks, commercials, and so on. With all these inputs, we are ultimately left to make our own choices about which values to follow. If you don't consciously choose the values you want to live by, you put yourself in a position where other people can exert undue influence over your choices, manipulating you to do things that are not in your own best interests.

The more you understand your values, the better able you are to make satisfactory choices and take appropriate action. Values clarification focuses on *how* you have acquired your values rather than *what* they should be. It is a method that lets you discover the values you're currently living by. More importantly, it creates awareness of what values you want to live by to be your best possible self in the future.[26]

How we spend our time and money provides clues about our values. As do the situations that get us riled up enough to take a stand or to take action. Our fantasies and daydreams derive from our desires to recreate positive experiences from our past. We feel most energized and alive when we're engaged in activities that we believe are valuable. And there are values clarification exercises—such as the one awaiting you in Chapter 13—that can aid in surfacing the values you feel most passionate about using to guide your day-to-day decisions.

## Visualization: The Second Step for Increasing Harmonious Passion

Once you understand what's most valuable to you in life, you can develop a picture of what your life would look like if you were more consistently living by your values. That congruence of your inner values and external actions is the core of harmonious passion.

To achieve that level of functioning, you must be able to picture the positive outcome you would like to attain. Literally picture yourself being in situations that would be immensely valuable and deeply gratifying. Imagining what your life could look like is necessary because of how your brain is wired. Change brings up fears and doubts, stimulating fight–flight–freeze reactions. To counter those responses, you must activate your left prefrontal cortex, which is accomplished by imagining what it will look like when you have reached your goal.

It's always helpful to *write down* your vision of how you want your life to be working if you were at your best. Post your vision statement someplace where you'll see it every day.

## Taking Action: The Third Step for Increasing Harmonious Passion

Simply fantasizing about a better future has been shown to alleviate stress in the short term, but it will promote discouragement in the long term if dreaming is all you do. Talking endlessly in committee meetings about what needs to be done is a sad fact of life in many hospitals.

Gabriele Oettingen, a psychologist at New York University, New York, has shown that merely talking about positive outcomes makes it much harder for people to tackle tasks that require a concerted effort. In numerous studies, positive imaging produced lower energy levels and lower levels of accomplishment. As a result of dreaming about losing weight, for example, people's brains told them that it wasn't necessary to exercise or eat well because their mind had already shot ahead to the end of the story in which success had been attained. Unwittingly, by picturing that they were already where they wanted to be, they had demotivated themselves from feeling the need to take action.[27]

Oettingen found that an effective method for getting people to take action after they had identified a goal was to immediately confront them with the realities of what was standing in the way. This technique, termed *mental contrasting*, gave people a surge in energy. They were able to instantly engage in working toward their goal—but it was only those subjects who believed they had a reasonable chance of success.

Subsequent studies have shown that mental contrasting paired with positive reinforcement leads to even better outcomes. Supportive relationships provide an amplifying effect that helps us achieve our goals.

"Dreaming a little and then imagining the obstacle lets you unlock new potentials inside of yourself, potentials that you scarcely knew existed," Oettingen writes. "Until now you have likely approached life using only part of your mind's latent capacities. Mental contrasting lets you finally engage in viable, heartfelt wishes with everything you've got."[28]

While Oettingen was conducting her research, her husband, Peter Gollwitzer (also a psychology professor at New York University), was studying how people can best achieve their dreams. He was interested in determining why so many people set goals but fail to translate their intention into action. New Year's resolutions are the prime example.

What Gollwitzer discovered was that creating "implementation intentions" makes it much more likely that people will take the necessary steps to accomplish their goals. Simply stated, an implementation intention is an "if _____ then _____" plan.

Forging explicit intentions about how to achieve a goal occurs in two phases: initially, you consider possibilities and decide to commit to a goal, and then you make a plan for what you'll do to achieve the outcome. Decades of studies have demonstrated that creating a strong intention to pursue a goal will greatly improve the chances of achieving a positive outcome.[29]

Gollwitzer identified two reasons people fail to follow through on their intentions: (1) They set a goal but never take any action (indicating the need for initiating a first step) and (2) they start to take action toward a goal but derail (indicating a need for assistance in maintaining the goal-directed behavior). These impediments account for the fact that most people never accomplish their intended goal.

A meta-analysis of nearly 100 studies revealed that using "if-then" statements resulted in significantly improving the odds that people would accomplish their objectives. If-then statements help you begin to take action on tasks, "whether getting started was an issue of remembering to act, seizing good opportunities, or overcoming initial reluctance."[30] Moreover, it protected against becoming distracted, overcame counterproductive habits, and helped sustain energy to tackle new tasks.

Experiments over the past 20 years have examined the positive effects of creating if-then intentions to successfully achieve a variety of goals, including New Year's resolutions, performing self-examinations to detect cancer and implementing workplace safety measures.

Oettingen and Gollwitzer combined their research into a single, unified tool that they termed WOOP—wish, outcome, obstacle, and plan:

- *Wish*: Visualize what it will look like to achieve your goal.
- *Outcome*: Imagine how it will feel when you're there.
- *Obstacle*: What is it within you that has been holding you back?
- *Plan*: *If* you experience that obstacle, *then* what's your plan for overcoming it?

In one study using WOOP to help healthcare providers cope with stress and improve engagement in difficult professional environments, providers who used WOOP reported that after 3 weeks they could significantly reduce their level of physical and mental distress by turning their energy into effective action.[31] Now that's a tactic you can use to generate the passion you need for acting on the values that are important in your life!

# Applying the PASSION Research: Developing Team Mastery

## Creating PROPEL Teams

In a PROPEL initiative, it is important to create a small, diverse group of five to seven representatives from the entire staff members—inpatient unit, outpatient clinic, administrative group, and so on. These individuals are selected by asking staff members and leadership: "Who are the people who have the most passion for their jobs, have the best relationships, and are most optimistic when dealing with setbacks?"

PROPEL teams undergo training on how to apply positive psychology principles by completing the exercises in the PROPEL Toolkit in Chapters 13 and 14. To get started, the teams develop three or four values that they have in common. Based on their shared values, the PROPEL team creates a vision of what it would look like if their entire staff members were performing at a more optimal level. It's a good idea for the team to keep track of the highlights of meetings and then send an e-mail to the entire staff members summarizing what was discussed. Inviting feedback encourages engagement with the larger group of employees.

Once armed with a working knowledge of optimal functioning and a new set of skills for influencing their coworkers, the PROPEL team develops ideas for making progress toward their vision. Each team member then takes the responsibility for encouraging others on the staff members to join in piloting a new behavior to determine if it improves performance. They must figure out how to overcome the unique obstacles they confront within their work environment. Incremental improvements are made based on the entire staff members' feedback until the team's vision has been achieved.

## Using "Smart Team" Research

PROPEL teams benefit from learning about the dynamics of optimal group functioning. Positive psychologists studying work teams have found three key characteristics of high-performing teams[32]:

- Generating more positive than negative interactions
- Using inquiry to learn more about a situation before advocating one's own position
- Understanding what others need before focusing on your own fulfillment

Originally, researchers thought there was a fixed ratio of positive interactions to negative interactions that were necessary to maintain optimal functioning. Subsequent studies have shown that people need more positive than negative exchanges; however, the amount of positivity required to maintain well-being is dependent on a number of variables such as the following:

- Personal circumstances that affect one's work life, and vice versa
- The level of intensity associated with stressful events
- The degree to which someone is vulnerable to negativity based on their background
- The individual's ability to adopt a growth mind-set when facing a challenge
- The amount of recognition and reinforcement each person needs to maintain motivation

Other studies of "smart teams" conducted by researchers at Massachusetts Institute of Technology and elsewhere found additional factors[33]:

- Equal participation of all members in discussions
- The ability to read the emotions of teammates
- High-quality communication

In smart teams, each team member is required to contribute equally—regardless of rank in the hospital hierarchy. If one or two people start to dominate the conversation, they are thanked for the contribution and asked (for the sake of the limited amount of time set aside for the meeting) to allow others to express their thoughts. Collective intelligence distinguishes high-performing smart teams.

Each team member of an optimally functioning team can read the emotions of everyone else on the team. This skill is necessary to generate enough positive emotions to maintain sufficient goodwill and avoid lapsing into fight–flight–freeze reactions. Having a good balance of men and women on teams was found to be extremely helpful in this regard as females tend to be better at reading facial cues.

Smart team members engage in high-quality communications, which involves the following:

1. Using more inquiry than advocacy to build better situational awareness
2. Stating your understanding of the person's point of view (before offering your own thoughts) to create feelings of respect
3. Generating multiple perspectives to provide more information, new ideas, and motivation for achieving mutually agreeable solutions
4. Arriving at mutually agreeable strategies for reaching the team's goals

## Applying the PASSION Research: Developing a Culture of Intention

### Passion Is More Important Than Employee Engagement

Passion is different from—and more important than—engagement, according to a 2014 report from Deloitte's Center for the Edge. "Employee engagement is typically defined," the report says, "by how happy workers are with their work setting, coworkers, organization-wide programs, and their overall treatment by their employer. Employee engagement is important, and improving it typically will give a firm a bump in performance. But engagement is often a one-time bump; employees move from unhappy to happy, bring a better attitude to work, and possibly take fewer sick days. However, workers who are merely engaged won't actively seek to achieve higher performance levels, to the benefit of self and firm; passionate workers will, though."[34]

Passion, in contrast, revolves around how employees respond to challenges. The Deloitte report designates an employee as displaying passion if they:

- Get excited by, and actively seek out, challenges.
- Enjoy solving problems.
- Like to learn, develop skills, and build their careers over the long term.
- Interact well with others to pursue their goals.
- Help themselves and their company develop the capabilities to constantly learn and improve performance.
- Deliver sustained and significant performance improvement over time.

What would a dream employee look like? The Deloitte report says, "She searches for new, better, solutions to challenging problems, takes meaningful risks to improve performance, performs at a higher level of performance with each passing year, works the hours needed to get the job done, is well connected to others internally and externally, and cuts across silos to deliver results."

The reality of today's workplace is the exact opposite, the report states, because around 88 percent of the workforce lack this kind of passion—and the enhanced productivity that goes along with it.

"The key message from our work is that workers of all types and in all locations have the potential to be passionate—it's not limited to a privileged few," the Deloitte report concludes. "Rather than focusing on recruiting more passionate workers, the big opportunity is to look at the existing workforce and create environments that can tap into, nurture, and amplify the passion of every worker already on the job. Without the right work environments, efforts to recruit additional passionate workers will likely be undermined as those new workers become frustrated in environments that do not support passion."

Unfortunately, many companies do not recognize the value of worker passion. In fact, they view it with suspicion. Hospitals, in particular, tend to emphasize processes and policies. To ensure rules will be followed, however, providers must also be motivated, which requires generating harmonious passion.

Gallup research reveals that "the efficacy of technological solutions and policy changes relies on whether people properly implement them. Nurses have been identified as a key connecting point through which systems, patients, and physicians work together to identify and prevent potential medical errors. They represent the key 'people factor' in controlling healthcare quality."[35]

"Cultivation of passionate workers internally is probably the most effective way to increase the proportion of passionate workers in your organization," concludes the Deloitte report. "Organizations should evaluate their work environments to understand where they cultivate or discourage passion. The right work environments will help attract, retain, and develop passionate employees."[36]

The Deloitte report goes on to identify strategies for finding and developing passion within the workforce, including tangible steps for how companies can create work environments that unlock worker passion at all levels of the existing workforce. These include the following:

- Encouraging workers to work cross-functionally and/or develop an understanding of other needs to function well in their role
- Encouraging workers to participate on projects they are interested in, even on those outside of their responsibilities
- Encouraging workers to connect with others both in the organization and in their industry
- Engaging with others—patients as well as coworkers—to innovate new product and service ideas
- Defining high-impact challenges by helping workers and teams focus on the areas of highest business impact, learning, and sustainable improvement
- Augmenting workers' impact with the right infrastructure, such as healthy work environments that enable collaboration both inside and outside the organization
- Recruiting workers who are more inclined to be passionate about their work

Passion at the organizational level must be intentionally created. Not by a board of directors who post a plaque declaring what they've decided should be the organization's values, but by executives getting out to talk to employees at every level about when they believe the organization is at its best—and worst. By integrating that input into a set of shared values, defining the behaviors that exemplify those values, and setting expectations that, to the greatest extent humanly possible, people will act accordingly.

The continuation of Curtis's story illustrates what PROPEL looks like in action.

## Curtis's Story: The Resolution

"My director and I discussed radiology participating in a PROPEL initiative," Curtis told me. "I understand that it helps create a more positive work environment, which we certainly need. But I don't know exactly what to expect, or how it's going to help."

"You and I will be getting together for one-on-one coaching as well as meeting with a select group of your staff members," I explained. "I'll be teaching you and your PROPEL team to use six positive psychology principles to help your staff members become more positive and higher performing. This evidence-based approach brings a fresh way of thinking as well as a new skill set, which has enabled many other teams to resolve the challenges they were facing."

The fact is that it's nearly impossible for any one person to be able to affect changes on their own. Leaders need to align with their staff members, starting with a small team that can work with them to influence the rest of their coworkers.

Limiting teams to five to seven people is important because to be effective everyone must be highly engaged—showing up for meetings, supporting their teammates, continuously offering their suggestions, and collaborating with their teammates between meetings to implement the ideas that are generated.

Curtis selected the staff members he thought would be most engaged. But he wanted to know what to tell them about the purpose of the team. Here's what we suggested:

> A PROPEL initiative brings leaders and staff members together to work on the unique challenges the team feels are preventing their unit from functioning at its best. As part of learning to use six positive psychology principles, the team comes together by first identifying unifying values and a shared vision. PROPEL teams set tangible goals that improve both the positivity and the performance of their unit. Over time they engage the majority of their coworkers to join their effort to achieve measurable results. At the end of the PROPEL initiative, managers will have learned to be more collaborative with staff members, PROPEL team members will have become highly influential leaders, and staff members will know they play a significant role in affecting changes on their unit.

Curtis recognized that he'd started out as a new nurse manager believing he could fix the radiology department's problem single-handedly. He simply wanted the professionals who worked for him to accept his ideas to resolve the issues of low volume, difficulty scheduling appointments, and poor patient satisfaction scores. The staff members quickly shot his plan down. So he joined forces with his boss, the director of radiology, in a top-down effort to mandate changes. Curtis discovered neither approach was effective.

"I was naive," Curtis grumbled. "And I hate to be wrong. I'm hard on myself when I know I've screwed up."

"Whoa! Time to tell yourself, 'no mistakes, only lessons'. Sounds like you need to show more compassion to yourself," I suggested.

"I'd love to know how to stop beating myself up," Curtis said with a small chuckle.

"Let me begin by asking what you're thinking when you become hard on yourself?"

Curtis paused for a moment, and solemnly replied: "I'm thinking that I'm not good enough to fix this problem."

"What's the strongest emotion you feel when you think that?" I gently probed.

"I'm inadequate," Curtis said, clearly irritated.

"Where in your body is this inadequate feeling located?"

"My stomach."

"What does it feel like? Burning? Tingling?"

"It's a sinking feeling, like suddenly dropping in an elevator."

"How can you soothe the sensation? Loosen its grip?"

"Breathing. When I breathe it's better."

"Then put your hand on the spot to soothe it and repeat to yourself: breathe 1–2–3–4. Count to 4 as you inhale, hold your breath for another 4 count, exhale to a 4 count, and hold the exhale for a final 4 count. Use a tone that works to soothe you."

After a minute, Curtis began to speak, a note of surprise in his voice: "Yeah, that really helps calm me down."

"Next, ask yourself what you'd say to a friend who came to you feeling this way about a similar problem."

Curtis took a minute to consider that question. "I'd tell him to get a grip. That this isn't about him. He's dealing with a huge hospital run by administrators who have enough trouble keeping their own departments functioning. Everyone's struggling with staffing, budgeting, scheduling, and dozens of other demands. They're too consumed with their own problems to see big picture solutions. And God bless those nurses on the frontline who—in spite of all the craziness—are trying to take good care of the patients."

"And does hearing that perspective change your feelings?" I wondered.

"Somewhat," Curtis said tentatively. "I still get a sinking feeling that I'll never be able to change it."

"Allow the emotion to be there without blaming yourself or anyone else," I suggested. "Let go of expectations of how you should be trying to fix it. What does it feel like to simply acknowledge your emotion?"

"Actually, it feels kind of liberating," Curtis sighed with relief. "I realize I can't fix it all on my own. It's not all on me. It's not about what's wrong with me."

"What is it about?" I inquired.

"It's about a desire to make a difference for the patients who have to wait too long to get their treatment. And a realization that I have to find kindred spirits who share that desire and are willing try to solve this problem." Curtis stated emphatically.

"How are you feeling now about doing this work?"

"Much better—I'm not down on myself," he replied. "I recognize the scope of the problem is more than one person can fix."

"Well, let's make this a part of your homework," I proposed. "Would you be willing to take 10 minutes during the day to identify a negative emotion that's getting you down and practice being more compassionate toward yourself?"

"I can do that," he agreed.

Curtis and his newly formed PROPEL team scheduled a kickoff meeting designed to rekindle their passion by uncovering the values that unite them and creating a vision that inspires them. The meeting started out with people remembering times they felt they had been at their best.

- *Carolyn:* For me it's important to feel connected to people—coworkers and patients alike.
- *Rick:* I get my energy from hearing people's ideas about how to solve problems.

- *Allie:* I like pulling people together that I have good relationships with—even if they're from different disciplines. We are usually able to figure out how to make the day work out.
- *Sandy:* I'm like Allie and Carolyn. I feel best when I'm working as part of a team.
- *Julie:* I agree. It feels good when someone asks my opinion and trusts my input.
- *Lauren:* I like fixing messes—talking about what's gone wrong and what we can do differently next time.
- *Curtis:* I feel good when I notice patients are having a problem and I step in to help them.

They also recalled times they felt bad about situations. One story was horrific. A team member told about receiving a call from a distraught mother whose child had surgery several years earlier for a brain tumor but was experiencing symptoms again. When told it could be up to 4 months before the department could get the child in for an MRI, the mother started sobbing. Everyone in the meeting teared up.

This mother's story represented a clear violation of the values that had led the people on the team to become healthcare providers. And sharing it opened up a lively discussion of what compelling values each team member held near and dear to their heart.

In the end, the radiology department decided that their core values were trust, teamwork, and pride. Importantly, they decided that they could begin to take action to fix the issue of excessively long wait times for pediatric patients. "We're better than this" was the attitude that was expressed. The PROPEL team's passion had been ignited.

They created a vision statement of what it would look like when the radiology department was living the values of trust, teamwork, and pride more consistently:

> We are an inspired team proud to provide safe, high-quality patient and family-centered care in an environment that fosters trust, support, collegiality, and positivity.

To prevent them from going down the road of "good intentions" that were never realized, we asked each person to do the WOOP exercise. Curtis set an example by going first:

> "My wish is for the staff in the radiology department to collaborate to find a solution to the problem of long pediatric wait times."

> "I'd feel proud of the people who worked together, and overjoyed when we could tell parents that we would be able to quickly get their child the MRI they need."

"What's been holding me back is fear. When I feel fearful, I resort to flight or fight. I give in to discouragement or I try to force the staff members to change."

"If I feel fear, then I will remind myself that I can turn to teammates who are as passionately committed as I am to finding a solution."

Each person on the PROPEL team completed the WOOP exercise. By the end of the meeting, the passion in the room was palpable, including with Curtis's boss. He had seen that strategies don't have to originate at the top. When action plans are harmoniously created, they're imbued with the entire team's heartfelt passion for helping make them successful.

Within days of having participated in the kickoff meeting, the staff members had scheduled times to meet with like-minded people on the nursing and radiology technician staff members. They also spoke to several of the more collaborative radiologists and anesthesiologists. The PROPEL team continued to collect and share stories about seriously sick kids having to wait—and the anguish that caused the parents. They asked coworkers to partner with them to involve other disciplines in the effort to fix the problem.

The discussions with these coworkers generated passionate conversations about the need to deliver better patient care, but not necessarily agreement regarding how to achieve that goal. Here's an example of a meeting with a physician:

*PROPEL team leader:* "Thanks for meeting with us. You're considered to be one of the most collaborative members of the physician group. We'd like to get your input on how we might solve the problem of long pediatric delays."

*Physician representative:* "I agree with the goal here, but the fact of the matter is that the doctors won't work late shifts. They're already burned out just trying to get all of their work done now. They don't want to take on anything more."

*Team leader:* "Sounds like you've had this conversation with your colleagues in the past. Tell us more about your experience talking to them about working later hours."

*Physician:* "They say that one of the reasons they chose this specialty was to have a better work–life balance than the physicians working on the inpatient units. They want to go home and be with their families, and that's hard to do now with all of the demands the hospital is putting on them."

*Team leader:* "Okay. So we need to honor their work–life balance value to be able to find an agreeable solution. I like to brainstorm solutions. Let's go around the table and get everyone's ideas."

After many others had shared their thoughts, one of the nurses on the PROPEL team suggested: "What if we created a schedule that had doctors working 2 hours late one night a week? That would get the physicians off 1 day every month so they could go visit their kid's school or have a long weekend."

*Physician:* "I like that idea. I could get behind trying to convince the other doctors in the group to at least try it."

*Team leader:* "Would you be willing to test market the idea with some of the doctors you think might be most supportive? Could you get their ideas about how this could work out for everyone and bring back those suggestions?"

*Physician:* "Yeah. Let me see if I can build a coalition. We might not even need every single doc to sign onto this plan if we could cover the schedule with volunteers. Then we wouldn't need unanimous consent, which has been a deal breaker in the past. Let me see what I can do."

*Team leader:* "You're terrific to work with. Would you consider becoming a regular participant in our PROPEL meetings?"

*Physician:* "Yes. You folks have something good going on. I'd enjoy being a part of making things better around here."

Over the next several months, the PROPEL team held regular meetings—all brief and action oriented. They slowly but surely ironed out a series of solutions, each one a piece of the puzzle. The most engaged and collaborative physicians, techs, and nurses conducted trials to determine what would work. Eventually the picture was complete. Ultimately even the less engaged providers saw that progress was possible. Their fears of being a part of a failed initiative had been mitigated; they joined the "winning" team to help realize the goals of the radiology department.

Curtis and his staff members achieved astonishing results: pediatric MRI wait times decreased from 16 weeks to 12 days. But the PROPEL team didn't stop there. Within a year, the extended hours for patients to schedule appointments had been worked out, and the volume of patients doubled.

Their passion for demonstrating trust, teamwork, and pride enabled the Radiology Department to improve their safety scores as well as their Press Ganey patient satisfaction ratings—and they hadn't even held meetings to discuss those issues.

The culture in Radiology changed, and almost everyone got on board. The few holdouts resigned and took jobs where being negative still got them an audience. Radiology became a premier place to work, and vacancies were never open for long.

"I don't solve people's problems anymore," Curtis said during our follow-up a year later. "I teach people how they can solve their own. We start by getting passionate about achieving our shared goals. Then the team finds solutions for working together to achieve them. I just get out of their way."

## Conclusion

Passion beats burnout—if it is harmonious with what is most valuable to you and your coworkers. Pushing for what you want is exhausting; aligning with others is invigorating. When you and your teammates create a shared vision of what's important for making your work meaningful and fulfilling, motivation to make it so is ignited.

# Chapter 8

---

# Relationships: Building
# a High-Performing Team

---

No matter how much passion you have, it will eventually wane if other people continually thwart your efforts. In this chapter, you'll find the story of a manager trying to relieve the frustrations of the staff members on her unit who were working in silos. You will learn, as she did, how to harness the research on creating high-functioning relationships to achieve an extraordinary accomplishment for your staff members—and your hospital.

## Rita's Story: The Problem

Rita looked beleaguered, slumped over her desk piled high with papers. Her posture suggested stress was taking a toll on this usually vibrant young woman. I noticed a flicker of fear in her eyes as she shifted her gaze from her computer to the office door where I stood. I wondered what was distressing her.

It had been about a year since Rita had become the nurse manager of the Blood and Marrow Transplant (BMT) case management program. Her group was responsible for clearing all the hurdles that had to be overcome for patients to receive lifesaving treatments.

At one of our initial meetings, she explained the details of the work her group was doing. "There are 100 hoops we have to jump through to get a patient a transplant," Rita said in a demure tone. "People are referred into our BMT program from around the world. They're very sick and urgently need our specialized treatments.

"But, a lot of stars need to align before it can happen. To give you the highlights: we need to get approval from health insurance companies, find time in a physician's packed schedule, meet research protocol requirements, insure the patient's and donor's lab reports indicate they're ready to undergo the procedure, and understand the unique needs of each patient and their family. If any one of those issues gets fouled up, we have to start the process all over again."

In subsequent meetings with staff members I heard a lot about how frustrated everyone became when cases failed to clear all the obstacles. In fact, Rita and her case managers described feeling disappointed on a daily basis. The staff members said they frequently felt they were letting patients down when all of their hard work failed to achieve the desired outcome.

Tears were shed in one of our meetings when a nurse recounted her efforts to get a BMT for a gravely ill mother of three young children. In a race against time, the case manager described her struggle to get approval from the woman's insurance company. "I was trying everything I knew to work through the appeal process. It didn't happen in time, and I felt horrible when the family called to tell me the patient had passed. Later that day, someone called me to complain that I hadn't gotten back to them on another case. I lost it. I'm sure others could hear me shouting but nobody said anything. Even though I sit next to five people in our tiny office, it's often lonely."

Screaming matches regularly broke out between staff members when tensions flared as people were desperately trying to meet deadlines. Rita frequently found herself playing referee, sending people to their respective corners of the ring to cool off. But it didn't take long until the stony silence was shattered and the shouting resumed. Although these were dedicated people, they had succumbed to the fight or flight reactions that often arise when people work in an extremely stressful environment. The group's focus on failure created an air of resentment that permeated the small room they shared.

The fallout from these clashes lead to another challenge for Rita. When frustration boiled over in her group, she would take the tough case herself to avoid further conflicts among the case managers. In conjunction with her managerial obligations, taking on many of the most difficult cases put her into perpetual overload. Conflicts and overwhelming workload were clearly the culprits driving her daily stress level through the roof.

Rita's story exemplifies what happens when relationships devolve into dysfunction. Negative emotions reign supreme. People harbor frustration and resentment, which drive them into their silos—until the pressure builds to the boiling point. Then conflicts erupt, causing further damage and creating despair for everyone involved. Fortunately, researchers have found the formula for developing deeply satisfying relationships.

# The Research on Creating and Sustaining High-Functioning Relationships

Human beings depend on relationships for nourishment as much as they do food and water. We all possess a deep desire to be loved, supported, and respected. Our happiness depends on the quality of our relationships. The sensory pleasures of life provide immediate, but fleeting satisfaction. Being positively engaged with our families and coworkers increases our happiness, as well as our physical health and psychological well-being.

## Most Relationships Flounder

Sadly, most people have not learned how to maintain good relationships. Over a span of 40 years, 67 percent of marriages will end in divorce. In failing marriages, couples handle conflicts poorly by lapsing into a doom loop that begins with criticism, escalates to contempt, arouses defensiveness, and ends with stonewalling. Being stuck in this pattern predicted divorce 82 percent of the time.[1]

Gallup surveys of employee engagement have found that more than 50 percent of American workers are disengaged. Almost 20 percent of employees admit to actively sabotaging their work environment. The reason people usually give for being dissatisfied at work—and the best predictor of someone leaving their job—is that they don't have a satisfactory relationship with their boss.[2] The biggest source of satisfaction and motivation for the 30 percent who are engaged (working with passion, making the extra effort, and feeling committed to the organization's values and goals) is having a good relationship with a coworker.[3]

There are common patterns that describe the downward trajectory of floundering relationships—personal or professional. Most people experience an abundance of positive emotions when they first connect, which can extend up to 2 or 3 years. But over time, frustration and disappointment inevitably occur.

Human beings make mistakes, experience stressful events, and display their downside characteristics. Communication breaks down, especially when people resort to the blame game. Over time, resentment, disengagement, and isolation build. In dysfunctional relationships, individuals develop a mind-set of "learned helplessness" if they repeatedly see their efforts to improve their relationships fail.

When conflicts remain unresolved, people increasingly focus on taking care of themselves. Some find their connections become characterized by cold civility punctuated by occasional hostile outbursts or passive–aggressive putdowns. Many give up trying to maintain positive relationships and retreat into a silo.

## Lack of Engagement in Relationships Degrades Healthcare Quality

Gallup surveys have found that healthcare workers' engagement levels closely parallel the American work force. More than half are disengaged—not doing anything more than what is required, including helping others in their workgroup. Another one in six staff members admits that they're actively undermining their coworkers. The consequence, Gallup concluded in a study of 200 hospitals, is that the nurses' disengagement level is the most significant variable correlating to patient mortality.[4]

"The commitment and emotional involvement of the nurses on staff members is even more important than their numbers. As it did for mortality rates, nursing engagement emerges as even more important than patient acuity or nursing staff size in explaining the variation in complication rates across hospitals," Gallup determined.[5]

In 2015, Jim Harter, Gallup's chief scientist for workplace management and well-being reported that "as much as 70 percent of the variance in the employee engagement of teams can be traced back to the influence of the manager."[6]

Nurses are disengaging in large numbers, which is curious because they chose a profession dedicated to helping people. But they're human, and when problems occur in work relationships—in particular, with bosses and others in authority—employees lose their desire to engage with everyone involved. And that includes with patients.

## What Role Do Physicians Play?

Relationship problems in medical settings have been well documented for decades, resulting in significant impairments in the performance of providers. Improving the quality of communication between physicians and nurses, nurses and techs, as well as leaders and staff members remains a central challenge for improving the quality of patient care.

The journal *Nursing* conducted a major survey of nurse–physician relationships and found that 43 percent of nurses report having unsatisfactory relationships with physicians.[7] Nurses mentioned several factors that influenced suboptimal nurse–physician relationships:

- Male physicians' perceptions of traditional gender roles
- Physicians' feelings of superiority combined with nurses' feelings of inferiority
- Hospital cultures in which nurses are seen as subordinate to physicians

The majority of the nurses in the study reported physicians had treated them disrespectfully. The RNs felt inferior in their relationships with physicians, mostly because their opinions were misunderstood or ignored. In addition, most nurses believed the culture in their healthcare organization would not enforce sanctions for physicians demonstrating disruptive behavior. A common complaint among RNs was that "older physicians and those from cultures characterized by male/female inequality were more likely to view nurses as subordinates." The report strongly recommended that efforts be undertaken to improve collaboration between physicians and nurses by enhancing interprofessional communication.

Increasingly, patient safety studies are emphasizing the importance of creating a *culture* of safety, one that expects all staff members to speak up when a patient may be harmed. A classic study performed 30 years ago in intensive care settings found that communication between physicians and nurses was the most significant factor associated with patient mortality. More recent studies have confirmed these findings.[8]

## Optimal Communication in Healthcare Teams

Astoundingly, medical and nursing schools "neither teach courses in error prevention nor offer training in the teamwork that's so necessary when members of varied disciplines must collaborate in a fast-paced, high-tech, risk-laden environment. Add to this mix the traditional hierarchy of an academic medical center—where nurses may hesitate to raise concerns with doctors, residents may feel uncomfortable about second-guessing attending physicians, and everyone may overlook the concerns of patients and families—and it's no wonder that faulty communication has been cited as a culprit in nearly 85 percent of medical errors," according to an article published in *Hopkins Medicine Magazine* in 2004. Patient safety expert Peter Pronovost, MD, was quoted as saying, "In almost all cases, someone sensed something was wrong but didn't speak up."[9]

Hospitals around the country are seeking new ways to enable employees to talk about medical errors—not only after the fact in morbidity and mortality conferences and hospital review committees, but in real-time transactions when a healthcare worker has a bad feeling about what is happening with a patient.

Johns Hopkins Hospital, Baltimore, Maryland, has become a leader in changing the culture of secrecy and blame that does little to prevent mistakes in the first place. Physicians, nurses, and the myriad others who contribute to patient care have been historically reluctant to speak openly. "We're trained from our earliest days in school that health professionals don't make mistakes, and if you do, you don't talk about it," says Beryl Rosenstein, Vice President for Medical Affairs at the hospital.[10]

## Improving Communication Improves Quality Healthcare

Studies by Dr. Peter Pronovost and his colleagues at the Armstrong Institute for Patient Safety and Quality at Johns Hopkins Hospital have examined the effects of improving communication between attending physicians, residents, and nurses. By collaboratively completing a daily goals form, the residents and nurses improved their understanding of patient care goals from below 10 percent to over 95 percent, resulting in a decrease in the patient's length of stay from 2.2 to 1.1 days. The study concluded that "nurses felt they were an active part of this patient care team; they partnered with physicians to achieve a common goal."[10]

PROPEL initiatives have demonstrated that when interdisciplinary rounds are implemented, both physicians and nurses feel their relationships become more respectful, collaborative, and friendly. Nurses report receiving return phone calls much more promptly from the doctors. Physicians appreciate the time they save when nurses with whom they have rounded become the professional contact communicating the plan of care to patients and their families. Satisfaction levels improve for everyone involved.

## *Courageous Communication in Relationships*

In 25 years of research with 20,000 people and hundreds of organizations, researchers have determined that individuals who achieve great results while maintaining good relationships have mastered the skills of how to have crucial conversations.[11]

Courageous communicators get issues resolved because they're able to have difficult discussions without allowing defensiveness, anger, disengagement, or outright hostility to defeat them. Instead, they focus on finding mutually agreeable solutions, which require listening, compassion, clarity, calmness, assertiveness, creativity, and negotiation.

Drawn from multiple studies, here is a summary of effective communication skills:

> *Courageous conversations defined*: A dialogue between two or more people about an important topic on which they have their different perspectives that must be understood and resolved for each party to attain enough of what they need to reach a win–win solution.
>
> *The goal of a courageous conversation*: Arrive at a mutually acceptable resolution of issues by gathering information from people with differing viewpoints. The goal is to make the best possible decision based on the input from a wide variety of individuals who are involved. Having input creates a willingness for participants to act on the decision, no matter what it is. It's important to make it clear from the start how the decision will be made (majority rules, boss decides, must be mutually agreeable, etc.)
>
> *The strategy for staying focused*: Know the outcome that you want—for yourself, the other person, the work group, and the relationships between everyone involved. Ask yourself what behavior you must demonstrate to achieve those results.
>
> *The two most important success factors—safety and awareness*: People need to feel safe to be willing to share information, so maintain a high level of awareness of the emotional cues signaling whether you and others are in dialog or distress.
>
> *The two safety warning signs—silence and violence*: When people become silent and stops sharing their perspective or they try to force you to accept their point of view, stop discussing the topic, and address the discomfort. Reassure the other person that you respect their point of view and intend to work out a win–win agreement.

*What to do when the conversation becomes adversarial*: Take a deep breath. Reflect on the story you're telling yourself that's driving you toward dissolution rather than a solution: Is the narrative making one person out to be a villain and the other a victim? Stop the blame game, refocus, and revisit what you each need to attain a mutually acceptable outcome.

*If the other person escalates the level of hostility*: State that you're uncomfortable with the tone of the conversation and insist they remain respectful for you to remain in the dialogue. Say something like: "Let's hit the reset button by powering down for a few minutes and try this again when we can stay focused on finding a solution that will work for both of us."

*If the behavior doesn't change after the timeout*: Take the issue to a higher authority who can mediate the conflict and help keep the tone civil.

*If the behavior does improve*: Return to developing an understanding of what the other person needs. Then clearly and concisely express what you need. Proceed by asking "What would it look like if we both got most of what we want?" Continue the conversation for as long as necessary until you find a mutually agreeable solution by saying "yes, and..." when you hear a partial solution being offered: "'Yes' that works, 'and' we still need to resolve _____."

*A win–win agreement is not a commitment to take action*: Once you've arrived at a mutually acceptable outcome, you can see how things could turn out. But you need to specify the first steps each of you will take and the timeline for taking action in order to build trust.

*Establish a time for progress checks*: Agree ahead of time there will be setbacks. Discuss how you'll make it safe to openly admit problems. Agree that you'll learn from setbacks and go on to try something new.

## Optimal Communication Dynamics

Research reveals that communication dynamics greatly impact the performance of a team. Communication in multidisciplinary discussions falls into four basic actions: move, follow, oppose, or bystand. But most team communication breaks down because people fear retribution if they offer opposing perspectives or objective bystander facts that contradict the proposed move.[12]

An attempt to *move* the group to take a specific action provides direction and generates momentum. For example, "I think we should start having huddles right after report, must be followed by action on the suggestion or it will wither for lack of support. An individual's *follow* response, such as "Great idea!" can create a sequence that solidifies the decision to *move*, but risks ignoring input from others on the team.

This *move-follow* pattern is particularly prevalent among leaders and their deputies, and effectively shuts down further discussion. Leaders often compound their mistakes by assuming that silence means everyone agrees, which is usually not the case. Almost always someone sees a problem or has a concern about the proposed *move* action. If they find the courage to *oppose* the idea, or the leader asks for dissenting opinions, the original move plan can be modified to take other perspectives into consideration. For example, "The nurses need to get the patients' medications distributed within an hour of the report. I think holding a huddle will make that difficult some days."

The *oppose* action is often seen as being negative, and no one wants to be seen as an obstructionist. So, often the flawed plan goes forward unopposed. In the huddle example, the *move* may be destined to fail if the nurses find the plan difficult to implement. When making an *oppose* comment, it's crucial to clarify your intent. For example, "I think this is an idea worth exploring but it may need more planning." Another tactic to use in conjunction with expressing an *oppose* concern is to offer a solution that improves the original *move* idea: "What if we huddled an hour after report?"

Finally, a *bystand* comment (not to be confused with staying silent on the sidelines) can be a way to bring more information into the discussion. To continue the example, "I read a study that said mid-morning and mid-afternoon huddles were most effective because those were times staff members were acutely aware of the challenges they were facing."

But again, a *bystand* contribution can be drowned out by others who react with frustration, criticism, defensiveness, exasperation, and so on. Healthy teams self-correct when they get stuck in negativity by recognizing that the value of vigorous debate is anticipating problems before they derail an initiative. As the old saying goes, "if you fail to plan, plan to fail."

Having team members who can encourage the group to use "yes, and…" communication can be crucial. Example: "Let's remember to use 'yes, and…' when responding to the concern about what time to hold huddles: "Yes, you have a point about needing to share information, and here's another consideration—it's nearly impossible to reassemble everyone on the shift once they're into taking care of patients."

Why are *opposing* and *bystanding* essential communication skills for healthcare teams? Because preventable medical errors are now the third leading cause of death in the United States—and, the majority of the time someone is aware that a mistake is being made but is afraid to speak up.[13]

## *Other Dynamics That Improve Relationships*

Positive psychology studies show that individuals who have the highest levels of success in life also have a large circle of friends, partners, coworkers, and others who provide abundant social support. And they are far more likely than the average person to be satisfied in their relationships at work, in their families, and in their social activities.[14]

Here's a summary of how people engage in highly satisfying relationships:

*Love*: People who are flourishing recognize loving feelings as the most powerful of all the positive emotions. They actively seek and maintain loving relationships to have a steady supply of this wildly happiness-inducing emotion.[15]

*Friendship*: The best relationships are built around being good friends. The universal rules for having great friendships include the following:
  – Standing up for people when they're not present
  – Keeping what they share in confidence
  – Never putting down other people
  – Always returning favors

*Mapping*: Another important method for maintaining close connections is the skill of mapping, the ability to understand what is going on in another person's world. By having a map of the highs and lows of another person's life, you are able to empathize when they are struggling and celebrate with them when they are successful.

*Coping*: When you have strong social bonds, you are able to give and receive support during times of distress. People in healthy relationships characteristically share their problems, listen to one another, empathize, share their perspectives, and seek solutions to resolve difficult situations. Being curious about what the other person believes will resolve a problem is by far the best way to start working toward a mutually acceptable solution.[16]

*Active Constructive Responses* (*ACR*): The best way positive psychologists have found to build positivity in relationships is to make ACRs when people are making a bid for your attention, especially when they share good news with you. Responding with positive energy, enthusiasm, curiosity, and heartfelt admiration is one of the best ways ever discovered for building a high-quality connections.[17]

*Appreciation*: Expressing your admiration when someone demonstrates being at their best does more than simply reinforce that behavior; it creates awareness of that person's top character traits. When we recognize people for doing well and let them know we are proud of them, it not only makes them happy but also inspires them to strive for even greater goals. In fact, in high-functioning relationships, people consistently bring out the best in each other by commenting on one another's efforts to live according to their core values.

*Gratitude*: Another strategy for creating an overwhelmingly positive relationship is to express heartfelt gratitude. It's easy to catch people doing things wrong and lapse into criticizing, lecturing, or nagging. Most of us could spend a lot more time catching people doing things right. A powerful positive psychology approach for generating fabulous feelings between yourself and another person you're close to is to sit down and write them a one-page gratitude letter.

But don't e-mail it. Read it face to face. Let that person know from the bottom of your heart how grateful you are to have him or her in your life.[18]

*Three blessings*: Research into relationships has revealed that after about 2 years people start taking each other for granted. Or worse, they start paying more attention to what is wrong with the other person. Arguments become power struggles when people try to change the other person's thinking and behavior. To counteract the tendency to develop a negativity bias, take a good look at your relationships and see with fresh eyes how terrific it is to have people fulfilling their roles to get the job done, make the family work, or be a supportive friend. Take a "timeout" from frenetically pushing to get things done; ask yourself what three good things happened to you in the past 24 hours. Redirect your attention to giving people kudos for what they're doing to make you feel blessed.

*Be the change you want to see*: Another secret of well-functioning relationships involves acting in a positive fashion in the middle of a tense situation to dissipate the negativity. For example, shifting away from hostile behaviors toward friendly behaviors such as expressing affection, being humorous, or saying something that shows acceptance of the other person's perspective are all extremely effective approaches.

*Curiosity*: Remember the old saying: "to make a friend, be a friend." Make sure that your communication is heavily weighted toward inquiry versus self-advocacy. When people disclose what's going on in their lives, be sure to make eye contact, give them your full attention, and acknowledge what they are telling you by summarizing what you've heard. Avoid giving unsolicited advice or turning attention back to yourself by shifting the focus to your own story. If the other person is going to turn out to be a friend, he or she will also be curious about how you're doing.

*Respect*: Even if you engage in using all of the strategies listed so far, it won't necessarily mean that you will have a fulfilling relationship. You must also develop enough trust and respect to share your dreams and most deeply held values. It is this level of connection—the willingness to be vulnerable—that allows you to grow together, make trial and error explorations, share responsibility, and provide support to each other to realize your life dreams. The strongest relationships are based on a commitment to support each other's efforts to live a life filled with purpose and meaning.[1]

*Circles of trust*: You don't have to be best friends with every person you know. In fact, in any given situation having three close connections with people who you can really count on is often sufficient. Think for a minute about three people at work who could offer you the highest quality communication, collaboration, and connection. Now do the same in your personal life. How could you make more time to interact with these people? When you are with them, how can you show interest in them? In what ways could you offer encouragement and support?

## Applying the RELATIONSHIP Research: Developing Personal Mastery

### Steps for Improving Positivity in Relationships

People with the highest levels of success and satisfaction maintain high-quality connections. Everyone experiences ups and downs, but in optimally functioning relationships, people have learned how to boost positivity and downregulate negativity.

Step 1: Maintain awareness of your own emotional state. If you're feeling negative, seek out a key person in your life who will give you support.

Step 2: Commit to generating many more positive than negative interactions with everyone, regardless of how they treat you.

Step 3: Make time to check in on people—especially those you want to have in your inner circle—so you know the "map" of their world.

Step 4: Pay attention to people who want your attention. Empathize if they are stressed and be enthusiastic if they are sharing good news.

Step 5: Develop deep connections with those special people with whom you can share your innermost dreams and values. Agree on goals that you can work together to achieve.

Step 6: Make it psychologically safe for others to express their differing point of view by understanding that there are always competing values in any situation, problems with any plan, and negative reactions to what you've said or done.

Step 7: Express your appreciation for people's kindness, collaboration, and commitment when you feel grateful.

## Applying RELATIONSHIP Research: Developing Team Mastery

### It's Important to Manage Negativity in Relationships

There are times when negative emotions cannot be avoided. Learning to effectively resolve conflicts, frustrations, letdowns, failures, and disagreements is crucial if you are to generate many more positive interactions than negative exchanges. Unmanaged anger can create a deficit in the positive-to-negative emotional ratio that is hard to overcome.

Some people are afraid to express their negative emotions because they are worried about what others will think. Bad feelings bring discomfort and vulnerability. Ultimately, disengaging from relationships is self-defeating because unresolved conflicts erode connections.

Researchers have explored how people in optimal relationships manage their negative emotions so they don't permanently damage their relationships. In fact, studies show that, expressed in the right way, negativity can be good for relationships. Astoundingly, two of the world's most prominent positive psychology researchers concluded[19]:

> Positivity alone is insufficient to the task of helping us navigate social interactions and relationships. Anger is a tool that helps us read and respond to upsetting social situations. As for its benefits, research overwhelmingly indicates that feeling angry increases optimism, creativity, and effective performance, and that expressing anger leads to more successful negotiations and a fast track for mobilizing people into agents of change.

## Steps for Managing Negativity in Relationships

Unmanaged anger can certainly be destructive. However, expressing intensely negative emotions can be done successfully. Here's a compilation of strategies from several sources that have been found to be effective:

Step 1: Breathe. To regulate the emotional flooding that accompanies negative reactions to other people, you must slow down your body's automatic release of stress chemicals. Special Forces troops are taught "4 × 4 breathing" to calm themselves in combat. Count to 4 when you inhale, count to 4 as you hold your breath, do another 4 count as you exhale, and count to 4 before you inhale again. Repeat until your breathing is under control, which means your brain has slowed down enough to be able to return to rational thinking.[20]

Step 2: Picture a positive outcome. Ask yourself, "What would it look like if this problem was resolved?" Become curious about what a win–win outcome might look like. Picturing the specific behaviors you hope to see activates the executive functioning part of your brain.[21]

Step 3: Assume a more powerful position. Be aware of your body language: averting your eyes, closing up, and crossing your arms send the message you are in a low-power position. Instead, assume a powerful posture, spreading out, looking the person in the eye, and leaning forward. Put your hands on the table or on your hips or make a fist. Do NOT demean the other person, scream, or use a hostile tone. DO assert your position forcefully.[22]

Step 4: Declare your distress. When you start talking about your negative emotions, warn the people involved that you're feeling extremely uncomfortable with what is transpiring. Tell them that you're intensely emotional, and that right now it's difficult for you to communicate effectively. Apologize for initiating a difficult discussion by saying something like, "I'm feeling upset right now, which is making it hard for me to express myself. But I feel it's important for me to address the situation because it's bothering me and I want to get it resolved."[19]

Step 5: Put anger to work. Remember that you are trying to influence what is going to happen. Speak slowly, pause frequently, and remain focused on getting to a positive outcome. State your objections to what is occurring and what you think is wrong with it. Then be as clear as possible about what you think would be fair, right, practical, and/or acceptable.[23]

Step 6: Monitor the situation. Is the situation escalating or is the tension subsiding? Are you maintaining your composure or do you need to slow down to stay in control? Is the conversation moving toward a solution? Whenever it is becoming too intense, go back to managing your breathing, recalling your outcome, affirming your desire to find a mutually acceptable result, assuming a strong position, and offering a win–win solution.

Step 7: Take a "timeout." If the conversation becomes gridlocked or hostile, say "Let's take a break and come back to this later." Allow at least 30 minutes for the stress chemicals to subside before returning to the discussion. It's essential to agree on a time to return to the conversation to continue seeking a mutually acceptable resolution.[24]

# Applying RELATIONSHIP Research: Developing a Culture of Progress

## Making Progress Makes for Good Days

Healthcare organizations must develop strategies to increase the number of employees who are more fully engaged in their jobs. The best approach for accomplishing this is to encourage coworkers to help each other every day.

For example, when nurse managers and charge nurses regularly round on the unit to see who needs help with patients, they're creating a working environment that encourages—even expects—that coworkers will pitch in when another nurse has an especially heavy assignment.

Making progress is the biggest determinant of whether an employee feels they've had a good day, according to studies conducted by Amabile and Kramer, two psychologists at Harvard University, Cambridge, Massachusetts.[25] And two-thirds of the time when people have had a good day, someone helped them or provided encouragement. Conversely, experiencing a setback will most likely leave someone feeling they've had a bad day on the job, especially if no one stepped up to provide assistance.

Figure 8.1 shows that 43 percent of the time during which a person makes progress, one or more teammates had become catalysts, directly helping make that progress possible. And 25 percent of the time, another individual provided nourishment in the form of positive social and emotional support. An astounding 85 percent of the days in which employees left work feeling great, one of these elements came into play.

Setbacks are primarily responsible for bad work days. However, Figure 8.2 shows the other two factors that are also prevalent: someone actively hinders your efforts or shows toxic disrespect.

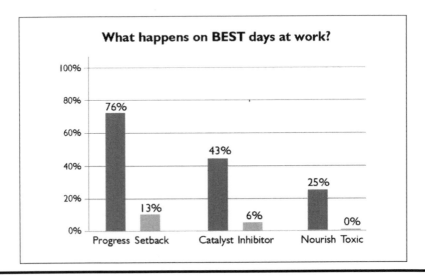

**Figure 8.1    Factors contributing to employees being productive.**

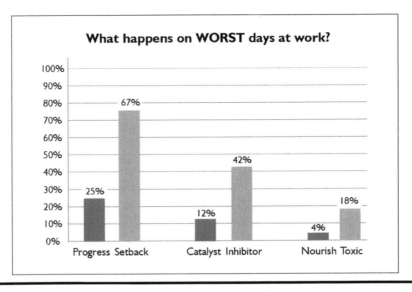

**Figure 8.2    Factors causing employees to underperform.**

Leaders in healthcare organizations can create institutional initiatives to encourage collaborative relationships that enable frontline staff members to figure out how to help one another take care of patients. It's important to make it a daily practice to recognize those who have helped their colleagues during a shift. Install a kudos board for staff members to write "thank-you notes" to the coworker who helped them. Mention their names at the end of shift huddle, and make sure everyone has gotten the help he or she needs so they can leave work at the same time everyone else does.

Rita's story illustrates how this process builds bonds and optimizes performance in the workplace.

## Rita's Story: The Resolution

Rita wanted to get her PROPEL team to envision how they would be better off if they improved their relationships. She scheduled a kickoff meeting to bring the Director of Nursing together with her team to create a shared vision of the future. Rita needed a forum for aligning her outcomes with the needs of the people in her the BMT unit. "No leader can affect change alone," I advised.

The team's first goal was to explore the possibilities for creating a more positive and productive work culture that enabled staff members to be at their best more consistently. At their first meeting, they were given four rules regarding how smart teams achieve superior results:

1. Commit to staying focused on creating a vision of a positive outcome everyone is passionate about achieving.
2. Engage with your teammates frequently; equal participation is expected during the meeting. Leaders are encouraged to let others express their viewpoints first.
3. Read the emotions of your teammates to create at least three positive interactions for every negative exchange.
4. Before advocating for your point of view, use inquiry to understand what others on the team think, believe, and need.

The team was asked to describe situations in which people felt they were able to be at their best. Several case managers spoke of having built good working relationships with people outside of their workgroup—a United Healthcare appeals supervisor, a lab technician, and so on.

One of the case managers reflected on how she had built a really good relationship with one of the physician's administrative assistant. She went out of her way to stop by the woman's office to see how she was doing and to offer help whenever she could. When problems arose, the two women would get on the phone to resolve the issue before it caused an explosion. Typically the two of them ended their day walking to the parking garage together, giving each other kudos for how well they'd handled one crisis after another.

Because the team had never spoken of successful cases, I was surprised when Sherry, the director of nursing for oncology, spoke up to compliment the unit on managing to get BMTs for an average of 20 patients every month. The workgroup received more than 600 referrals every year, and 240 were making it through the complicated process. When I asked how they celebrated success, I was astounded to hear that there was absolutely no discussion, much less appreciation, of their accomplishments.

When asked about what happened when the workgroup was at its worst, the team described tension that would build until it finally erupted. Coworkers sat a few feet apart, but barely spoke for the entire day. One senior staff member was famous for angrily throwing her papers into the air when her frustration level boiled over.

The team began to open up about having jobs in which they encounter one obstacle after another, with little or no support from anyone else.

From these experiences of peaks and valleys, a few common denominators became apparent. The team determined that they were at their best when "we have passion about our work, we collaborate, and we make progress toward our goals." Distilled down to three words, the team's shared values became passion, collaboration, and progress, which are defined as follows:

*Passion*: Being committed to our patients and to the quality of our work; taking ownership of the work; engaging in creative problem solving; feeling we make a difference

*Collaboration*: Communicating with each other in our unit and our department, and with other departments; functioning as a team within our unit and our department and with other departments; being able to access the appropriate data from various sources; trusting others to do their part

*Progress*: Being goal oriented; taking pride in our results; being proactive and empowered to achieve great results; leaving work at days-end feeling pleased with the results

Extrapolating from this common set of core values, the team went on to create a vision of what it would look like if they were living those values more consistently:

We come to work smiling each day, making eye contact, checking in with patients and colleagues, and responding to staff members and patient needs. Staff members will have all they need to do their jobs well—including help from teammates. We'll work together to get patients their BMTs so everyone can leave smiling at the end of the day.

Everyone agreed to become proactive by taking one small step. Each person at the table made a statement that started with "You can count on me to ...."

*Sue:* When I encounter unhappy colleagues, ask what I can do to help.
*Stephanie:* Express appreciation for help I receive.
*Rita:* Ask, "What will it look like when we've solved this problem?"
*Sara:* Express gratitude for three good things that happened that week.
*Kathy:* Start each staff meeting with "at our best stories."
*Sherry:* Share our vision with all of the stakeholders we work with.
*Bernie:* Start each day with "What will it look like if we make today a good day?"

The team was told that future PROPEL meetings would start with a progress report to follow up on each individual's pledge to be proactive every day. "Make 1 percent progress every day and—thanks to the magic of compounding—you'll improve your situation significantly in a short amount of time."

The subsequent PROPEL team meeting started out with a progress check: "You told your teammates they could count on you to introduce more positive behaviors into your workdays. Tell us about your experience doing that."

*Stephanie:* Every day I made a point of catching people doings things right and complimenting them. It was wonderful to see how people in the office responded. There were big smiles, nice hugs, and lots of "thank you!" It was like they were starved for positive feedback. And I noticed that the person I commended usually gave someone else kudos later that day.

*Sue:* I committed to asking coworkers how I could help them if I thought they were getting stressed. All I can say is "Wow." It's only been 2 weeks, but more and more of the staff members are also asking if they can help. Practicing "be the change you want to see in the world" is really working well.

*Sara:* I was going to be grateful for three goods things that happened every week, but it was harder to do than I thought. I found myself dwelling on what had gone wrong at work. So I started focusing on doing it at home. I told my husband about three things that happened with the kids and him that had made me feel good. You know, this stuff works really well at home, too! He likes hearing it and tells me what he loved as well.

*Kathy:* I started out the last two weekly staff meetings by asking people to share good stories about what happened during the week. So far only those of us on the PROPEL team have offered anything, but I did notice that the meetings haven't devolved into bitch sessions the way they usually do.

*Bernie:* I've had a similar experience with starting the day asking "what will it look like if we make this a good day?" Only a couple of PROPEL team people were responding until a couple of days ago when several other nurses chimed in. But it's helped me to ask because I've been reminding myself that I want to walk out at the end of the day with a smile on my face. And I'm happy to say that's been the case most days.

*Rita:* I've been asking people "what will it look like once we've solved this?" every time someone brings me a problem. Most people have an idea of what would help resolve the issue, and they leave my office with something *they* can do. It's making my life a lot better because *I'm* not taking on so many of the problems that need to be addressed. I circle back to staff members to see if the problem was resolved and almost always they were able to fix it. It feels a lot better to be praising people than to be taking on their problems.

"And I spoke to Sherry," Rita added. "She wanted me to tell you that she spoke to the physician group about the impact on patients and staff members when they cancel a surgery that was scheduled. Believe it or not, they had no idea that we had to start the approval process over nearly from the beginning when they do that. The doctors thought it was just making a couple of phone calls to reschedule the patient. We'll see if her talking to them makes a difference."

After receiving a resounding round of compliments for their progress, the next step in each of the PROPEL team meetings was to ask what challenges they would like to discuss to find the next steps the team could take. One of the first issues raised was staff burnout and trying to keep up the pace.

"All I do is work, eat, and sleep," Bernie reported.

"I agree," Kathy added. "I feel frayed around the edges, with no off button."

"Because the nursing staff are not hourly employees, we're not paid for all the hours we work," Sara complained. "Resentment builds, and I think sometimes we take it out on each other."

"To make matters worse, we can't take comp time because we are too busy," Sue added.

"We're expected to do more with less; and because we get it done, nothing changes," Stephanie observed.

Like all human beings—even the most positive among us—negative emotions fired up quickly when the PROPEL team began to discuss a troublesome topic.

Rita's initial reaction was to try to quell the flood of negativity by defending why the problems had persisted: "I've told you that you should take time off when you need to, but you rarely do it—so you can't blame me. Or the fact that this has been going on for a long time, even before I took over as nurse manager."

"Let's pause the conversation for a moment," I advised, "so we can understand what's happening. It's obvious that the staff feels overwhelmed by the workload. They can't get on top of it—even by putting in extra uncompensated time. And Rita's feeling bad that she hasn't been able to fix the problem in spite of her best efforts. Can we all agree that's what going on?"

There was unanimous agreement.

"I'm really sorry that you've been struggling so much for so long," I empathized. "And your unhappiness is certainly understandable. I also learned in our kickoff meeting that every one of you wants to improve the situation. But right now your negative emotions are limiting your brain's ability to see past the problems. Let's all take a few deep breaths."

"I have an idea about what we could do," Sue chimed in shortly thereafter. "What if at the end of the week we shared something we learned that made our job easier. For example, sharing the contact information for someone in another department who is helpful."

"Oh, I like that idea," Kathy responded enthusiastically. "And we could make it part of a celebration for having been successful at getting a patient their transplant."

"So does everyone agree that we'll start an end-of-the-week-celebration during which we share something we learned?" Bernie asked.

And so the PROPEL team started the process of addressing problems each week by understanding people's feelings but not staying stuck in them. Instead, they reoriented to their vision and took a few minutes to contemplate possible solutions.

Another issue surfaced. A disruptive employee, Lynn, was throwing her papers all over the office when she became exasperated. Rita had put her into discipline, which only curtailed the outbursts until her probation came to an end. Because she was the most experienced and productive person on staff, Rita didn't want to terminate her. After learning more about high-quality communication, Rita committed to having a courageous conversation with her.

Rita began the conversation with Lynn by saying: "Today I'd like to talk as colleagues who have the same goal—reduce some of the sources of frustration and help you manage your reactions when problems do arise. Can we agree that we'll both speak respectfully and constructively about what might work better for you and the other people sitting in your office going forward?"

"So you're not going to fire me today?" Lynn asked.

"No," Rita replied. "In fact, I want to have this conversation so you never have another angry outburst. You're too valuable to lose. Think about all of the patients you've helped. Don't you want to be able to do more of that?"

"Yes, but that's why I get so frustrated," Lynn explained. "I blow up when there's a patient I really want to help, like that father of three young kids. I lose it when I run into too many roadblocks and the patient runs out of time. I hate trying so hard and failing to get patients what they need."

"That makes perfect sense to me," Rita responded. "That passion is another reason I want this situation to work out. Can you understand the impact your outbursts have on the other people sitting in the room with you?"

"Yeah, I guess it gets them upset as well," Lynn acknowledged.

"And how do you think that impacts their work?" Rita inquired.

"I never really thought about it. I guess they go about their business while I pick up my papers," Lynn assumed.

"Actually, no one can concentrate for a day or two. Your emotions are contagious, and the rest of the group becomes discouraged as well," Rita explained. "It takes several days before they're able to get back on track and put another patient through the process. We lose patients that way. Not just yours, but some of theirs too."

"Oh. I never thought about that." Lynn was horrified.

"Let's agree that our goal is to get transplants for as many patients as possible, and that we're not going to let setbacks or letdowns stop the work our group is doing to make that happen," Rita proposed.

"I wholeheartedly agree," Lynn stated emphatically.

"If you become frustrated, then what do you think your plan could be to handle the situation more effectively?" Rita asked.

"I'm not sure," Lynn reflected. "I guess I should ask for help, but I'm supposed to be the most knowledgeable person in the office."

"None of us can solve problems well when our emotions flare up," Rita empathized. "And do you think your coworkers would have less respect for you because you asked for help instead of firing off in frustration?"

"I never thought about it that way," Lynn sheepishly admitted. "If I get frustrated, I'd rather ask for help than cause the entire work flow to come to a halt."

After that conversation, Lynn never threw her papers around the office again. In fact, she became one of the leaders in the effort to provide more help for one another.

Over the next 6 months, the team discussed and took action to resolve many other issues:

- *Frustrations with other departments*: The BMT staff members worked in concert with other departments (pharmacy, social work, MDs, lab). They needed to receive timely responses in order to schedule transplants successfully. The PROPEL team developed a script: "What we do to save patients' lives hinges on our ability to work together. Will you help me right now so we can save this patient's life?" Who could say no to that???
- *Lack of physician awareness*: Doctors cancelling surgeries at the last minute was a major obstacle. The team developed another script: "There are 200 patients on the waiting list. We've done the work, and now you want to reschedule the case. Are you aware that if you cancel the scheduled procedure, then we'll need to start all over again? And your patient goes to the bottom of the list." Becoming assertive in direct conversations with the doctors had a major impact. Most of them said they had no idea about the ramifications of their request to reschedule. Those who tried to bully the staff members to get their way were referred to the chairman of the department. After a few months, that disruptive behavior stopped, and so did cancellations.
- *Implementation of a new electronic medical records system*: Staff members were still using both electronic and paper charting. With the tremendous pressure to get all of the pieces in place, this was considered "a monumental waste of precious time." The staff members asked Sherrie, their director, for additional short-term resources to aid in the EMR transition. Request granted.
- *Respect issues*: There was perceived disparity between inpatient and outpatient nurses: "It feels like the outpatient nurses are second-class citizens and are underappreciated compared to other departments." The BMT staff members

began to round on the inpatient unit to meet the patients whose transplants they'd made possible. They received a great deal of much needed appreciation from the patients, families, and other staff members.

■ *Stress over staff members workload*: "It's hard to take the day off or even take lunch or, for that matter, be able to leave my desk to go to the bathroom." The team learned that managing energy rather than time was the best way to achieve success. Breaks became the norm, and productivity increased as energy levels were enhanced.

■ *Disruptive behavior*: The BMT group worked closely in a small area, and lack of consideration created additional stress. "Some people blurt out whatever comes into their heads, with no thought for how that might affect the rest of the group." The PROPEL team took the lead in recognizing that stressful comments were a signal that someone needed help. The new rule is: if someone's bothering you, ask how you can help them.

Week after week, the PROPEL team would develop action steps to overcome these challenges. Each person on the team would commit to making 1 percent progress every day.

Many of the innovative ideas the BMT developed to overcome their challenges worked incredibly well:

■ A ceremony was held every week during which each staff member placed a pearl hued marble in a beautiful glass vase for every case they successfully got through the process. They took turns describing the unique difficulties they had faced, shared strategies they had developed and described what they had learned from the experience. And last, but certainly not least, they spoke about the difference the transplant had made in the patient's life to remind everyone that their work was profoundly meaningful.

■ The case managers developed a daily ritual of expressing profound gratitude to their coworkers who took time away from their own heavy case load to help staff members who became distressed. They worked together to get all the phone calls made, or whatever else needed to be done to meet a deadline.

■ When a staff member had a meltdown, a coworker would stand up, face their colleague, and say "I'm feeling uncomfortable right now, but need to let you know your behavior is disrupting our whole office. If you're frustrated, please ask for help. We want to be able to tackle problems as a team."

■ Rita changed the agenda in staff meetings from feeding people information to active discussions of current cases. Problems with each case were identified, and the entire group took part in identifying strategies to resolve the issues. Coworkers offered to help where they could. For example, "I have a contact at the insurance company. Let me make a call and see if I can get that person to help."

■ As the team began to experience progress, they put a picture of a train on the door to their office with the caption, "We're the little engine that could!"

## The Bottom Line

After a year of using the PROPEL Principles to improve their working environment, the BMT group was able to increase the number of patients who got the lifesaving procedure from 20 to 30 per month. And they did it with the same number of staff members! That was an additional 120 patients whose stories the staff members were able to share and celebrate in the marble ceremony.

Increasing the number of transplants by 50 percent represents a substantial increase in revenue for the hospital. According to the National Foundation for Transplants, the average cost of a BMT is $800,000. That is an additional $96 million a year in revenue.

The value to those patients who were given a chance for survival? That can't be calculated.

# Chapter 9

# Optimism: Changing Your Thinking to Generate Gritty Determination

Anyone who's tried instituting changes in a healthcare facility knows it is a daunting task to achieve significant improvements in a timely manner. Sustaining employees' efforts long enough to get impressive results is rare. In large part, this is due to the difficulties involved in overcoming people's frustrations and discouragement when setbacks occur and mistakes are made.

Most people want to believe that they are optimists who can maintain their positive attitude and motivation, but the facts show otherwise. Most people who diet end up gaining weight. Most marriages end in divorce. Most healthcare employees are disengaged.

This chapter will teach you how to think about problems to give you the best chance of solving them. You will also learn how to teach optimistic thinking to the people you are counting on to help you succeed.

## Terri's Story: The Problem

The door to the Postoperative Transplant Unit's (PTU) nurse manager's office was wide open. I peered in and saw a slightly built, dark haired woman in her mid-thirties staring intently at her computer. I was struck by how orderly, but sparse, her office was.

Knock, knock. Terri took a moment to break away from her computer screen before turning around to greet me. It was more of a questioning look than a greeting. After introducing myself, I got a weak smile and an invitation to grab a seat. She put up her finger to indicate she needed a moment and finished up some work on her computer. "Sorry. I have to get payroll done today," she explained when she'd finished. "With all of the budget cuts, I don't have an admin anymore."

"Sounds like you've got a lot on your plate," I responded. "I'm Dr. Tom Muha, your PROPEL coach, and as you're aware, we'll be working together to figure out how to make your job more manageable."

"Good luck with that," Terri replied wearily.

"One of my favorite quotes defines good luck as the intersection of preparation and opportunity," I offered. "I'm prepared to teach you a new evidence-based approach for managing people. Are you open to the opportunity?"

"Oh yeah," Terri replied, explaining she'd been a nurse manager for 7 years, or as she put it "seven long, hard years." She was an unassuming person, humbly describing the ups and downs of keeping the PTU functioning. "The population of patients coming to our unit makes our job especially challenging. They're younger than most hospital patients, and typically they've received a liver or kidney transplant because their abuse of drugs or alcohol destroyed theirs.

"Our patients are often drugged up on so much pain medication they're rude to the nurse," Terri said ruefully. "That hostile behavior has caused a serious turnover problem. Two years ago, I was blindsided when suddenly more than half my staff members left for other, less demanding jobs. I had to hire 20 new nurses, adding a massive amount of time to my already jam-packed schedule. If that wasn't bad enough," Terri said with a glum look, "I was getting—still am for that matter—a lot of pressure from the director of nursing to reduce patient falls."

I wasn't surprised to hear that her boss was focused on the fall rate. When a hospitalized patient falls, particularly patients as vulnerable as the ones on the PTU, the effects can be serious. Broken bones that require surgery, lacerations that become nonhealing wounds, or trauma that causes neurologic damage are the most common results. Being confined to bed because of a fall increases the likelihood of pneumonia, pressure sores, blood clots—the list goes on.

Falls are devastating for the nurse who was responsible for keeping the patient safe; it's infuriating to the admitting physician; and it's confounding to the family. The average cost to a hospital of one fall is in excess of $13,000 and adds more than 6 days to the patient's stay, according to the Joint Commission. No wonder the unit's patient satisfaction scores were low, averaging below the 70th percentile.

"And what would it look like if the PROPEL program helped you and your unit?"

"Where to begin?" Terri reflected. "There are a number of issues I'd like to see resolved. First, I'd like to see my staff members less frustrated. The physicians meet off the unit and send their nurse practitioners (NPs) over to convey their orders. My nurses have no direct input to the docs. And the communication from the NPs is usually brusque, delivered with an attitude of 'this is what the physician has decided, so do what you're told'.

"There's no sense of teamwork, even among the nurses. What I'd like to see are nurses helping each other rather than being on Facebook," she stated emphatically.

With a note of sadness in her voice, Terri confided: "I'd also like to feel less frustrated. I hate having to stay so late to get everything done and going home exhausted. It's taking a toll on my relationship with my husband because I don't have any energy left for him."

"Those are all serious challenges we can address. PROPEL offers you and your staff members the opportunity to implement some strategies that lead to better outcomes for staff members and patients alike. Would you be willing to do some homework for our next session? Specifically, I think you'd benefit from thinking more about what those positive outcomes will look like," I explained.

"I'll do that. But the truth is, I don't always know what's going on with the staff," Terri confessed. "I'd like you to talk with them to get their perspective."

## *Meeting with the PTU Staff*

I was taken by how young the staff members was. Typically there is a wide age range among the staff members on units. "Tell me how long you all have been nurses," I asked. The answers from the 20 or so people ranged from 6 months to 3 years, except for one RN who'd been on the unit for more than 10 years.

Next I wanted to know, "What would I see happening if I were observing you during a good shift." Several people responded simultaneously: "We'd be helping a nurse who was overloaded."

"The physicians would be communicating what was happening with their patients," chimed another group.

"We'd have more staff members, but everybody knows that's not going to happen," said one of the 3-year veterans. "For that matter," she continued in a derisive tone, "the docs 'won't' start communicating and the nurses aren't able to help out more than they already do."

I didn't have to ask what a bad shift would look like; the floodgates had been opened.

"And when a doctor does talk to you, it is one-way communication," added one of the nurses indignantly. "Even when the patient's having problems, like incontinence, it's impossible to ask their physician about a plan for dealing with the issue."

"Another problem we have with patients is our high fall rate," one of the millennials pointed out. "We need more training to deal with uncooperative or confused patients. And we need the physicians to stop writing so many prescriptions for pain meds. Some patients have so many painkillers in them they can't even stand up. Others become nasty when we try to deal with them."

"These transplant patients are manipulative when it comes to getting pain medications. To make matters worse," one of the fresh faces offered, "they're young and they don't believe they need nurses helping them get to and from the bathroom. That's why the PTU always has the highest patient fall rate in the hospital."

"It's not just difficult asking the physicians for help with patient problems," suggested one of the newer nurses. "I feel bad asking another nurse for help—even when I've got two or three problems happening with patients at the same time."

"We have a number of nurses with bad attitudes," stated one of the young charge nurses. "They have a negative effect on your whole shift. I try to avoid them, but they have a way of getting to you."

"What would I see if I were observing someone with a 'bad attitude'?" I inquired.

"They roll their eyes if you ask for help with something" was the response. "Or, they flat out say, 'I'm too busy'."

I asked the group what they believed would improve the situation.

"Getting a lunch break would help," one of the nurses said sarcastically.

"We've talked about starting to round with physicians. But we need the docs to see the benefits of two-way communication," suggested one of the nurses who had been quiet until then.

"Maybe it would help if we could tie improved communication to increased patient safety," offered the newest nurse on the staff members.

My final question: "Who do you think would be good at building on these ideas and would be willing to work hard to figure out how to implement them? Feel free to nominate yourself." In about a minute 14 names had been offered as potential PROPEL team members.

# The Research on Optimistic Thinking

## Change Initiatives Usually Fail

Typically 75 percent of change initiatives fail.[1] The reasons most often cited are poor communication and skepticism.[2] The truth is that it takes weeks to get employees on board and often months to make real progress toward a goal. Then, just when you think you have some momentum, a setback occurs that can derail your project.

Is this any way to start a chapter on optimism? Yes. Optimism isn't about becoming a Pollyanna—quite the contrary. The power of positive thinking is a myth. *Imagining* the outcome you want to see is merely wishful thinking. The truth is that it takes hard work to overcome the complex challenges that must be tackled to achieve change. Most often pessimistic thinking undermines the staff's ability to persevere long enough to overcome the obstacles they face.

To be clear, it is important to consider the possibility of failure and to identify the pitfalls that could contribute to a poor outcome. In the past few years, renowned optimism researcher Martin Seligman was asked about his current views on optimism: "The idea that optimism is always good is a caricature. It misses realism, it misses appropriateness, and it misses the importance of negative emotion."

While still an advocate of optimism, he says it must be paired with "reality testing—conscientious checking on the results of our efforts—to make sure that overly positive expectations are not leading us astray."[3]

Our thinking needs to have a mix of optimism and realism; but pessimistic thinking has been linked to prematurely giving up when setbacks stall change initiatives. Optimistic thinking gives us the ability to develop realistic strategies that enable efforts to work *around, through, and past obstacles.*[4]

## Defining Optimistic and Pessimistic Thinking

Optimism and pessimism are both learned ways of thinking. We develop habitual ways of viewing the world based on our past experiences. Our "explanatory styles" are stories we've learned to tell ourselves to explain *why* things happen and *what impact* they will have. Every situation is unique, and even people in the same situation will have differing explanations.

Our mind is "a machine for jumping to conclusions," warns Nobel Laureate Daniel Kahneman in his classic book *Thinking, Fast and Slow.*[5] Instead of accurately assessing the challenge we're currently confronting, we frequently fill in a lot of blanks using our old habitual explanations. Because we make assumptions based on what's happened to us in the past, we frequently fail to gather sufficient information for making a sound decision about what to do in the present.

Martin Seligman's research shows that when people are trying to make meaning of events in their lives, they unconsciously define the problem according to three elements that comprise their explanatory style[6]:

- *Personalization*: Who caused the problem? *Me/someone else.*
- *Permanence*: How long will this problem last? *Always/not always.*
- *Pervasiveness*: How much of my life does this problem affect? *Everything/not everything.*

Whenever negative encounters, setbacks, or challenges beset people with an optimistic mind-set, they frame them as temporary ("other units have overcome their patient fall problems"), specific ("tough day at work, thankfully there's someone at home who loves me"), and situational ("tomorrow I'll get ideas from my team about what new actions we can take to resolve this problem").

No matter the setting, individuals who give up demonstrate one trait in common: pessimistic thinking. This explanatory style depicts failure as permanent, pervasive, and personal. If a problem is permanent, it is pointless to try: "Patients seldom listen to our warnings about fall risk, and the younger generation always thinks they know best." If the problem is pervasive, it contaminates every aspect of life: "I feel terrible when patients fall, and that affects the evening with my family." If the problem is personal, it must be somebody's fault: "I'm not good at getting my nursing staff to do what's necessary to prevent patient falls."

Fundamental attribution error is the tendency to explain other people's behavior by placing an undue emphasis on their character or intention rather than external factors.[4] However, when attributing causation to our own behavior, we typically attribute situational factors as an explanation for why we acted as we did.

A classic example would be a scheduled noon lunch meeting to which one party arrives 20 minutes late. If it's the other person who's tardy, we will likely attribute it to personal factors such as poor time management skills. If we're the late one, we'll almost certainly attribute it to some situation out of our control such as heavy traffic.

Rather than getting stuck in the mind-set of learned helplessness or faulty attributions, *optimistic thinking* activates your left prefrontal cortex, allowing you to engage your brain's "executive functioning" capabilities to think about how to change your situation. This mental shift enables you to overrule catastrophic thinking and distressful emotions that are characteristic of *pessimistic thinking*. Choosing to explain situations using an optimistic mind-set breaks the downward spiral into worry and discouragement, or worse—anger and conflict. Optimistic thinking focuses attention on a realistic assessment of the present and possibilities for the future.

## The Benefits of Optimistic Thinking

By challenging pessimistic explanations of negative events and reinterpreting them in optimistic terms, anyone can maintain hope, commitment, and resolve. And, because optimistic thinkers learn to handle problems without taking them personally, they are far better equipped to contend with critics, naysayers, and bullies. People can increase the probability of being successful by first managing their thought process, as that's the mechanism by which they decide how to respond to challenging situations.

Optimism enables hope. Not the wishful thinking kind of hope that says, "maybe tomorrow the weather will be better." But the gritty brand of hope that tells us, while there's nothing we can do about the weather, there are things we could do to make tomorrow a better day.

In addition to having better mental health, optimists perform better in school and on the job. They're more satisfied with their marriages. People who practice optimistic thinking when facing challenges have been shown to be healthier physically and live longer than pessimists because their psychological responses strengthen the telomeres protecting their DNA.[7]

Humans are hardwired to scan for threats, but we need to train our brain how to shift into possibility thinking. When we seek solutions to improve our situation, there is a chance we will find one. When we stop searching, we guarantee we won't. Henry Ford captured it perfectly when he said, "Whether you think you can, or you think you can't—you're right."

## The Downside of Pessimistic Thinking

*Pessimistic thinking*, however, leads to suffering. People who feel they have no control over their situation reliably develop symptoms of depression, including sleep problems, poor concentration, sadness (often in women), irritability (typically in men), changes in appetite and physical activity, and feelings of lethargy.[8]

Believing that you can't change a situation results from having a fixed rather than a growth mind-set, according to Carol Dweck.[9] This Stanford psychologist's research has focused on determining why some people turn out to be optimists and others pessimists. One of her first studies put children into two groups that had to solve progressively more difficult math problems. Half of the kids participated in a success-only program in which they received praise for how well they solved problems no matter how many they completed correctly. The other half were assigned to an "attribution retraining program" that challenged the children's explanations of why they had not solved enough problems correctly by occasionally telling them that they should try harder.

Dweck was testing whether providing only positive reinforcement would prevent prior failures from producing learned helplessness and pessimistic thinking. Or would teaching the children how to interpret their failures by attributing them to lack of effort be more effective at boosting motivation and optimistic thinking? When she retested the children, the success-only group showed no difference in how easily they gave up when facing difficult problems. The attribution retraining group, however, tried harder when challenging problems were presented. The kids in the second group learned to explain failure optimistically as a matter of effort rather than ability.

## Defining Fixed and Growth Mind-Sets

When you experience setbacks, a *fixed mind-set* presents problems because the story you tell yourself focuses on not having what it takes to reach the next level. Your pessimistic explanation will likely focus on your weaknesses, leaving you feeling too discouraged to continue making an effort. A fixed mind-set automatically assumes you're not good enough, and leads you to conclude it's best to cut your losses and give up.

*A growth mind-set*, however, makes the assumption: "I can change. We can improve." Believing that you and your team can grow leads to much different behavior. You'll look for the opportunity to get some mentoring and you'll make a concerted effort to apply what you learn. You'll believe that your team can learn how to achieve outstanding outcomes with proper support and determination.

# Applying OPTIMISM Research: Developing Personal Mastery

## Mind-Sets—Attributions That Affect Performance

Optimism is a key factor in being able to attain optimal functioning—it can make you more powerful, more resilient, and more successful. To increase our optimism, we need to challenge our explanatory styles on each dimension by thinking accurately and flexibly about each situation we encounter.

## What's Your Explanatory Style?

Reflect on these questions:

- In times of stress, do I often blame myself for not reacting well? ("Me" thinking)
- Do I often blame other people for problems that occur? ("Someone else" thinking)
- Do I often feel as if problems are not likely to improve and will adversely affect other aspects of my life? ("Always/everything" thinking)
- Do I typically look at how to start solving a problem, limit its impact, and improve the situation? ("Not always/not everything/not personal" thinking)

## Do You Have a Fixed or Growth Mind-Set?

Studies have shown that people (individually and in teams) explain their talent as fixed at a certain level, or they believe it's possible for them to grow their capabilities. Dweck uses four statements to distinguish between the two groups.[9] Consider your answers as you read each statement:

- Your intelligence is something basic that you can't change much.
- You can learn new things, but you can't really change how intelligent you are.
- No matter how much intelligence you have, you can always change it quite a bit.
- You can always substantially change how intelligent you are.

If you agree with the first two statements and disagree with the last two, Dweck's research suggests that you likely have a fixed mind-set. But if your answers were the opposite, you probably have a growth mind-set.

## Grit—The Secret to Success

Angela Duckworth, a positive psychologist at the University of Pennsylvania, Philadelphia, Pennsylvania, is considered by many to be one of the world's foremost authorities on how to achieve success. She discovered that having "grit"—a combination of passion and perseverance—is the best predictor of who will succeed. Her studies show that people who predictably achieve positive results have optimistic thinking skills which enable them to persevere over adversity.[10]

In contrast, people with a fixed mind-set regarding their abilities were found to be prone to pessimistic self-talk, which caused them to either avoid challenges or give up when confronted with them.

With this framework in mind, Duckworth offers three recommendations for improving the chances of success. First, she suggests updating beliefs about intelligence and talent by learning how the human brain works. Recent research from Alex Korb, a neuropsychologist at the University of California, Los Angeles (Los Angeles, California), who uses functional magnetic resonance imaging to study brain circuits, has proven that you can rewire your brain to combat pessimism and strengthen your optimism pathways. Korb's research reveals two steps a person can take to change his or her brain in ways that promote positive responses[8]:

> The first step is to simply imagine the *possibility* of positive future events. You don't have to believe they will happen, just that they *could* happen. It's possible that you could find true love tomorrow. It's possible that you could find a better job. It's possible that things won't turn out in the worst conceivable way. Recognizing that good things are possible activates the lower (ventral) anterior cingulate. Importantly, the ventral anterior cingulate helps regulate the amygdala, so admitting the possibility of good things helps control the brain's negativity bias.

> The second step to strengthening optimism circuits is not only recognizing that good things *could* happen, but also expecting that they *will* happen. Expecting positive events also activates the ventral anterior cingulate, as well as prefrontal areas that also help control the amygdala.

The second Duckworth recommendation is practicing optimistic self-talk to grow "grit" from the inside out. To motivate yourself and your teammates to change old, habitual ways of thinking requires first understanding why it will be worth the effort.

- How would you personally benefit from becoming more optimistic?
- What difference will becoming more optimistic make at work?
- What new behaviors will you see when you've changed your thinking?
- How will those changes make you feel?
- When have you been at your best at learning new things?
- Who could support your growth into a more optimistic thinker?

Third, Duckworth says you can grow grit from the outside in by asking for help. She cites research showing that people develop mind-sets based on how the people around them respond to their success and failure, particularly those in a position of authority. Find people who believe that you can learn and grow and ask them to help you accomplish a goal. Create PROPEL teams who can develop personal mastery for themselves and then teach it to other staff members.

## Applying OPTIMISM Research: Developing Team Mastery

### Does Your Team Have a Growth or Fixed Mind-Set?

In teams, mind-sets are reflected in statements such as the following[9]:

- It's not possible to change someone's nasty personality.
- You can make someone do their job, but you can't make them have a good attitude.
- No matter how negative someone is, they can always change their mind.
- You can always change your attitude about work.

### Create "Tipping Points" to Engage the Disengaged

Our research in implementing PROPEL has revealed that the attitudes of the middle 50 percent of underengaged employees are influenced by whichever side is winning—the positive people or the pessimists. When the 15–20 percent of staff members who are actively disengaged are able to control the climate by spewing negativity, the middle group "tips" into learned helplessness because they believe their pessimistic coworkers are right—things will never get any better. BMWs (blame, moan, and whiners) control the culture with their infectious negativity, focusing coworkers' minds on what is wrong—and derailing any efforts to improve their situation.

But when there is a group of people willing and able speak up and express an optimistic perspective, the 50 percent of staff members who blow in the wind can "tip" in the other direction. Fashioning PROPEL teams of seven or more of the most highly engaged staff members and training them to use optimistic thinking skills provides an extraordinarily effective force that can counter negative influences. Employees who are already performing at a high level are capable of creating a vision of an optimally functioning culture for the entire unit. In addition, this optimistic group believes that their coworkers can learn and grow. Because they're hopeful, they willing to make an effort to create a high-performing unit.

PROPEL teams often start by finding ways to increase positivity in their work-group. Increasing positive emotions initiates an upward spiral of increased optimism and engagement by expanding our cognitive capabilities and triggering our action repertoire, according to the "broaden-and-build" research of psychologist Barbara Fredrickson.[11]

Getting more employees positively engaged eventually brings enough people on board to help create a tipping point in which the majority of employees support the new behaviors the PROPEL team is promoting. Studies show that at least 65 percent of employees must be engaged to create a high-performing culture; anything less indicates a workforce that is, at best, indifferent to the organization's success.[12]

In a typical work setting, 30 percent of employees are already engaged. PROPEL teams recruit them to be "early adopters." When the disengaged see the top 30 percent of their coworkers taking action to improve the working conditions, they come to believe they could do so as well. Our studies show that it typically takes 6–12 months to achieve a tipping point in which at least two out of three employees have joined the effort.

This method stands in stark contrast to the standard approach of trying to fix the problem by changing the behavior of the most negative employees. Of course, negative behaviors cannot be ignored, especially if they involve harm (physical or psychological) to patients or coworkers. But discipline should come quickly and be matter of fact. The goal is to take away the power of negative people by denying them their pessimistic platform—no arguing, debating, attention, or audience for those with a fixed pessimistic mind-set.

Change is achieved incrementally. Progress checks in regularly scheduled meetings sustain optimism that the goal can be attained. Using appreciative inquiry allows for a root–cause analysis of success and offers a safe environment to discuss what has been learned from setbacks.

Keep in mind, however, that persistent problems are not solved easily. No single intervention is sufficient to overcome complex, chronic issues that are rooted in human behavior. Cultivating grit by establishing a positive outcome a PROPEL team is passionate about pursuing encourages persistent effort and offers the best chance of success.

## Applying OPTIMISM Research: Developing a Culture of Influence

There is a tool PROPEL teams have found to be extraordinarily effective in getting their coworkers engaged: the six sources of influence. The research supporting this model demonstrates that effective influencers rely on six different sources to drive change. They are 10 times more likely to succeed at achieving a "tipping point" when they've learned to simultaneously use at least four sources of influence to produce significant and sustainable change. This method of motivating larger groups of people is described in the *New York Times* bestseller *Influencer: The New Science of Leading Change.* The authors write[13]:

> Unless and until we develop far more effective ways of thinking about and exerting influence on human behavior, we will never solve the most profound and persistent problems in our organizations, our personal lives, and our world.
>
> Unfortunately, we live in a quick-fix world full of people who are gimmicked into believing that a simple solution exists for their monumentally complex behavior problem. This goes for both business and personal challenges. We want one trick to get employees to improve quality or one trick to help us shed thirty pounds.

Patrice Putman, director of employee development at MaineGeneral Health, wanted to improve patient safety and employee satisfaction.[13] She knew that employees would need to radically improve their confidence level to be able to speak up candidly at critical times.

Putman "overdetermined success" by implementing a multipronged influence effort. Her first step was to identify the behaviors that needed to change. She knew from experience that training people to assert themselves in order to increase their ability to speak up would be necessary but insufficient. She provided plenty of deliberate practice so that staff members could learn to voice concerns with ease.

Another source of influence was garnering the support of key opinion leaders. Based on those conversations, changes to policies, work layout, and organizational structure were made. In addition, Putman aligned the performance review systems with the target behaviors. By taking a multifaceted approach that harnessed individual, social, and structural influence sources, Putman completely transformed the organizational culture. The results would be as follows: Staff satisfaction scores improved on 41 of 42 questions on the annual survey, and there was a 53 percent increase in staff willingness to address dangerous behaviors and ability to learn from mistakes in patient care.

Figure 9.1 graphically displays the six sources of influence that are demonstrated by the MaineGeneral Health story.[13]

As Terri's story continues, you'll see how a PROPEL team is able to influence the development of optimistic thinking and behavior change.

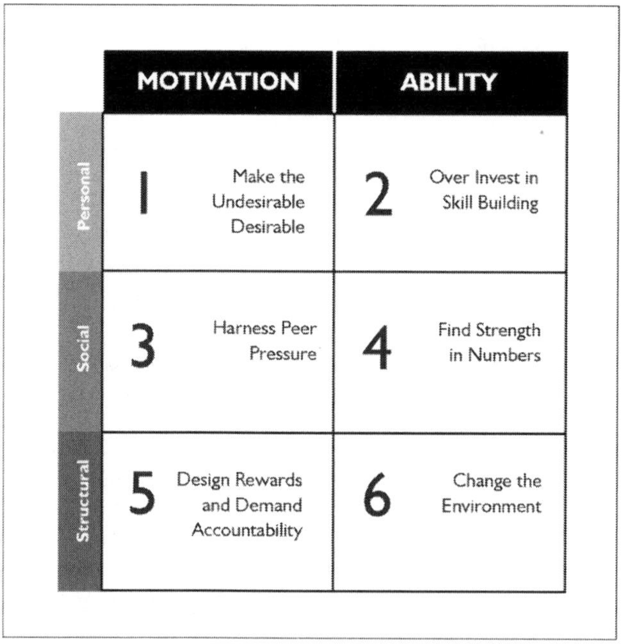

| MOTIVATION | | ABILITY | |
|---|---|---|---|
| **Personal** | **1** Make the Undesirable Desirable | **2** | Over Invest in Skill Building |
| **Social** | **3** Harness Peer Pressure | **4** | Find Strength in Numbers |
| **Structural** | **5** Design Rewards and Demand Accountability | **6** | Change the Environment |

**Figure 9.1　The six sources of influence.**

## Terri's Story: The Resolution

"To start every session, I'll be asking you for a progress report," I told Terri at the beginning of our session. "Today I'd like to check on how you did developing a picture of the behaviors you'd like to see if your staff members were functioning at their best. I'm also curious about how imagining the possibilities for a better future impacted you."

"Sure," Terri responded. "I found it much harder than I expected to state the outcome in terms of what I 'do' want to see with my staff members. My mind kept focusing on the problems rather than the positive outcome. And even when I wrote down things like 'better teamwork,' I realized that I needed to add the observable behaviors that would constitute great teamwork."

"The exercise was eye opening," she continued. "I've always thought of myself as a positive person, but this helped me realize that I tend to focus on what's wrong rather than picturing the changes I want us to work toward. As positive images came to mind, I felt differently. Instead of overwhelmed, I felt hopeful. And I automatically began to think about how I could get my staff members to work in new ways. I even ran some ideas by a few of the staff members who I think may work well on the PROPEL team. I wanted to know what they thought we could do to reduce the number of patient falls."

"And how did they respond?" I asked.

"They believe that providing more help to a nurse who's overloaded could make a difference. Patients get impatient waiting for someone to come when they want to get out of bed."

"That's progress. I'm happy to hear that you've already discovered a useful tool. I applaud your efforts," I said, giving her two thumbs up. "Sounds like you're ready to select a group of your most motivated staff members for your PROPEL team. We'll begin with a kickoff meeting to hear what they believe will make the PTU a better unit. We'll align their vision of the future with yours."

"Let's schedule something soon," Terri replied. "But I want to know what you learned when you met with the staff members."

"I was somewhat surprised to discover that most of your staff members have been nurses for less than 3 years," I admitted. "Several of them mentioned they're afraid to ask for help when they get swamped for fear of looking incompetent. And they're not even getting a real lunch break, which is contributing to their feeling overloaded.

"They're particularly dissatisfied that they have so little opportunity to talk to the physicians," I continued. "They see the patient fall problem as a function of the physicians overprescribing pain meds and the younger patient population being unwilling to listen to their warnings about fall risks. We'll have to help them expand their explanation of the problem. Right now they're focusing exclusively on how the MDs contribute to the fall problem. We'll need to help them look at what they might do to improve the situation.

"The good news is...they also see some possible solutions," I added. "I heard the same thing when I spoke to the staff members—they need to learn how to help one another. They're optimistic about getting multidisciplinary (multi-D) rounds started soon. The nurses are eager to discuss patients with the physicians."

"Well, you did a good job with your homework as well," Terri said with a wry smile.

When a group of the most engaged staff members met with Terri in a 2-hour kickoff meeting off the unit, they were able to reflect on when they were at their best—and worst. From that discussion, the PROPEL team was able to agree on what consistently high performance would look like: RNs and MDs communicating daily, staff members helping each other on every shift, and patients *always* getting the assistance they needed to get out of bed safely.

Terri disclosed that she had been discussing the research on multidisciplinary rounds with the physicians and nurse practitioners. She had been able to show them the evidence that bedside rounds typically improve patient care and increase patient safety. After many meetings, the physicians and nurse practitioners had finally agreed to give them a trial. The PROPEL team was eager to support implementation of the first part of their vision.

But when the time came to start the multi-D rounds the doctors became resistant. Terri and the six other members of PROPEL team lapsed into pessimistic explanations regarding the struggle:

> The docs and NPs don't respect us.
>
> They don't care about our input regarding the patients.
>
> It's been this way for years—it's never going to change.

"Let's look at this problem through the lens of optimistic versus pessimistic thinking," I advised. "Are you making this personal, pervasive, and permanent? Or are you explaining the challenge as situational, specific, and temporary?"

The team universally agreed they were thinking pessimistically—and feeling discouraged as a result. As soon as they recognized their explanations were self-defeating, they began to reframe their thinking to more optimistic explanations.

> Change is always difficult in the beginning. We just need to try harder and longer.
>
> How could we change the situation to make multi-D rounds easier and faster?
>
> What do you think will motivate the providers?

We also discussed tipping points: "Think about recruiting a few of the docs and nurse practitioners with whom you have good relationships to help with this effort. They, in turn, can help their peers see that multi-D rounds can work well. Once you get to two-thirds participation, you'll have reached the tipping point and most everyone will get on board." The PROPEL team quickly shifted to possibility thinking:

> Who are the most positive physicians and NPs we could approach to request support for getting the multi-D rounds launched?
>
> How could we show appreciation for the one or two people who have been willing to get the multi-D rounds started?

The session ended with everyone having homework. Each person chose a doctor or nurse practitioner to approach, and the team developed an elevator speech to deliver:

> We know you're as concerned about patient care and safety as we are. We're making an effort to reduce patient falls, and we need your help. Getting multi-D rounds going would enable us to work together to conduct a fall risk assessment and create a plan for each patient, including a discussion about medications. What can we do to get your support?

At the following week's PROPEL team meeting, I learned that about a third of the physicians and nurse practitioners had started participating in the multi-D rounds. We were a couple of weeks into it, but the team was feeling good about finally making progress. A few early "wins" were what they needed to give them an initial boost of confidence. Overcoming an obstacle was just what they needed to prepare them to persevere through the months of ups and downs that they would likely encounter.

Riding their initial wave of encouragement, the group considered next steps to build on their success. There was a widespread agreement that they needed to shorten the time spent with each patient because the rounds were taking too long.

> When I was in the military, we had a script for rounds. Well, we had a script for everything, but it worked really well for efficient rounding.
>
> Yes, many of us are new nurses and we get nervous or talk too much.
>
> If we had a script, it would clarify what's important to cover and at what level of detail.

The team came up with a short script for the nurses. Homework: each PROPEL team member would test the script during the next week and ask another nurse to try it as well.

The following week's progress report revealed that the team's trial-and-error effort to evaluate and revise the script had uncovered some shortcuts. Bouncing ideas back and forth, the team created an even more efficient script.

The PROPEL team wondered if they would be able to get the rest of the nurses to use the script in multi-D rounds. I suggested we use the six sources of influence model and pulled up the "All Washed Up" YouTube video on my laptop for them to watch. After seeing little kids become convinced to use hand sanitizer after being exposed to four sources of influence, the PROPEL team knew they could use a similar approach with their peers. They quickly became immersed in a discussion of how to impact the other nurses' willingness and ability to use the newly developed script:

> We need to help people see why this is important—for themselves as well as our patients. Let's create a one-page list of the benefits of efficient multi-D rounds.
>
> We were influential in our one-on-one conversations with our top docs. I'll bet that'll work with our best nurses as well.
>
> That's a good idea. And we could ask that same group to help us do a few practice sessions with some of our new nurses.
>
> As the nurse manager, I can impress upon people the importance of this initiative in our next staff meeting. And I can join the multi-D rounds to encourage the nurses to use the script.

Over the next few weeks, the PROPEL team commandeered a bulletin board, putting up a poster extolling the benefits. They hosted "Chat & Chew" lunches, luring staff members with free food and—once ensnared—getting them to practice using the script. True to her word, Terri was encouraging with the staff members, sending out e-mails, talking up the plan in staff meetings, and "catching them doing things right" during rounds.

Six weeks after starting the multi-D rounds, the PROPEL team declared victory. The docs and nurse practitioners were consistently participating, and the nurses' script worked well to keep their input brief and focused. And some hoped-for benefits came to fruition as everyone became better informed; the provider group started cutting back on pain meds, and the nurses had a much better sense of the patients' treatment plans.

The PROPEL team was feeling empowered. That was the good news. The patient fall rate, however, remained stubbornly high. When Terri shared the news with the PROPEL team, they were surprised, then saddened, and finally, dejected. These swings of up and down emotions are characteristic of the teams who take on long-standing challenges. The process is always more complicated than they expect, takes longer than they want, and requires more perseverance than they thought they had.

This group, however, was like most PROPEL teams: they were staff selected because their peers and manager believed they were especially resilient. They needed some help getting past their negative reaction and putting their thinking caps back on. "What have you learned as a team about how to make significant improvements on your unit?" I inquired. The switch to optimistic thinking enabled them to rally:

> Change requires trial and error. Some ideas work right off the bat, but most need tweaking before they're effective.

> Don't start by trying to change the most negative people. Begin with like-minded colleagues who are already engaged and get them to help create a "tipping point" where the majority are working together to change things up.

> Be the change you want to see. Try out new activities yourself, like we did with testing the script we use with the providers. Not only did we learn how to improve the script, but a lot of the staff members were curious about what we were doing and shared their ideas.

> The six sources of influence is one of the most amazing things we learned. It's incredible how people comply when they have multiple reminders of what they need to be doing differently. Much more effective than "holding them accountable."

As the PTU PROPEL team mentally changed gears, their restrictive negative emotions subsided. They were able to engage in possibility thinking. "You've overcome one obstacle by getting the providers more engaged, but there are obviously other challenges that need to be addressed to continue progressing to your goal. What else will the team need to tackle in order to reduce the patient fall rate?" I inquired.

> We could get better bed alarms. The ones we have set off too many false alarms, so staff turns them off or doesn't respond as quickly as they could.

> We could increase the frequency of checks on high-risk patients, but we're already overloaded so I'm not sure how well that will work.

> Yes, all of those things are true. And early on we talked about helping each other out when someone's overloaded.

> Another piece of this is getting the patients to take more responsibility. I'm not sure how successful we'll be if they're not more willing to contribute to keeping themselves safe.

"That's the way to sort through the complexities," I encouraged. "How could you explore these ideas and seek other possible solutions?"

The PROPEL team quickly coalesced around a plan to go to the staff members to ask the same questions they were pondering: What worked to get us this far? What problems remain and what solutions can you suggest? For homework, each of the team members agreed to conduct a mini appreciative inquiry with three colleagues. That would result in a total of 21 staff interviews.

"Progress report?" I ask at the following week's meeting. The energy in the room was back:

> I heard from several people that they really liked having a script for multi-D rounds and that we should devise a script for talking to patients.

> I had staff members tell me they thought signs in the patient rooms could be an effective reminder. They even know where to go to get them translated into Spanish and Arabic.

> Someone suggested signs for the staff members on the patient's door that have big block letters saying HIGH RISK FOR FALL!

> I had a tech come up with an interesting idea: paint the strings on the call bell cords in bathrooms red so they stand out against the white walls.

> And we could put up a sign in there saying "Call, Don't Fall!"

Another good idea came from a charge nurse who thought getting families to help might make a difference. He suggested putting a sheet entitled "Fall Risk Information—What You Can Do to Help" in the welcome packet given to patients and family members.

It took another 6 months for the PROPEL team to implement these ideas. The signs for staff members went up first: (number) days without a fall. The PTU went from 5–7 days to 30, then to 45, and eventually to 80. Each time there was a fall the entire PROPEL team did a debriefing instead of Terri calling the nurse into her office for a one-on-one conversation about her individual performance. Because they looked at the entire situation to determine the all of the factors that contributed to the fall, they were able to create a multifaceted solution. The PROPEL team would then explain to the rest of the staff members how they could play a role in preventing a fall when a similar situation arose.

The RN script for talking to patients evolved slowly. At first just the PROPEL team tried various versions to gauge patient reactions. Once they had revised the script to their liking, the team would take it to a few of the coworkers they thought would give it a fair test and provide good feedback.

More revisions followed, the most important of which was the discovery of how important the nonverbal communication was when it came to gaining the patient's compliance. Going into each patient's room and rattling off a rehearsed script the way flight attendants do was a bust. The nurses found that what worked best was looking the patient in the eye. Then they had a genuine conversation about how important it was to both of them that the patient does not have to spend an extra couple of weeks in the hospital because of a fall.

And the cords got painted red. The signs went up in patient rooms and next to the toilets. The HIGH RISK FOR FALL door signs got the staff's attention. Family members were also more motivated to read and follow the "How You Can Help" instructions in the welcome packet.

After 9 months of persistence, the PTU's patient fall rate dropped 70 percent. Although it varies from month to month, the fall rate has remained one of the lowest in the hospital.

Optimistic thinking has three elements, the PTU PROPEL team reported at the end of the initiative:

- *Realistic* assessment: "We need to understand all aspects of the situation that contributed to the problem, not focus on who's at fault."
- A *growth* mind-set: "We need to learn new behaviors to overcome the old patterns that perpetuate this problem."
- A *grit* mentality: "We have to find multiple methods for creating and sustaining passion in order to persevere to a tipping point."

## Chapter 10

# Proactivity: Using Your Best Traits to Achieve the Best Results

Optimism changes how you think, enabling you to see possible solutions to problem situations. You must take action, however, to get to the positive outcome you desire. Fearing failure and doubting your abilities triggers negative reactions when it comes time to act, bringing out your worst characteristics. Choosing to be proactive when facing challenges is the opposite of being reactive. People who are most successful at achieving their goals proactively play to their strengths—consciously deploying their best attributes in order to perform at their best.

## Steve's Story: The Problem

When I first spoke with Steve, a psychiatrist and Medical Director of the Psychiatry inpatient unit, he explained that his staff members were embroiled in constant conflict. "They're frequently at each other's throats, and relationships between the Psych unit and staff members in the ER are even worse. We can't get Psych patients onto our unit fast enough for Bill [the ER Medical Director]. My pager is going off constantly," Steve lamented. "My staff is beyond stressed. There's a lot of yelling going on."

"And I'm frustrated that patient care is suffering as a result," Steve relayed with dismay. "Some days it seems like we've become a holding tank rather than a treatment facility. Our unit is a revolving door for severely disturbed patients who are with us for less than a week. As soon as they're somewhat stable, the insurance companies say they've got to be released. But they're usually back in a matter of months. I can understand why my staff is discouraged."

Psychiatric patients are difficult to manage for a lot of reasons. In an Emergency Room (ER), doctors and nurses stand at the ready to foil a heart attack, diagnose pneumonia and get the antibiotics started, clean out and sew up a deep cut, X-ray a limb and fix a fracture, or stop a stroke in its tracks. They specialize in emergency medicine because they like to identify a problem and fix it—fast. Immediate gratification. Patients are in and, as quickly as possible, out; discharged home or admitted to a floor for further treatment as a hospitalized patient.

Mental illness is a different animal. The problem can't be seen with an X-ray or a blood test. These patients tend to be disruptive and, sometimes, violent. The ER wants to get them out quickly so they can get back to doing what they do best— taking care of physically ill and injured patients. This was the source of Steve's problem when we first met. Patients on stretchers, waiting to be admitted to the Psychiatric unit, were clogging the ER hallways and stretching thin the capabilities of the ER nurses. Steve and his staff members felt the pressure constantly, yet they couldn't seem to devise a better process.

When I met with Bill, the medical director of the Emergency Department (ED), his anger was palpable. "Diversions of ambulances coming to our ER have been necessary because there are times psych patients take up all the available space in the ER. We're averaging 168 hours of diversion every month," he fumed. "All while there are beds available in the hospital that remain empty because we're turning away ambulances!"

"I know you want to help, but this problem has been going on for years and I don't see how this 'positive psychology' stuff could possibly change anything," Bill stated emphatically. "We've had other consulting groups in here over the years and nothing changed. The staff members on the Psych unit can't get their act together. I'm sorry, but I don't have the time for PROPEL right now."

"I understand that many of your ER staff members are feeling frustrated about making changes after other initiatives failed to remedy the problem. Steve is interested in seeing if PROPEL could help his Psych unit, which could also benefit the ER. Would you be willing to allow a few of your staff members who are interested to meet with Steve's staff members to explore possible solutions?" I asked with as much courage as I could muster.

"Yeah, sure, whatever. If you can find anyone who wants to do it on their own time, that would be okay with me," Bill said with a wave of his hand as he ushered me out of his office.

Robert, the president of the hospital, was putting a lot of pressure on Steve and Bill to fix the patient flow problem. He wanted to maximize the number of patients admitted through the ER because they represent a major contribution to the revenue stream. He explained to me that when Bill declares a "diversion," new patients are transported to other medical centers. "Here's something I'd like you to read about the cost of diverting patients," Robert said, sliding a 2013 article from *Emergency Physicians Monthly* across his desk:

To calculate the cost, one might count the average number of EMS patients arriving during the busy hours of the day (not including the middle of the night, when diversion rarely is utilized). Assume that arrival rate is a modest two EMS patients per hour. Count the average revenue for ED services for those patients for the hospital. Many hospitals use a direct revenue figure per patient of $500. Calculate the average rate of admission for arriving EMS patients. In the 2012 ED Benchmarking Alliance survey, it is 40 percent. Calculate the average contribution to overhead for a patient that is admitted. Many financial officers report that an admitted patient contributes $6000 above the direct cost of service. If that is the case, every 10 patients diverted costs the hospital 4 admissions, or $24,000. Calculating an economic loss for 10 patients then equals: $500 times six patients ($3000) plus $24,000 for admissions, totaling $27,000, or $2700 per patient. So the cost of an hour of diversion for an ED that greets two EMS patients per diversion hour is $5400. This is direct revenue loss only, not the loss of the patient for future visits and admissions, and loss of relationship with EMS.[1]

When I finished reading, I looked over at Robert and shared one of my favorite quotes: "Harvard psychologist Rosebeth Moss Kanter once wrote that 'The happiest people I know are dedicated to dealing with the most difficult problems'. You're making me a very happy man."

"Keep my hospital from losing $5400 an hour, and I'll be a happy man too," Robert retorted.

This is the type of complex and costly problem that healthcare executives contend with every day. There are lots of moving parts, contentious relationships, failed change initiatives, and feelings of frustration. All of the ingredients that bring out the worst in people and limit effective action.

# The Research on Proactivity

## *Defining Proactivity*

The opposite of reacting negatively to a problem is responding proactively by engaging your best qualities—your strengths. Even though they feel pressure, high performers learn to rise to a challenge. Like all human beings, their brain initially floods with stress chemicals and they feel the same wave of fear that drives fight–flight–freeze reactions in all of us. But they have trained themselves to overcome those base instincts and have rewired their brains so they can routinely respond effectively. Athletes call it "being in the zone."

Creating an optimal response to a problematic situation starts with changing your thinking. You must be able to picture a positive outcome, and then align it with what other stakeholders need in order to motivate the majority of the people involved in the change initiative. The team leading the effort must remain optimistic in order to persevere past opposition and setbacks.

Positive thinking without action, however, is merely wishful thinking. The most effective way to take action, researchers have found, is to consistently use your *strengths*.

## What Are Strengths?

When it is time to take action, knowing and using strengths is the easiest, least stressful, and most effective way to successfully achieve a goal. Strengths, functional Magnetic Resonance Imaging (fMRI) studies show, are natural talents we have developed to such a high degree they've become hard-wired in our brains. They enable us to perform at our best. Employees who use their strengths at work are *six* times more likely to be engaged in their jobs, have lower turnover, higher productivity, and greater patient satisfaction.[2]

Alex Linley at the Center for Applied Positive Psychology defines a strength as "a pre-existing capacity for a particular way of behaving, thinking or feeling that is authentic, energizing to the user, and enables optimal functioning, development and performance."[3] Linley's research has revealed that learning to use your strengths is "the smallest thing you can do to make the biggest difference."

Strengths are on display when you are doing something at which you are good and find enjoyable. Almost everyone has had times when they were looking forward to engaging in an activity and found themselves completely absorbed when doing it. When the activity was over, they felt an increased sense of confidence, energy, and satisfaction.

When you are using your strengths to perform a task, your actions are effortless because they have become second nature. After years of practice, your brain has become hardwired to engage these patterns of behavior automatically. Think of signing your name: You don't have to consciously tell your dominate hand how to write your name; however, it takes conscious thought to sign with your other hand.

## Two Types of Strengths—Internal and External

Your *inner character strengths* align your values with your actions. When your deepest personal beliefs are consciously connected to your behaviors, your choices have clarity and your actions feel authentic. Research reveals that learning to use your character strengths reduces stress and builds confidence, increases energy and engagement, and boosts both happiness and job satisfaction. Developing the use of your inner strengths promotes personal well-being *and* is intrinsically motivating.[4]

Your *externally applied strengths* were defined by Gallup psychologist Don Clifton as "the consistent near perfect performance in an activity that leads to high achievement."[5] Clifton's 30 years of research led him to conclude that strengths are based on natural talents that are developed early in our life and are our most productive way to function. Because we receive recognition, reinforcement, and rewards when we perform at our best, using talent-based strengths is extrinsically motivating.

For example, some people have a knack for developing close connections with others and with practice they develop the strength of "Relator." Once established, this strength can be amplified by becoming more knowledgeable about how relationships work, practicing skills that build connections, and learning lessons from life experiences. The better someone becomes at using their Relator strength, the more likely that he or she is to be selected as a class president, a team captain, or a leader in their organization.

## Internal Strengths

When positive psychology was emerging as a science in the late 1990s, Martin Seligman and Chris Peterson set out to discover those inner character traits that—when used consistently—enabled people to attain the highest level of life satisfaction. These two positive psychology pioneers researched human history and cultures around the world to identify the characteristics that are universally recognized as worthy attributes. They identified 24 personal qualities and referred to them as VIA (values in action) Character Strengths. When these positive traits are exercised, they produce feelings of invigoration and excitement, a desire for further development and additional deployment, and a sense of "This is me at my best."

Knowing your Character Strengths and using them frequently, numerous studies show, leads to a personally fulfilling life. In particular, people who routinely utilize the strengths of hope, love, curiosity, and gratitude report having the highest levels of happiness and long-term life satisfaction.[6]

## The 24 VIA Character Strengths©*

Here is a description of each character strength:

1. *Wisdom and knowledge*—Cognitive strengths that entail the acquisition and use of knowledge
   - **Creativity** (originality, ingenuity): Thinking of novel and productive ways to conceptualize and do things; includes artistic achievement but is not limited to it
   - **Curiosity** (interest, novelty seeking, openness to experience): Taking an interest in ongoing experience for its own sake; finding subjects and topics fascinating; exploring and discovering
   - **Judgment** (critical thinking): Thinking things through and examining them from all sides; not jumping to conclusions; being able to change one's mind in light of evidence; weighing all evidence fairly

---

- **Love of learning**: Mastering new skills, topics, and bodies of knowledge, whether on one's own or formally; obviously related to the strength of curiosity but goes beyond it to describe the tendency to add systematically to what one knows
- **Perspective** (wisdom): Being able to provide wise counsel to others; having ways of looking at the world that make sense to oneself and to other people

2. *Courage*—Emotional strengths that involve the exercise of will to accomplish goals in the face of opposition, external or internal
    - **Bravery** (valor): Not shrinking from threat, challenge, difficulty, or pain; speaking up for what is right even if there is opposition; acting on convictions even if unpopular; includes physical bravery but is not limited to it
    - **Perseverance** (persistence, industriousness): Finishing what one starts; persisting in a course of action in spite of obstacles; "getting it out the door"; taking pleasure in completing tasks
    - **Honesty** (authenticity, integrity): Speaking the truth but more broadly presenting oneself in a genuine way and acting in a sincere way; being without pretense; taking responsibility for one's feelings and actions
    - **Zest** (vitality, enthusiasm, vigor, energy): Approaching life with excitement and energy; not doing things halfway or halfheartedly; living life as an adventure; feeling alive and activated

3. *Humanity*—Interpersonal strengths that involve tending and befriending others
    - **Love**: Valuing close relations with others, in particular those in which sharing and caring are reciprocated; being close to people
    - **Kindness** (generosity, nurturance, care, compassion, altruistic love, "niceness"): Doing favors and good deeds for others; helping them; taking care of them
    - **Social Intelligence** (emotional intelligence, personal intelligence): Being aware of the motives and feelings of other people and oneself; knowing what to do to fit into different social situations; knowing what makes other people tick

4. *Justice*—Civic strengths that underlie healthy community life
    - **Teamwork** (citizenship, social responsibility, loyalty): Working well as a member of a group or team; being loyal to the group; doing one's share
    - **Fairness**: Treating all people the same according to notions of fairness and justice; not letting personal feelings bias decisions about others; giving everyone a fair chance
    - **Leadership**: Encouraging a group of which one is a member to get things done, and at the same time maintaining good relations within the group; organizing group activities and seeing that they happen

5. *Temperance*—Strengths that protect against excess
   - **Forgiveness**: Forgiving those who have done wrong; accepting the short-comings of others; giving people a second chance; not being vengeful
   - **Humility**: Letting one's accomplishments speak for themselves; not regarding oneself as more special than one is
   - **Prudence**: Being careful about one's choices; not taking undue risks; not saying or doing things that might later be regretted
   - **Self-regulation** (self-control): Regulating what one feels and does; being disciplined; controlling one's appetites and emotions

6. *Transcendence*—Strengths that forge connections to the larger universe and provide meaning
   - **Appreciation of beauty and excellence** (awe, wonder, elevation): Noticing and appreciating beauty, excellence, and/or skilled performance in various domains of life, from nature to art to mathematics to science to everyday experience
   - **Gratitude**: Being aware of and thankful for the good things that happen; taking time to express thanks
   - **Hope** (optimism, future-mindedness, future orientation): Expecting the best in the future and working to achieve it; believing that a good future is something that can be brought about
   - **Humor** (playfulness): Liking to laugh and tease; bringing smiles to other people; seeing the light side; making (not necessarily telling) jokes
   - **Spirituality** (faith, purpose): Having coherent beliefs about the higher purpose and meaning of the universe; knowing where one fits within the larger scheme; having beliefs about the meaning of life that shape conduct and provide comfort

## External Strengths

Over the past 25 years, the Gallup organization studied millions of managers searching for those who consistently perform at the highest level. Gallup has uncovered 34 strengths that top performers use in the workplace, not only to enhance their own performance but also to bring out the best in their team.

> People who use their strengths every day are six times more likely to be engaged on the job. Research has established a compelling connection between strengths and employee engagement in the workplace—a connection that has the power to accelerate performance when companies work on enhancing both simultaneously.[8]

Another compelling finding from Gallup is that the most successful leaders do not treat everyone the same way. Quite the opposite, in fact. They pay attention to each employee's unique talents and match their job to their strengths. Rather than trying to fix someone's weaknesses so they function in their role, the best managers find a job that is the right fit for the person. Does it make a difference?

Gallup conducted a meta-analysis of 50 years of their polls delineating the world's most admired leaders. Their analysts combined 20,000 in-depth interviews with senior leaders with studies of more than one million work teams. Three key success factors characterized the leaders who were most effective because they spend their time[9]:

1. Investing in strengths.
2. Surrounding themselves with the right people and maximizing their team.
3. Understanding their followers' needs.

The *first success factor* enables leaders to match employees' best talents to the task at hand. When a leader fails to focus on how a person can best apply their strengths, the odds of that individual being engaged in their job is only 9 percent—that's only 1 in 11 employees! No wonder leaders who ignore strengths need to spend so much time following up to be sure people are getting their work done. Contrast that with leaders who do focus on helping their employees' use their strengths: nearly three out of four (73 percent) of their workers are engaged in doing a good job.

The *second success factor* is recognition that you personally do not have every skill set required for effectively achieving goals. The advantage of focusing on coworkers' strengths is that you don't have to be perfectly well rounded; you can create a team that is. By surrounding yourself with people who compliment your own strengths, you can create teams that have strengths in all four of the domains required for optimal performance—executing, influencing, relationship building, and strategic thinking.[9] As seen in Figure 10.1, a team that has strengths in all four domains can take the pressure off you to perform well in areas that are not your strong suit.

Optimal teamwork requires individuals who can contribute in all four domains. People with executing strengths are skilled at making things happen and work hard to implement solutions. Those with influencing attributes speak up to promote a team's ideas in a workgroup and within the larger organization, making sure the team's message gets shared with the broadest possible audience. Team members with relationship building strengths supply the glue that bonds a group of individuals, demonstrating their unique abilities to help a team be much more than the sum of its parts. And people who bring strategic thinking skills keep teams focused on what could be, enabling them to analyze data to make the best decisions to reach their goals.

The *third success factor* defining great leaders is that they have fantastic followers. When Gallup asked 10,000 followers what they want and need from their leaders, four basic needs emerged: trust, compassion, stability, and hope.[10]

## The Four Domains of Leadership Strengths

| Executing | Influencing | Relationship Building | Strategic Thinking |
|---|---|---|---|
| Achiever | Activator | Adaptability | Analytical |
| Arranger | Command | Developer | Context |
| Belief | Communication | Connectedness | Futuristic |
| Consistancy | Competition | Empathy | Ideation |
| Deliberative | Maximizer | Harmony | Input |
| Discipline | Self-Assurance | Includer | Intellection |
| Focus | Significance | Individualization | Learner |
| Responsibility | Woo | Poisitivity | Strategic |
| Restorative | | Relator | |

**Figure 10.1    Gallup StrengthsFinder constellations of strengths.**

- *Trust*, along with honesty and respect, were found to be the filters employees use to determine who they will spend time with at work. The most productive days on the job come when coworkers help each other achieve their goals.

- *Compassion* comes when employees feel their manager cares about them. When asked what their leader contributes to their life, employees most often used the words "caring," "love," "friendship," and "happiness." There is clear evidence that positive emotions between leaders and followers are crucial for satisfaction and success.

- *Stability* allows followers to feel that they can count on their leader in times of need. The most stable leaders were those who were clear about their core values. When leaders consistently live by their values, employees know what to expect. A stable set of values provides the security, strength, support and peace of mind that followers need to experience to make the best decisions, particularly in a crisis.

- *Hope* is the single most important ingredient of leadership in determining whether employees feel enthusiastic about the future. It helps people see their way through the chaos and complexity of the challenges their organization is facing. It provides powerful motivation to help make the future better. Sixty-nine percent of employees who felt hopeful were engaged in their jobs, compared to 1 percent who had lost faith in their organizations future.

Gallup researchers discovered that the majority of leaders they interviewed spent almost all their time reacting to the pressing problems of the day instead of deliberately initiating discussions to create optimism about the future. Leaders who are reactive versus proactive convey a sense of being out of control.

There are substantial benefits to healthcare teams when leaders focus on employee strengths. Gallup reports impressive results in a hospital that implemented a strengths-based employee development initiative[11]:

1. *Employee engagement skyrocketed*: Between 2010 and 2013, the hospital's overall engagement score jumped from around the 20th percentile to above the 70th percentile.
2. *Turnover dropped significantly*: In that same timeframe, the hospital's overall turnover rate fell from 22 percent to 15 percent. RN turnover was reduced from 25 percent in 2010 to 13 percent in 2013.
3. *Workers' compensation claims decreased substantially*: Between 2010 and 2013, workers' compensation claims dropped from 18 per year to only 7 per year.
4. *These changes have had a significant impact on the hospital's bottom line*: From 2010 to 2013, the hospital's RN turnover costs have decreased by $1.7 million, and the hospital increased its operating margin.

## The Problem Is...

Most people have not learned how to tap into their strengths to optimally engage and achieve peak performance. This tendency can be especially true in healthcare settings where professionals are trained to diagnose what is wrong with people. With a highly developed mind-set that scans for dysfunction, healthcare providers often automatically look at themselves and their coworkers through that lens.

Unfortunately, most people believe that focusing on flaws and weaknesses is the best way to improve performance. Renowned strengths researcher Marcus Buckingham found that 61 percent of Americans *mistakenly* believe that focusing on weaknesses is the best way for people for people to grow.[12] Although you will need to develop some basic competency in your weaker areas to function in life, you'll never be at your best if that is where you devote most your time and attention.

Your weaknesses limit you; your strengths amplify you.

## Blocks to Applying Strengths

Linley observed that even when people have the opportunity to use their strengths, they exhibit "blockers," which interfere with the knowing and growing of strengths. The most prominent blockers are as follows[3]:

■ Reluctance to embrace positive feedback
■ Unfavorable comparisons of ourselves to others which undermines self-confidence and performance

- A fixed versus growth mind-set
- Failure to practice and refine strengths by creating habits and rituals

Even when you are dedicated to deploying your strengths, you may find times you revert to ruminating on a problem and dwelling on your shortcomings. The diagnostic term for such people is "human being." Welcome to the club.

Researchers originally believed that simply telling people to start using their strengths more often would enable them to become high performers. It turns out that it wasn't that easy; moderation and timing make all the difference.

Linley has studied the most effective methods for learning to apply strengths. "We all have a symphony of strengths that advance into the foreground or recede into the background as the situation requires," he writes in *Average to A+: Realizing Strengths in Yourself and Others*. "To use strengths optimally, we need to do so according to the golden mean: the right strength, to the right amount, in the right way and at the right time."[3]

As seen in Figure 10.2, Linley classifies strengths into one of the four quadrants. Sometimes we realize what strengths we can use well; other times our strengths are unrealized. We are usually aware of our weakness, but not always cognizant of which behaviors we have learned to use that will lead to burnout.

1. *Unrealized strengths* are the actions you find energizing and perform well, but don't use often. Maximize to spur your personal development and career advancement, and to reach your goals.

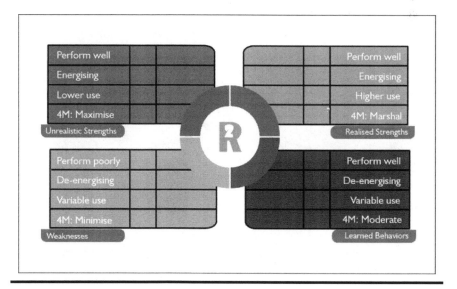

**Figure 10.2   How strengths and weaknesses are managed.**

2. *Weaknesses* are the activities you find hard to do well and find draining. Minimize their use to make them irrelevant by knowing what to work on, what to avoid, and what to pass on to others.

3. *Realized strengths* are the things you find energizing, perform well, and use often. Marshal them for outstanding performance by dialing them up and down, depending on your situation.

4. *Learned behaviors* are the actions you have learned to do well, but are extraordinarily energy depleting. To prevent burnout, moderate their use and work from your strengths more frequently.

## Benefits of Using Strengths

Numerous fMRI studies have shown that it is much easier for your brain to expand the use of existing neural pathways than it is to forge altogether new ones. And your motivation remains much higher when you are doing what you enjoy rather than trying to force yourself to act outside of your comfort zone. Your confidence level is much higher when you are using your strengths, enabling you to remain optimistic and resilient when facing challenges.

Figure 10.3 shows the multiple benefits arising from the use of strengths.[3]

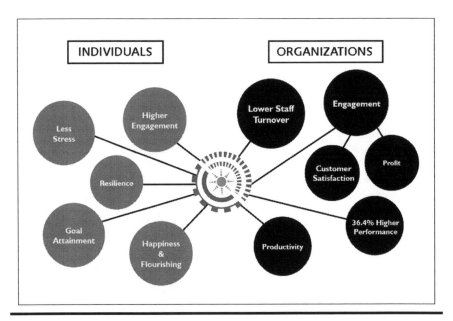

**Figure 10.3  Linley's benefits of using strengths.**

## Applying PROACTIVITY Research: Developing Personal Mastery

To discover the traits that enable you to be at your best, visit the websites listed in Figure 10.4. Take the surveys you'll find there (some are free and all are worthwhile), and take time to reflect on the results. Awareness is the first stage in the growth process.

Gallup publishes two books I recommend: *Now, Discover Your Strengths* (an excellent introduction to understanding individual strengths) and *Strength-Based Leadership* (a framework for categorizing the strengths of a team). Each book contains a code that allows you to take the StrengthsFinder survey at no additional cost.

The VIA Institute on Character website (www.viacharacter.org/survey) includes a free test that identifies your Character Strengths. After completing the 10- to 15-minute survey, you will receive a report listing your most prominent character strengths. Remember that learning to use your best qualities more often is far more effective than focusing on traits at the bottom of the list.

Once you have identified your strengths, you will need to learn which strength to deploy at what time, in what amount, and in what situation. To begin to cultivate your ability to use strengths, start to observe yourself in action. Make notes as you go through your day, on paper or on your phone, about situations in which you feel you did well and those in which you struggled. Once you're aware of those times you were particularly effective, reflect on which of your strengths you used to be at your best.

Next, consider those situations where you found yourself struggling, underperforming, or detesting the task. How could you deploy your strengths to improve

**VIA CHARACTER STRENGTHS:**

*www.viacharacter.org*

**GALLUP STRENGTHFINDER:**

*www.gallupstrengthscenter.com*

**R2 STRENGTHS PROFILER**

*https://assessment.r2profiler.com/*

**Figure 10.4    Strengths tests websites.**

your performance? What unrealized strengths could you bring to bear? Imagine what your strengths-fueled future could look like.

Unfortunately, it's not just a matter of simply switching gears and suddenly using your strengths at full throttle. Changing behavior requires small incremental improvements. Think about the fact that 80 percent of New Year's resolutions fail. Sheer willpower doesn't last long enough to sustain change. Researchers have found that willpower is like a muscle; the more you use it, the quicker it wears out.[13]

Duke University researchers have found that 40 percent of your behavior—that is 6 hours every day—is not controlled by conscious choices, but by established habits.[14] Fortunately, MIT studies have shown that there is a neurological loop that is at the center of every habit: a cue, a routine, and a reward.[15] Habits are born when this loop is repeated enough times for the behavior to become automatic.

There are three methods for creating a cue. The first is anchoring—timing the new habit to follow an existing one. For example, practicing your new routine of rounding on your unit to express gratitude to your staff members could come just after you have had your first sip of coffee in the morning.

The second cue building technique is embedding—tying one habit to another. You put a reminder in your electronic calendar to signal you at lunch to go check on your charge nurse and tell her you appreciate her efforts.

The third approach is one you already know, if–then plans—"*If* I see a staff member helping a coworker, *then* I'll walk over to praise them."

VERY IMPORTANT: As soon as the cue triggers your new routine, imagine the reward you will get for being proactive. "When I go to sleep tonight, I'll be able to drift off feeling good about three good actions I took to create a more positive work environment." Then be sure to give yourself the reward. Receiving the reward is crucial because it fires off a flood of dopamine, the neurotransmitter that makes you feel good. You will actually create a biologically based craving to take action by repeating this cue–routine–reward cycle.

## Applying PROACTIVITY Research: Developing Team Mastery

The majority of employees say they do NOT use their strengths throughout the day to do what they do best.[3] Occasions when people perform at their best are usually random—a lucky set of circumstances that enabled the person to be extraordinarily productive, pleased with their team, and proud of their accomplishments.

Unfortunately, most managers spend 85 percent of their time telling their employees what to do or "holding them accountable" for not doing as they were told. This command and control style of leadership is the least effective approach for influencing the performance of direct reports. It has a profoundly negative impact on the quality of the leaders'—as well as their employees'—work life.

When you and your staff members need to overcome blocks that are preventing people from using their strengths, Linley suggests using these strategies[3]:

1. Giving positive feedback that is specific, is targeted, and provides evidence
2. Using positive roles models who inspire the feeling "I want to be like that"
3. Adopting a growth mind-set: believing it's possible to grow and improve strengths
4. Recognizing strengths and finding a niche where they can be applied
5. Discussing strengths, which makes it far more likely people will be willing to talk about their weaknesses as well
6. Creating daily rituals to deliberately practice using strengths

Applying these suggestions will transform your role as a leader. Figure out how to get everyone on your staff members to take a strengths test. Post the results and have meetings in which coworkers can discuss how they have seen each other use their strengths. It will be incredibly uplifting. Start complementing staff members when you see them using their strengths. It will supercharge their engagement.

## Applying PROACTIVITY Research: Developing a Culture of Engagement

In a study of nearly 20,000 employees from seven different industries, including healthcare, the Corporate Leadership Council found a profound impact on performance when organizations systematically emphasize strengths.[16] When annual reviews specifically examined an individual's use of personal strengths, performance was 21.3 percent higher. And when people's reviews emphasized the use of performance strengths, the employee performed 36.4 percent better than previous reviews. Focusing on their best qualities resulted in increased grit—employees were willing to try harder and were more committed to the goals of the organization.

By comparison, organizations that focused reviews on performance weaknesses experienced a 26.8 percent drop in employees' performance. Focusing on personality weaknesses resulted in a 5.5 percent decline in productivity.

Several Gallup studies have reported similar findings.[17] In one study of over 65,000 workers, turnover was 15 percent lower in organizations that gave their employees feedback about their strengths. Another study of 530 work units found that managers receiving strengths feedback had 12 percent higher productivity than those who received no feedback and were 86 percent more likely to receive above average performance levels.

Receiving no feedback, which is to be ignored, is a fate worse than hearing about your weaknesses. The Gallup studies found about 25 percent of the workforce in hospitals feels ignored by their manager, and 40 percent of those employees report being actively disengaged (Figure 10.5).[18]

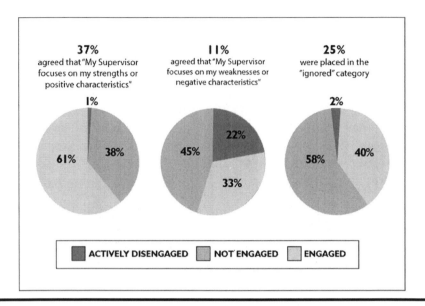

**Figure 10.5   How to reduce disengagement.**

The Gallup Employee Engagement Science website states "actively disengaged employees are more or less out to damage their company. They monopolize managers' time; have more on-the-job accidents; account for more quality defects; contribute to 'shrinkage,' as theft is called; are sicker; miss more days; and quit at a higher rate than engaged employees do. Whatever the engaged do—such as solving problems, innovating, and creating new customers—the actively disengaged try to undo."[19]

That description should send a shiver down the spine of every healthcare leader whose "customers" are people putting their lives in the hands of these employees. When you look at Figure 10.5, consider the differential impact on the number of preventable medical errors occurring in your healthcare organization if you have only 1 percent of your employees actively disengaged versus 40 percent.[20]

The power of being proactive can be harnessed when organizations develop expectations and leaders create intentions to focus on employee's strengths. Baking a strengths approach into the organizations culture involves training, policies regarding performance reviews, and recognition of teams who achieve remarkable results using their combined talents. A strengths-based culture enables organizations to face the future with confidence because they know their employees are engaging the best qualities they possess to overcome challenges.

# Steve's Story: The Resolution

"Explain to me how making hospital units more positive can possibly help our ER diversion problem," Robert asked with the skeptical tone of a chief executive officer who doesn't care about fluff, just the financial bottom line.

"Robert, I've been reading some positive psychology studies," Steve, his Chief of Psychiatry, responded. "It's not your old-time power of positive thinking, but real research using fMRI. Studies are coming out of labs in some prominent universities. My people have some good qualities. They're just not bringing their best stuff as often or as effectively as we need them to. I'm hoping that this work will teach us how to consistently function at a high level.

"Reducing holding times in our ED will be well worth the effort," Steve asserted. "You shared some research with us during our last meeting. I also looked into the research on ED crowding and found an NIH study of two New York urban hospitals. They calculated that improving movement from the ED to an inpatient setting would save a county hospital $9.8 million and a university hospital $3.9 million per year."

"Steve understands the science supporting our approach, Robert," I asserted. "We're going to build capacity from the inside out with his staff members, developing their existing skills and adding some new knowledge about how, when, and where to apply their strengths."

"Let's get started and see if we can change what's happening here," Robert said in concluding the meeting.

The Psychiatry unit started its PROPEL experience with a kickoff meeting that included the staff members who were interesting in learning how to apply positive psychology to their personal and professional lives. Fourteen of the 16 staff members expressed interest in participating.

Steve was unhappy that the two people creating the biggest problems had opted out. "I want to mandate that they attend," he insisted "because they cause the most disruption with their constant complaining and conflicts with the other staff members. They're the ones who most need to learn how to be positive."

"That seems logical," I replied, "but it's probably not 'psychological.' Have you already initiated performance improvement counseling with these two individuals?"

"Several times. Too many times. The amount of time the nurse manager and I have spent talking to these two has been inordinate! Worse, it's been a waste of time," Steve snapped. "They behave a little better for a couple of months until they're off probation, and bang! They're right back to their old tricks. This has gone on for years."

"And do you imagine that their listening to me talk is going to turn out any better?" I countered.

"No," Steve said sullenly.

"And what happens in your staff meetings when these two tag-team you with their opposition to whatever plan you're trying to advance?" I inquired.

"The whole meeting ends up being a disaster as other staff members feel defeated before we even get started," Steve acknowledged.

"So why would we want to insist they join the discussion if they're likely to be openly defiant and bring the whole group down?" I wondered aloud.

"But how will we ever be able to change the dynamics on the unit if the two problem people aren't part of the solution?" Steve rejoined.

"As the majority of staff members learn to proactively engage by using their strengths," I explained, "they'll discover that they have the power to determine what kind of shift they'll work. The difficult employees will realize they have a choice about how to manage their negative reactions. As their ability to stir up trouble becomes greatly diminished, they will have to make a decision to get on board with their coworkers who are using their strengths or get off the bus."

"From your lips to God's ears," Steve responded with a wry smile.

At the kickoff meeting the staff members chose compassion, responsibility, and positive outcomes as their three core values. The vision statement the group chose was as follows:

> We enjoy coming to work because we make a difference in the lives of
> our coworkers and our patients. We are at our best most days because
> we know and use our best qualities—our strengths.

When the Psych unit reviewed the Strengths Matrix for their staff members (see Figure 10.6), it became clear why those values felt right to them—they reflected the most common qualities possessed by the group.

When the staff members reviewed occasions when they'd been at their best using their strengths, it was revealing—and somewhat sad—to hear that those times occurred mostly outside of work. People shared stories of using their strengths to help a neighbor who was distraught, a child who was struggling in school, or an elderly parent who was in hospice. At work, staff members felt they were rarely able to use their strengths to help patients.

The PROPEL team could, however, recall innumerable stories of disputes with coworkers, both on the Psych Unit and with staff members in the ER. Some of these disputes had turned into screaming matches in front of patients. Staff members spoke of the "cold war" climate that pervaded most shifts—come in, keep your head down, and do your own thing until it's time to leave. The worst part of the job, the team said, were encounters with patients that turned out poorly. Those incidents usually resulted in the staff members having to physically pin the patient down and put them into restraints.

The contrast heightened the team's awareness of the abundant opportunities to use their strengths at work. Each team member agreed to find at least 11 minutes on every shift to practice using their strengths. They also were to note any situations in which they believed they had underplayed or overplayed their strengths.

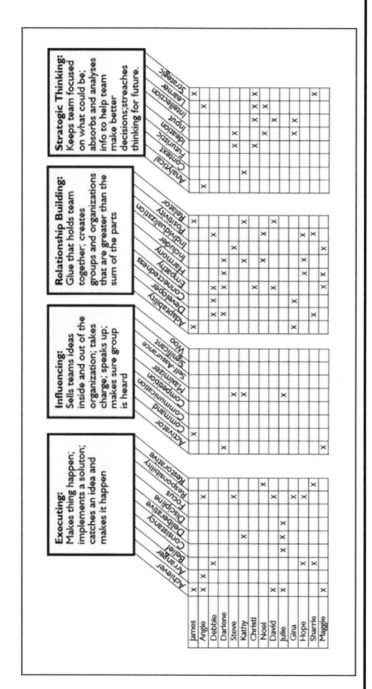

Figure 10.6 Strengths matrix for psychiatry unit. (Adapted from Rath, T. and Conchie, B., *Strength Based Leadership: Great Leaders, Teams, and Why People Follow,* Gallup Press, New York, 2008.)

An awakening occurred as the team members began to use their strengths more frequently on the job. At our next meeting, we discussed how each person assessed their ability to use their strengths in work situations ranging from the worst-case scenario to the best-case scenario. Most people said they had found a time or two on each shift to put their strengths into play. Here are a few examples:

*James:* I can see now that I was overplaying my *Command* strength. I started using my *Achiever* and *Strategic* strengths by talking to my teammates at the beginning of each shift about what we could do to leave work feeling good.

*Angie:* I spent my 11 minutes getting *Input* from patients about which of our treatment strategies worked best for them. I was able to *Learn* what I could do to get patients to be more engaged in the activities I run.

*Steve:* I love that *Idea*—ask the patients for their *Input*. I have an intern who will be here for a few weeks, and I'm going to have her contact patients a few weeks after they've been discharged to ask them the same question. In the meantime, would each individual on the PROPEL team take *Responsibility* for doing a short appreciative inquiry with one patient every day?

By the next meeting, the staff members had gotten some wonderful feedback from patients. Steve was able to share some input that his intern had been able to gather from recently discharged patients about what treatment approaches had been most effective for them. However, the staff members reported that they found it hard to use their strengths in difficult situations when negative emotions were ramping up. For their next assignment, each one wrote a version of the WOOP exercise: "*If* I notice I'm feeling negative emotions during my shift, *then* I will …."

Debbie offered a great example of how she could use her strengths to deal with difficult situations:

*Debbie:* If I see someone feeling badly about a negative exchange they had during a shift, then I will *Connect* to my teammate and *Empathize* to help them regain a *Positive* feeling.

At the next team meeting, the positive emotions had become contagious. They had used their relationship building skills to turn toward each other for support when troubles arose. By referencing the team's strength matrix, they knew who they could turn to for support.

*Darlene:* I've become a very quiet person on the unit over the past few years. I realize now that I'd stopped using my four relationship building skills. But over the past month, I've come alive. I'm *Empathizing* with coworkers when they're criticized and helping them *Develop* an effective response. I'll *Include* other supportive PROPEL team members; together we'll figure out what *Arrangements* we can make to restore *Harmony* on the unit.

When most staff members were able to maintain a higher level of positivity, their creative and collaborative capabilities were abundantly available. Building on Steve's request to gather input from patients regarding the most effective treatment strategies, and broadening the use of the staff's strengths, the PROPEL team decided to totally redesign its treatment approach.

Steve, in his role as the medical director, realized that he'd over used his Responsibility strength in the past by designing the Psych unit's treatment program primarily on his own. By switching his focus to Individualization, he understood that staff members could design a treatment strategy that allowed them to meet patient needs more effectively by harnessing their strengths.

*Steve:* I'd like each of you to figure out how you can use your strengths to incorporate the patient feedback to create a more effective treatment program.

Like almost all change initiatives, it threatened to derail before it even began to get traction. Right before the next meeting, I received a call from Steve. "My really negative people have become particularly vocal, ridiculing the staff's efforts to try to make each other feel good during their shift. I don't know what to do to help them."

"Do you think you could be overplaying your Responsibility and Maximizer strengths?" I asked.

"Oh, I hadn't looked at it that way," he exclaimed.

"Which of your other strengths might be more appropriate in your current situation?" was the question I posed.

"I'm pretty good at seeing the Individual qualities that each of my staff members possess," Steve reflected. "And I'm really good at getting Input from people. Perhaps I could start asking staff members how it's going, and then use the strategy you're using with me—suggesting which of their strengths might work well for them to deploy in those situations where they're struggling."

"Sounds like an excellent plan. What do you think about making that your 11-minute daily routine for building your strengths?" I encouraged.

"Yes, absolutely," Steve said with a renewed energy.

At the following meeting the PROPEL team reported they were taking small steps to use their strengths more often. The problem was the negative encounters continued to occur with the two contentious coworkers. We discussed what could be learned from these unsatisfactory experiences and what was needed to stay energized while making slow but steady progress.

Steve shared how well it was working to take a few minutes during his lunch break to talk to a staff member about how he or she might be able to help develop his or her strengths. The group decided they'd do a mini appreciative inquiry with each other at the end of each shift. They would start asking one another what had worked well and what was still presented a challenge. They agreed to give each other suggestions as well as positive reinforcement for their efforts.

Particularly difficult were the discussions about how to deal with the two negative staff members. The team tried everything they could think of to bring those folks on board, but to no avail. Finally, they decided to ignore their negative comments, complaints, and criticisms. "I'm not going there with you" became the common refrain.

It became glaringly obvious why the two staff members—who had no relationship-building strengths—were seen as being difficult to deal with. But an interesting shift in perception occurred. Rather than shunning the "negative" coworkers, the rest of the team began to use those colleagues' strengths to accomplish tasks like getting medications to patients done in a timely manner.

After several months, the PROPEL team members were able to maintain a positive approach on almost every shift. They converted the ideas that surfaced from patient feedback into innovative ideas for improving their treatment regimen. They were able to run therapy groups and develop patient activities that the staff members and the patients both enjoyed.

Once the PROPEL team was able to make the Psych unit positive most of the time, they invited several staff members from the ER to meet with them. Three ER staff members began to join the biweekly meetings, and they quickly learned about how the Psych staff members had been developing strengths to improve their ability to work together well. These 3 ER staff members took the strengths assessment. Lively discussions ensued about what it would look like if the ER and Psych staff members were at their best when dealing with patient flow issues.

The team began working with their newfound collaborators in the ER. They discussed how to achieve a "tipping point" by building and broadening positive working relationships between the two departments.

## Six Months Later

"A miracle occurred!" Steve startled me. "Both negative staff members resigned and we hired two new exceptionally positive staff members. What a change in the culture on our unit! And with our redesigned program our quality indicators are much improved. We were putting patients into restraints at least once a week for years but now we haven't used restraints at all for the past 3 months.

"Patient satisfaction has soared," Steve shared, "and I've been making it a habit to express my gratitude to staff members when I hand out the positive feedback cards from patients. It's really making the staff members feel that their work is meaningful. And as you'd predicted, it's improving our performance metrics—our length of stay has gone from 6 days to 5, which is helping alleviate the ER crowding.

"That data has brought Bill around to seeing the value of what we're doing," Steve exclaimed. "We've expanded the number of people from his staff members who join our regular meetings. We're sending our staff members down to the ER to help do triage. That has expedited identifying psych patients who can be released with a change in medication as opposed to those who need to be admitted.

"By tweaking what we're doing every couple of weeks, we've made steady progress at getting the Psych patients out of the ED," Steve proudly announced. "Robert is very pleased with the results of our collaborative effort to free up space the Psych patients had been taking up in the ER. We've virtually eliminated diversion, reducing it from 168 hours per month to 3 hours in the past 3 months. Robert calculated that at $5400 per hour, the cost of diversion over the past 3 months dropped from $907,200 to $16,200. We're projecting the hospital will realize a nearly $3.5 million benefit to the bottom line this year!"

Steve concluded with a heartfelt appreciation: "Tom, I never would have believed that the PROPEL program could make such a difference. We're deeply grateful for your help. We've learned how to enjoy our day-to-day working relationships—with each other and our patients—which has enabled us to make a significant difference."

*Lessons learned*: Human beings often react negatively to problems. People at the optimal end of performance have learned to use their strengths to respond proactively when facing a challenge. Strengths are like muscles—the more you use them, the more powerful you become.

# Chapter 11

# Energy: Refueling Your Internal Engine

You might think that those who devote their professional lives to improving the health of others would themselves be models of good health and good habits. You'd be wrong. Study after study finds that healthcare providers are pretty terrible about looking after their own health; actually, they have a surprising inclination toward unhealthy habits. Ironically, the passion and training that drives them to want to give the best care humanly possible does not carry over into their off-hours. Anyone who knows what a day in their shoes looks like can see why.

Caring for the sick, injured, dying, or even those recovering from an elective surgery is draining. And hospital environments—for the people who work in them, that is—have not done a great job in promoting good health. The soda and candy machines on every floor offer a quick caffeine fix or sugar jolt. Missed lunches are not unusual, particularly when there is a staff shortage. Patients' needs don't take a break. Fresh air and the great outdoors are usually not accessible for hospital workers, so shift after shift is spent cooped up indoors. Then there is the stress inherent in multidisciplinary teamwork and the unpredictable demands of patients and their family members. It is clear why those who provide care to others often have little energy left for themselves.

## Raquel's Story: The Problem

"Juanita, slow down and tell me again what's going on," Raquel told the nurse on the other end of the phone.

"Missy crashed her car into a tree on her way home," Juanita sobbed. "She died at the scene."

"Oh my God. I can't believe it. She just left the hospital a little while ago. Are you sure it was Missy?" Raquel mumbled in disbelief.

"Yes, yes, yes," Juanita insisted. "The police found her driver's license and went to her house. Her husband was about to take their two kids to school. The officers told him that they think she fell asleep at the wheel because there were no skid marks. He called me because he knows I'm her best friend on the unit."

Raquel sat in stunned silence, barely able to hold onto the phone she was shaking so hard.

"Are you still on the line," Juanita asked.

"Yes. I'm sorry," Raquel told her. "I don't know what to say. I need to call you back."

Normally a stoic person, Raquel hung up and burst into tears. One of her worst fears had come true. A 33-year-old nurse who had worked a 12-hour night shift had left so exhausted that she had a fatal accident on her way home.

Waves of sorrow washed over Raquel as she thought about Missy's children. An undertow of guilt pulled her down into despair. She tried to fight her way back to the surface, but her emotions overwhelmed her. It took almost an hour before she could pull herself together and tell the rest of the staff members.

For over a decade, Raquel has successfully managed more than 70 people on a 32-bed unit that provides postoperative care to inpatients undergoing surgical procedures. In spite of the fact that her unit has a heavy workload—they average 16 discharges and admissions every day—the statistics for her unit are impressive: patient satisfaction in the 80–90 percent range, a low number of patient safety problems, staff turnover well below 10 percent, and staff engagement over the 70 percent mark. Raquel's leadership style is exemplary. She is able to get nearly all of her staff members to participate on committees, assuring that the nurses and technicians are heavily engaged in scheduling, safety, education, research, practice, quality, and peer review. Every 6 weeks she devotes a day to 90-minute meetings with small groups of staff members. By holding four meetings with 15–20 of her staff members, she creates a safe space for them to have real discussions to surface issues and develop solutions. Raquel is the personification of a transformational leader.

But in the days after Missy's death, Raquel reflected on what had contributed to such a tragedy. She experienced moments of anger over how changes in healthcare reimbursement and a shrinking budget had led the hospital administrators to expand the nurse:patient ratio. Now her nurses have to care for more patients, elevating the demands to a point where they have to push themselves for 12 straight hours. At other times, the emotional whiplash would spiral Raquel down into depression when she realized that even the top leaders in her hospital were struggling to find solutions to the huge budget problem their organization was facing.

# The Research on Energy Replenishment

## *How Well Do You Take Care of Yourself?*

Could you be doing a better job of replenishing your energy so that you can thrive as a healthcare provider?

- How are your current habits of exercising, eating, and sleeping affecting the amount of energy you have available?
- How much of your energy is being expended in negative activities such as complaining, experiencing frustration, expressing anger, worrying, ruminating on resentments, feeling inadequate compared to others, or fearing that you're not good enough?
- How satisfied are you with the amount of energy you're devoting to others versus how much energy you're investing in taking care of yourself?
- How often do you direct your energy in the direction of issues or people beyond your control, rather than spending energy on actions that you can take to make a difference?

Your work can become so consuming that you might not take the time to replenish your own energy, and sooner or later you'll pay a price for neglecting yourself. You'll become physically exhausted, mentally drained, emotionally spent, and spiritually depleted. You could burn out.

## *Physician Burnout Rates Continue to Climb*

Taking care of patients is our mission in healthcare. But when we don't take care of ourselves, we run out of energy to take care of others. That's when bad things can—and do—happen to us.

The 2016 Medscape physician survey, echoing other recent national surveys, strongly suggests that burnout among U.S. physicians has reached a critical level. More female physicians (55 percent) reported burnout symptoms than their male colleagues (46 percent). These percentages have trended up for both men and women since Medscape's 2013 survey in which 45 percent of women and 37 percent of men reported burnout. Burnout was defined as "loss of enthusiasm for work, feelings of cynicism, and a low sense of personal accomplishment." Figure 11.1 reveals what issues MDs identified as causing burnout.[1]

The 2015 Mayo Clinic Proceedings also compared burnout rates between 2011 and 2014. They observed an increase in the percentage of physicians reporting at least one burnout symptom, a jump from 45.5 percent to 54.4 percent.[2]

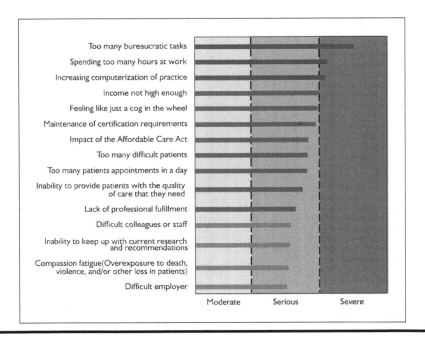

**Figure 11.1   Causes of burnout.**

Consider these startling statistics from the American Foundation for Suicide Prevention[3]:

■ Male physicians have a 70 percent higher suicide rate than men in other professions.
■ Suicide deaths are up to 400 percent higher among female physicians compared to females in other professions.

Depression is a major risk factor in physician suicide. Other factors include bipolar disorder and alcohol/substance abuse. Women physicians have a higher rate of major depression than age-matched women with doctorate degrees. Medical students have rates of depression 15–30 percent higher than the general population.

If your energy for dealing with life has dropped to this level, you should contact a mental health professional or an employee assistance program immediately.

## Nurse Burnout Rates Are Even Higher

The situation is even worse for nurses. Three out of four nurses cited the effects of stress and overwork as a top health concern in a 2011 survey by the American

Nurses Association.[4] Work schedules and insufficient staffing are among the factors driving many nurses to leave the profession.

Although 12-hour shifts are increasingly common among hospital nurses, a 2015 study found that such long shifts can have adverse effects. Shifts lasting 12 hours or longer were associated with a 40 percent greater level of job dissatisfaction and a 31 percent higher risk of planning to quit. "Job satisfaction and burnout in the nursing workforce are global concerns, both due to their potential impact on quality and safety of patient care and because low job satisfaction is a contributing factor associated with nurses leaving their job and the profession," the study reads.[5]

Besides driving nurses out of the profession, burnout can compromise the quality of patient care. For example, a 2012 survey of Pennsylvania hospitals found a "significant association" between nurse burnout and increased infections among patients. The authors concluded that a reduction in burnout is good for both nurses and patients.[6]

## Stress vs. Energy Management Mind-Sets

Do you believe stress is harmful to your performance, health, and well-being?

Or do you think that stress is a helpful resource that needs to be utilized and embraced?

If you're like the vast majority of people, you have a "stress is harmful" mindset. In 2014 National Public Radio (NPR), the Robert Wood Johnson Foundation and the Harvard School of Public Health conducted a survey that found 85 percent of Americans believe that stress negatively impacts their health, relationships, and work performance.[7] The American Psychological Association's Stress in America annual survey has shown that since 2007 a growing majority people have been perceiving their stress level as unhealthy.[8]

These surveys reflect outmoded perceptions for dealing with stress. Most people tell themselves stress is bad, impairing their performance, happiness, and health. They believe that experiencing stress and anxiety is bad for the body and the mind, and is responsible for making them miserable, ruining relationships, and draining their spirit.

*News flash*—Those results only occur if you think they are the inevitable consequence of stress.

Recent research has shown that not everyone suffers adverse effects from stressful situations. In fact, people who perform extraordinarily well under pressure have the same physiological responses as those whose performance declines under stress. But their bodies are healthier than most, as are their relationships. And their motivation levels are much higher than people who have debilitating stress reactions.[9]

What sets these high performers apart is a different mind-set—one that enables them to recognize stress sensations as a sign that they have abundant energy available to help them do extremely well.

What about all those studies showing that stress causes our blood pressure to rise, our mind to flood with anxiety, and our immune system to be compromised leaving us vulnerable to everything from colds to cancer? Those outcomes are only true for people who try to suppress their stress reactions.

The evidence supporting the shift in our understanding of how people successfully deal with stress began with a shocking finding from a 1998 survey of 30,000 adults in the United States who were asked two questions[10]:

1. How much stress have you experienced in the past year?
2. Do you believe that the stress is harming your health?

When the researchers reviewed the public records 8 years later to determine who had died, they found that high levels of stress increased the chances of dying by 43 percent if—and only if—they were in the group that had indicated they *believed* stress was hurting their health. People who had similarly high stress levels but didn't think of stress as being harmful had the lowest risk of death of any group in the study, even those with low levels of stress.

The researchers considered a multitude of factors that might explain their finding—race, gender, age, ethnicity, income, education, smoking, physical activity, marital status, work status, chronic health problems, and health insurance coverage. Nothing predicted mortality except stress level coupled with the belief stress was bad.

People who believed they could direct the energy generated in stressful situations were extraordinarily effective at succeeding in challenging circumstances. These high performers believed stress occurred when something they cared about was on the line. Stress gave them the energy they needed to summon their courage, develop connections with allies, and learn new skills.

## What about All the "Bad" Chemicals Stress Produces?

"You always think about stress as a really bad thing, but it's not," said Daniela Kaufer, associate professor of integrative biology at the University of California, Berkeley, Berkeley, California. "Some amounts of stress are good to push you just to the level of optimal alertness, behavioral and cognitive performance."[11]

You may be thinking "Is this really possible?" Yes, according to Stanford psychologist Kelly McGonigal, who brilliantly debunks our myths about stress in her groundbreaking book *The Upside of Stress: Why Stress Is Good for You, and How to Get Good at It.*[11] She explains the state-of-the-art research on two stress hormones—cortisol and DHEA—that are released when we are under stress. Cortisol converts sugar and fat into energy that our body and brain can use when reacting to a stressful event. DHEA is a hormone that helps our brain grow stronger from stressful experiences, much like testosterone helps our body to grow stronger from physical exertion.

Both of these hormones serve a good purpose as long as the amount of DHEA to cortisol remains high. When stress is chronic, an imbalance in the ratio of DHEA to cortisol can lead to long-term consequences. Too much cortisol has been linked to depression and suppression of the immune system. Maintaining a high ratio of DHEA to cortisol—referred to as the *growth index*—has been shown to reduce the risk of stress-related disorders such as depression, anxiety, and heart disease. Moreover, studies show that having a high growth index (more DHEA than cortisol) predicts that you will perform well under stress. It's been associated with higher levels of resilience and persistence, better focus, and superior problem solving.

When people were taught how to develop a "stress enhances performance" mind-set rather than thinking "stress is debilitating," their adrenal glands released more DHEA, thereby giving them a higher growth index. Seeing stress as being helpful changes people's biology and their brain's ability to function at an optimal level.

Amazing to think that a different mind-set can have such a powerful impact. But numerous studies have confirmed these findings.

## How Do You React to Stress?

What do you think when you feel your body is getting tense, your breath is quickening, or your palms are sweating? Do you usually feel a stressful situation poses a threat? Do you feel like your stress is causing you to become angry, anxious, or discouraged? Do you feel like you just need to get away? Or get into somebody's face? Or do you simply feel overwhelmed?

How often do you recognize the signals that indicate your body is mobilizing to take action? Do you consider what the most effective response would be? Do you figure out how to slow down, ask questions, seek support, or learn something new when you encounter a problem?

## How to Change Your Stress Mind-Set

To change your pattern for dealing with stressful situations, use your body's reactions as a signal to focus on how you want to respond going forward, not how you've reacted in the past. What would it look like to stand up for yourself? To ask for help? To practice a new behavior to attain a different result?

These strategies have been proven effective. Becoming resilient begins by stepping into your courage—which you're able to do when you've developed a mind-set that enables you to grow in response to stressful circumstances.

McGonigal has found that individuals who thrive in stressful conditions embrace stress as "an act of bravery, one that requires choosing meaning over avoiding discomfort. This is what it means to be good at stress. It's not about being untouched by adversity or unruffled by difficulties. It's about allowing stress to awaken in you those core human strengths of courage, connection, and growth."[11]

Although we can't control the challenges that occur in our lives, McGonigal says, we can choose our relationship to stressors when we experience them.

McGonigal's latest scientific findings indicate that with the proper mind-set, stress can make you more successful, smarter, and stronger. Changing your beliefs about stress has been shown to make people happier and healthier. Developing a new mind-set regarding stress has been shown to improve everything from having better cardiovascular health to a more meaningful life.

Now, you're probably curious about what exactly a stress mind-set is and how yours may be affecting you. Consider how many moments during the day you tell yourself, "this is stressful." How often do you feel the effects of stress in your body or in your ability to concentrate?

Every time you become even vaguely aware that you're experiencing stress, your mind automatically triggers your underlying beliefs about how stress will affect you. Your mind-set alters your biochemistry and determines how you will respond to the stressful situation. Becoming conscious of your mind-set allows you manage it. When you become aware of feeling stress, reframe your thinking to "I have energy available for dealing with this situation."

## *Energy Expenditure and Replenishment*

Since stress is simply energy you can use to take action when facing a challenge, use the PROPEL Principles to give yourself an optimal mind-set: Envision outcomes that ignite *passion, relationships* that provide support, *optimistic* thinking that enables solutions, and *proactive* responses that harness strengths.

But all of these efforts drain our energy.

"Every one of our thoughts, emotions, and behaviors has an energy consequence, for better or for worse," say Performance psychologists Jim Loehr and Tony Schwartz.[9] Drawing on years of experience helping some of the world's greatest athletes perform at their best, they developed a system to effectively replenish energy. Their studies show that managing energy, rather than time, is the key to high performance and full engagement. This finding is based on understanding the human as an oscillatory, rhythmic being who, by his or her physiological nature, must oscillate between periods of energy expenditure and energy renewal.

The opposite of a balanced rhythmic life is a highly linear life where "we assume that we can spend energy indefinitely in some dimensions—often the mental and emotional—and that we can perform effectively without investing much energy at all in others—most commonly the physical and the spiritual. We become flat liners."[9]

Because energy capacity diminishes with both overuse and underuse, we must learn to balance energy expenditure with intermittent energy renewal. Loehr and Schwartz's *The Power of Full Engagement* research reveals four core energy management practices[9]:

1. To be fully engaged requires drawing energy from four separate but related sources: physical, emotional, mental, and spiritual.
2. Energy diminishes both with overuse and with underuse; therefore, people need to balance their energy expenditure with intermittent energy renewal.
3. To build one's capacity, people must push beyond their normal limits, engaging in deliberate practice in the same systematic way the top athletes do.
4. To create specific energy replenishment rituals enables full engagement and peak performance.

## Applying ENERGY Renewal Research: Developing Personal Mastery

### Is Poor Energy Management Impacting Your Life?

Improving your work performance, physical and emotional health and personal happiness requires the skillful management of energy. "Energy, not time, is the fundamental currency of high performance," says Loehr.[9]

| How many signs of poor energy management do you have? | |
| --- | --- |
| ☐ Lack of energy | ☐ Mistrusting people |
| ☐ Feeling defensive | ☐ Trouble making decisions |
| ☐ Impatience | ☐ Negative attitude |
| ☐ Difficulty listening | ☐ Criticizing others |
| ☐ Overreactions | ☐ Not asking for what you need |
| ☐ Feeling unfocused | ☐ Overcontrolling |
| ☐ Irritability | ☐ Compassion fatigue |
| ☐ Poor teamwork | ☐ Overly anxious |
| ☐ Workaholic | ☐ Inflexibility |
| ☐ Insecurity | ☐ Disengagement |

### Renewing Physical Energy—Fueling the Fire

Physical energy is the fundamental source of fuel in life. If you don't have enough physical energy, you won't have adequate emotional and mental energy. That's why it is imperative to eat right, get enough rest, and exercise regularly. Making that commitment will give your body and mind the fuel, it needs for you to achieve success and satisfaction.

Because physical energy derives from the interaction of oxygen and glucose, the two most important elements for generating it are breathing and eating. Therefore, to increase the amount of physical energy you have available, follow these recommendations:

- Eat five to six low-calorie, nutritious meals a day, which ensures a steady supply of fuel.
- Drink 64 ounces of water daily.
- Get 7–8 hours of sleep per night.
- Go to bed early and wake up early to optimize performance.
- Exercise 3–5 times per week for a total of 150 minutes.
- Use interval training rather than steady-state exercise to build physical capacity and to make recovery more efficient.
- Take a recovery break every 90–120 minutes when working to stretch and do deep breathing.

## Renewing Emotional Energy—Transforming Threat into Challenge

Your self-confidence, self-discipline, sociability, and compassion are all influenced by your level of emotional energy. Frustration, fear, sadness, and anger are emotionally toxic to your well-being. Each negative emotion you experience must be counterbalanced by a least 3 positive emotions to perform at your best.

- Start every day thinking about the positive emotions you would like to experience: love, gratitude, enjoyment, challenge, adventure, and opportunity.
- Build your positive emotions like you would your muscles; make them stronger through regular exercise.
- Make the conscious choice to let negative emotions pass rather than giving them a home in your head; stop them from draining your energy.
- Limit TV watching—particularly the news—to avoid the illusion that you're doing something that will rejuvenate you.
- Engage in activities that you find enjoyable, fulfilling, and affirming as your way to achieve emotional renewal.
- Cultivate meaningful relationships at work to boost your performance.
- Generate positive relationships: use reflective listening skills, active constructive responses to people's good news, and be empathetic to their difficulties.

## Renewing Mental Energy—Appropriate Focus and Realistic Optimism

Both physical and emotional energy are prerequisites for good mental functioning—the ability to organize our lives and focus our attention. The mental energy that best serves full engagement is *realistic optimism*—seeing the world as it is, but always working positively toward a desired outcome or solution.

- Balance the time you're fully engaged with time set aside for recovering mental energy.
- Use periods of recovery to cultivate your best ideas, for example, while walking, gardening, or meditating.
- Picture positive outcomes to open your brain's pathway to higher mental functioning.
- Identify potential obstacles and make a plan to overcome them.
- Develop positive self-talk regarding how to best use your strengths.
- Schedule time to practice new skills you wish to learn.
- Challenge your brain all of your life to protect against age-related mental decline.

## Renewing Spiritual Energy—Having a "Why" to Live

Spiritual energy provides the force for action in all dimensions of your life. It fuels your passion, perseverance, and commitment. Spiritual energy is cultivated by connecting your deeply held values to a purpose beyond your self-interest. Character is the courage and conviction to live by your deepest values. Your spirit sends you strong signals when your values are violated.

- Post your values where you'll see them every day, such as on your mirror or computer.
- Develop a vision of what your life would look like if you were living your values more consistently.
- Identify what purpose your life will serve if you make a valuable contribution to the world.
- Increase awareness of opportunities where you can share your spiritual energy to empower others.
- Draw on your spiritual energy to provide the courage you need to make values-based choices when facing life's most difficult challenges.
- Make it a bedtime ritual to reflect on the three good things that you did during the day.

Choose one daily ritual to practice in each of the four dimensions to maintain better energy. Select the most modest activities you believe will give you the biggest boost to your energy. Schedule the precise time that you'll set aside to complete your routine. Decide who you will ask to support you. Identify how you'll handle obstacles that may derail you. And don't forget to pick your reward.

## Applying ENERGY Renewal Research: Developing Team Mastery

### What Is Your Staff's Mind-Set about Stress?

Stanford psychologist Alia Crum developed a Stress Mind-set Measure to help employees assess their view of stress.[12]

#### Mind-set 1

- The effects of stress are negative and should be avoided.
- Experiencing stress depletes my health and vitality.
- Experiencing stress inhibits my learning and growth.
- Experiencing stress debilitates my performance and productivity.

#### Mind-set 2

- Experiencing stress facilitates my learning and growth.
- Experiencing stress enhances my performance and productivity.
- Experiencing stress improves my health and vitality.
- The effects of stress are positive and should be utilized.

Crum and her colleagues worked with the financial firm USB following the 2008 economic collapse. The financial industry was an excellent test ground for studying stress mind-sets. Studies had shown that within a decade of entering the profession, nearly 100 percent of investment bankers demonstrated the symptoms of burnout—depression, insomnia, alcoholism, and so on. The great recession only exacerbated their stress levels.

Crum's research project randomly divided the employees into one of three groups.[12] The first group received the traditional "learn to manage your stress because it's bad for you program." The second group received a mind-set intervention which taught them that people under stress have been able to strengthen their commitment to personal values, build better relationships, improve their focus, and increase their physical resilience. The third group was put on a waiting list.

There were no improvements in groups one and three. The mind-set intervention group, however, was able to shift their view from "stress is harmful" to "stress has both good and bad aspects." This group of employees became far less anxious and depressed than their coworkers. They experienced fewer health concerns such as insomnia and back pain. In the midst of an immensely stressful time, they reported being able to focus, engage, collaborate, and perform at levels far above their peers.

Changing stress mind-sets has a powerful effect on how people think, feel, and act. If your staff members believe stress is harmful, then they will try—and fail—to avoid it. McGonigal found that typical stress-is-harmful reactions include[11]

- Distracting yourself from what's causing the stress rather than focusing on it.
- Trying to alleviate your stressful feelings rather than using the energy that's being aroused to take action to deal with the situation.
- Using alcohol or other substances to relieve your stressful feelings.
- Disengaging from the person, problem, or obstacle that's causing your stress.

However, people who have a stress-is-helpful mind-set are more likely to respond by:

- Accepting the reality that a stressful event had occurred.
- Seeking help, advice, or information regarding how to handle the situation.
- Planning a strategy to become proactive in dealing with the source of the stress.
- Taking action to change the stressful situation.
- Making the best of a bad situation by using it as an opportunity to learn and grow.

Which mind-set staff members embrace makes a huge difference. By facing stressful situations head-on, they build their capacity for dealing with life's difficulties. As they develop more resources for handling problems, people, and setbacks, their confidence level for being able to overcome challenges grows. Staff members come to respect one another's ability to address and resolve issues, enhancing the workgroup's social support network. Your staff's stress-is-helpful mind-set—like most mind-sets—becomes a self-fulfilling prophecy.

## Applying ENERGY Renewal Research: Developing a Culture of Abundance

### *What Is a Culture of Abundance?*

"Organizations that flourish have developed a 'culture of abundance,' which builds the collective capabilities of all members. It is characterized by the presence of numerous positive energizers throughout the system, including embedding virtuous practices, adaptive learning, meaningfulness and profound purpose, engaged members, and positive leadership," writes renowned positive psychologist Kim Cameron, cofounder of the Center for Positive Organizational Scholarship at the University of Michigan, Ann Arbor, Michigan.[14]

The Center for Positive Organizational Scholarship conducts a rigorous research to understand the characteristics of the best workplaces—which are defined as those exceptional organizations whose outcomes significantly exceed standard or expected performance. Cameron and his colleagues have collected a mountain of empirical evidence demonstrating that organizations displaying a culture of abundance achieve radically better results.

The three key characteristics found in an abundant culture are positive deviance, virtuous practices, and affirmative bias.[14] These attributes contrast with most organizations that focus primarily on preventing bad things from happening and eliminating the deficits believed to be producing poor performance: errors, inefficiencies, mistakes, and disreputable behavior.

## Positively Deviant Organizations

All healthcare organizations want to have excellent performance. At one end of the continuum are institutions that believe they can best accomplish that by building their employees' ability to provide consistently exceptional patient care. These organizations find providers who are acknowledged as being the best at delivering great care. They recognize them and promote them as models of excellence. They teach other employees to emulate their exceptional behavior. And they design their reward and incentive programs to reinforce the employees who ascend to that level of excellence.

At the other end of the spectrum are those institutions that focus on employees who demonstrate poor performance. These organizations make examples of people who commit mistakes (even honest mistakes). They threaten groups of employees who are struggling, for example, nurse managers who score low on performance metrics. In strict "hold them accountable" organizations, individuals who try to stand up to senior leaders for what they believe is right are publicly humiliated and shunned.

## Affirmative Bias in Organizations

Whether organizations focus on the best versus the worst performers hinges on whether leaders in the organization have a growth or fixed mind-set. An affirmative bias indicates the leaders have a growth mind-set. They believe their employees can learn from mistakes, grow their capabilities, and develop their strengths to become high performers.

Unfortunately, most people don't know how to function in an optimal fashion. So it is easy to fall into the trap of believing that what you see among low-performing employees is what you get—and all you'll ever get. That cognitive bias puts the "superiors" in a mind-set that they need to direct employees' behavior, scan for signs that they're failing to comply, and administer consequences when they fall short. Threatening or punishing people for not being able to live up to expectations only drives people further into dysfunction because it evokes flight or fight reactions. Or as Gallup would term it—disengagement or active disengagement.

Fortunately, positive psychology provides the knowledge and skills that people need to acquire to elevate themselves to higher levels of personal and professional functioning. Leaders with a growth mind-set affirm their employees' ability to grow into being a staff that's able to deliver excellence. Positively deviant organizations recognize that it's more effective, motivating, and self-reinforcing to promote programs that enable people to learn how to perform at their best.

## *Virtuous Organizations*

Creating an abundance culture requires lots of virtuous acts—being helpful to one another, giving generously to strangers who are struggling, sharing information, forgiving people who make mistakes, and coaching people who need wise counsel. Increasingly, studies show that although we don't benefit directly from the people who are aided by our virtuous actions, our lives are richer as a result of our good behavior: better health, more satisfying relationships, and higher confidence.

A culture characterized by support, compassion, forgiveness, hope, integrity, and optimism frees people from having to direct their energy to defending themselves, justifying mistakes, managing their fear of failing and not being forgiven, and protecting themselves from unjust accusations. Instead, their energy can go to determining what went wrong and what lessons they can learn to improve their performance in the future. Employees can use their energy to develop their strengths rather than disguising their weaknesses. When they work in a culture that generates energy through actions that create positive emotions, people are able to vigorously engage in the pursuit positive outcomes and remain resilient when experiencing setbacks.

# Raquel's Story: The Resolution

To say Raquel was stressed over Missy's death would be quite an understatement. "I hit bottom the other day," she told me. "I've been spending more time out on the floor over the last couple of weeks talking to staff members, trying to help them with their reactions to the loss. But this has hit me hard as well, and I don't always know what to say when people ask me if working here is really worth it. I was already putting in over 50 hour weeks and struggling to get home at a reasonable hour to be with my husband and two teenage sons. Dealing with Missy's death has put me over the edge."

"This has got to be incredibly difficult for you—as it would be for anyone in your position," I empathized. "I'm so sorry...for you...for your staff members... and most of all for Missy's family. How has this been affecting you?"

"I've been worrying a lot more," Raquel responded. "I worry about the toll this is taking on my staff, my family, and myself. It's on my mind when I try to go to sleep, and it makes it hard to get out of bed in the morning. I've been too tired to do my morning workout—not that I would have the time even if I had the energy. I just drink more coffee and Coke to keep going, but that's putting me into a miserable 'wired and tired' place."

"Sounds like you're lapsing into a downward spiral," I cautioned. "Your reactions are affecting your sleep and causing you to miss your morning exercise routine. Without exercise to burn off the extra stress chemicals, you're primed to ruminate about your problems even more."

"Yeah," Raquel nodded, "my cortisol levels must be going through the roof."

"In a strange way worrying works to make you feel better because of how your brain is wired," I explained. "Dwelling on a problem soothes you because your brain is engaged in examining the problem and figuring out what else could go wrong. That gives you the feeling that you're doing something to address the issues, but you're not taking any action to change the situation. So the threat remains, and as a result, the worrying gets worse.

"But stress can be a good thing if you recognize that it's a source of energy," I explained to Raquel. "If you take action rather than ruminate, you'll be harnessing your energy to effect a change on your unit."

"So how do I make that happen?"

"You need to change your mind-set," I suggested. "What outcome have you become passionate about achieving?"

"I never want to lose another one of my staff members like this again," she stated unequivocally.

"What could you do to achieve that?"

"I'm not sure. I need to ask my staff members what they think would need to happen."

"What specifically do you want to ask them?"

"First of all, I'd like to know how many people are getting their break, and how many others are leaving exhausted. Then I'd like to know if my staff believes we could turn our stressful reactions to losing Missy into energy for improving our situation."

"When can you put out a survey?" I inquired.

"Today!" she said emphatically.

"And in the meantime, what are healthy ways of replenishing your energy?"

"I know I have to get back to exercising," Raquel acknowledged.

Raquel and I covered several key questions to help her develop a specific plan:

"What will you do?"—"Run on the treadmill."
"When will you do it?"—"After I have a cup of coffee in the morning."
"What will motivate you?"—"I'll put a picture of Missy next to the coffee pot."
"Who will provide support?"—"My husband."
"What are the obstacles?"—"Early morning meetings."
"If that happens, then what?"—"Get someone else to cover them for me."

The following week I checked in with Raquel to see how she was doing and to learn about the results of the survey. "How did your exercise plan work out?"

"Good and bad," she replied. "I was on the treadmill almost every day. I'm feeling much better, mostly because I'm sleeping better. But I'm even more concerned about my staff members than I was last week."

"Kudos to you for getting back on track with your exercise and sleep routines. Sounds like that's helping replenish your energy," I offered. "What did you find out about how your staff is doing?"

"It's worse than I thought," she said, shaking her head. "Thirty-seven percent of my staff members reported that they *never* get their 30-minute break." She handed me the results showing the rest of the results: 21 percent of her staff members said they only *occasionally* get their break and another 21 percent indicated they *typically* get a break on about 50 percent of their shifts.

"Wow, I understand why you're concerned," I affirmed. "What were their suggestions?"

"When you total it up, nearly 80 percent of my staff members struggle to get breaks to eat, rest, or even use the bathroom. They feel strongly it's taking a toll on them and their ability to perform at a high level. But they're telling me that the heavy workload makes it impossible for things to change," Raquel revealed. "I see what you mean about mind-set. They believe it's bad and likely to get worse."

"We're turning over half of the beds on our unit most days, and there's a lot of pressure from bed management to get a patient discharged so another can be admitted. A few people thought that a better teamwork would help. Frankly, most of the comments were pretty pessimistic about the situation ever improving."

"This is troubling in a number of ways," I observed. "You have such a dedicated staff who are doing a great job of taking care of their patients. But the pace they have to keep is putting them—and their patients—at risk. You seemed to indicate that there were a few people who had some positive suggestions. Do you think they'd be willing to join a PROPEL team to work on overcoming the exhaustion issue?"

"Yes, absolutely," Raquel responded. "I've got some great staff members I've been talking to since Missy died. I know they're as concerned as I am and want to see things change. In fact, I'm getting the message that if we don't make changes, people will start to leave."

In keeping with her management style, Raquel showed her staff members the disturbing survey results: 37 percent of them were leaving work exhausted. She asked her staff members who they thought would be well suited to a PROPEL team—their action learning group that would focus on getting staff members their breaks.

I was impressed by the insight of the seven people who had accepted their coworkers' nomination to participate on the PROPEL team. Most people work in silos, they told me, putting their head down and going full steam ahead to get everything done to take care of their patients during their shift. But with high acuity patients and a large number of admissions and discharges, it was nearly impossible to keep up with the demands.

When staff members came onto their shift, they usually found that the supplies they needed were not in the patient rooms or on their carts. That's when the grumbling would typically start:

> What's wrong with people? They didn't do anything to restock supplies and they left the patients rooms a mess. Now I'm starting my shift behind because I have to do their work. And the patients are already starting to complain because I can't get to every one of them fast enough to give them their pain meds or get them to the bathroom!

"Of course, there's always a few staff members who go beyond grumbling. They complain as long and as loud as possible. If you have to work next door to someone like that, it makes your day miserable," lamented one of the PROPEL team members.

"Well, they do have a point," another team member reminded the group. "This isn't how we should be working. And let's remember what happened to Missy. We can do better than this."

"What would it look like if you were doing better?" I ask the team. They responded with a torrent of ideas:

*Jan:* It would be OK to ask for help because you'd know a colleague would help.

*Marita:* We'd be reading what's going on with the people working in proximity to us. You can tell when somebody's feeling stressed out. We could ask what we could do to help.

*Shantel:* Charge nurses could do a better job of anticipating who's got a heavy load and what patients are going to need. They could communicate what's going on and coordinate who could help out.

*Larry:* And the charge nurse could round on the unit to find out what's going on and who needs help.

The PROPEL team discussed the underlying values that were reflected in the positive outcome they wanted to experience, and chose *empathy*, *caring*, and *trust* as their three core values. Here's their vision of the unit they wanted to create:

> We listen and understand what our teammates need in order to take a break. Being aware of what's needed allows us to take action to help one another.

"It sounds like you all agree on the kind of unit you wish you worked on," I reflected. "How would it feel if you were able to make this outcome a reality?"

*Marita:* Personally, I like helping other nurses...especially the newer ones. I remember that there were some other staff members who went out of their way to look after me when I first started. I'd like to pay it forward.

*Larry:* I run charge a lot of the time. I'd like to see us develop a new mind-set regarding how to make every shift go well.

*Jan:* I think it would feel great to leave work knowing we took care of each other, no matter what the acuity or the number of admissions and discharges.

*Lucinda:* The patients would be expressing thanks more often—and that would be making the staff members feel great.

"What obstacles are standing in your way of achieving this vision?" I inquired.

The responses came rapid fire: "High acuity...staff who criticize...bad attitudes... I can do it myself mentality...chaos when supplies haven't been restocked...unwillingness to help others... inconsistent quality of charge nurses...burned out staff."

"How many of those factors are under your control?" I questioned.

"None" was the unanimous answer.

"Let me rephrase the question," I posed. "What obstacles within yourself are holding you back from taking action to start moving toward your vision?"

Silence.

Raquel, bless her nurse manager heart, stepped up to own the source of her reluctance: "I'm afraid of asking the staff members to do more when they're already working so hard."

"And what do you fear would happen if you did ask them," I queried.

"I guess I'm afraid they'll all quit," she responded. "But I heard on the staff survey that they're likely to quit if things stay the same. So I guess I've got nothing to lose by trying to make things better."

"What would be a plan for overcoming your fear of a mass resignation?" I wondered.

"I can think of several things I can do," Raquel replied. "First, I can send out the minutes of this meeting to the staff members explaining our vision for getting people breaks—and ask for their ideas and help. Second, I can approach people individually and let them know how important they are to the unit—and to me personally. I can let them know I'm concerned about their well-being."

"That sounds like a great plan," I enthused. "Put it into an 'if–then' statement, please."

"If I feel afraid that someone might resign, then I'll talk to them about how they can help make our unit better."

"I have an idea—what if you spoke to some of your staff members proactively?" I suggested. "Specifically, if you approached those people you suspect were the 'positive deviants'—the ones who said on your survey that they 'often' or 'always' got a break during their shift. If I recall correctly, around 8–9 percent were in that category. Out of a staff of 60, that means there are 5 people who've already figured out a solution to this problem."

"I'm not sure who those people are," Raquel confessed.

The PROPEL team pounced on the idea: "We know who they are because we're working next to them. We'll whisper some names in your ear."

"OK. If I get the names of those exceptional people, then I'll find out what they're doing differently," Raquel agreed. Other team members volunteered to join in the effort to find out what was working for a few of the top nurses.

At our next meeting, Raquel had some good feedback from the appreciative inquiry: "I learned that our 'positive deviants', as our coach calls them, always find someone working nearby, and they start finding ways to help that person early in the shift—answering a call bell if they know that nurse is tied up. Then when they need a break, they feel comfortable asking that person if they could watch their patients for a few minutes."

"I asked a few questions as well," Rose chimed in. "Another thing they do is set a schedule for themselves. They know what time they want to be done giving out meds, for instance. Because they're super organized they can stay on track most of the time. Then when it's their break time there's nothing the nurse who's covering for them needs to do other than answer the call bell."

"I heard that as well," Larry added. "But what intrigued me the most was that the nurse covering for them rarely got called. They go to each of the patients and tell them they're going on their lunch break. They make sure their patients' needs are taken care of using the five P's rounding script: PAIN—'How is your pain?', POSITION—'Are you comfortable?', POTTY—'Do you have bathroom needs?', PERIPHERY—'Do you need me to move the phone, call light, trash can, water cup, or over bed table?', and PUMP—'Check the IV pump'."

To get started, each person on the PROPEL team selected one of the staff members they believed would support the initiative to get a break. They asked that person at the beginning of the shift if they would be willing to be "buddies" who covered for each other in order to get a lunch break. They tried it for 2 weeks, and it worked wonderfully well. Their pilot program also got the attention of a number of other people. Within a few weeks, nearly everyone was on board.

The build and broaden plan worked pretty well, but not perfectly. In spite of several setbacks such as especially high-acuity shifts, the PROPEL team learned from each situation and adapted. As you can see in Figure 11.2, within 5 months, breaks had become much more common. A year later, the results were sustained.

The buddy system that the PROPEL team established continued to pay dividends beyond the ability of staff members to get their break. Figure 11.3 shows that there has been a steady increase in how often staff members helped each other.

Another important finding can been seen in Figure 11.4; this graph shows how staff members feel about their ability to accomplish what they set out to do at the start of their shift. Note that the nearly 30 percent increase in the number of staff members who say they often leave with a feeling of accomplishment 9 months after the PROPEL initiative officially concluded. This is what happens when the staff moves from a pessimistic, fixed mind-set—"there's nothing we can do to change our unit"—to a growth mind-set—"there are problems we can't change, but we can change the way we respond to them."

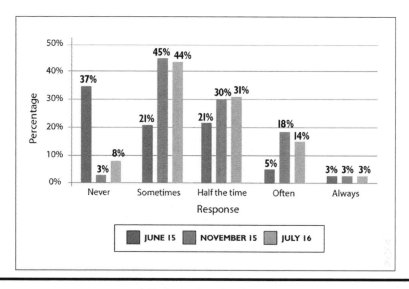

**Figure 11.2    On an average shift, how often do you get an uninterrupted 30-minute break?**

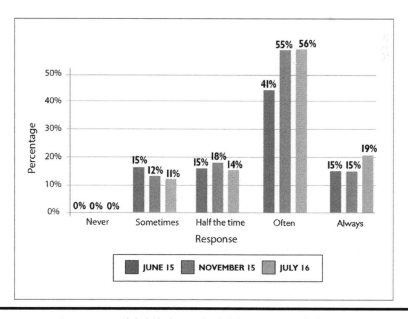

**Figure 11.3    On a successful shift, how often did you receive help from a coworker?**

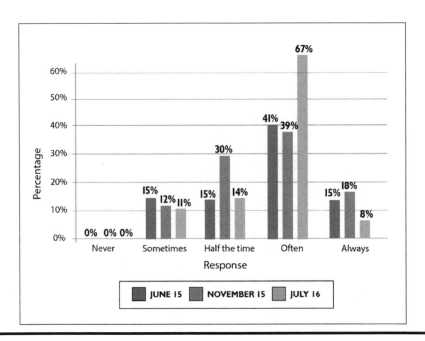

**Figure 11.4   How often do you leave work feeling like you accomplished what you set out for the shift?**

At the end of the PROPEL initiative, Raquel shared with me that among the many valuable lessons she had learned, two stood out:

First, the widespread belief that nurses—and nurse managers in particular—have to work themselves into exhaustion is a myth. She had discovered that it is essential to take the time to rejuvenate. When she faces challenges at work, she's able to direct her energy into effective action rather than worrying.

Second, the belief that there's nothing the staff can do to improve their situation is simply a self-fulfilling prophecy based on an outmoded mind-set regarding stress. Raquel told me that she never lets anyone complain anymore. They can share their concerns, but they must be willing to take action to improve the situation.

## Chapter 12

# Legacy: Empowering Others to Make a Meaningful Difference

Legacy—empowering people to make a difference—makes or breaks a healthcare system. Some organizations are renowned for building a staff dedicated to insuring that patients' best interests are served. Too many other treatment facilities, however, find many of their staff lapsing into disengagement—or active resistance—because they succumb to the belief that there is nothing they can do to improve the complex system the patients must navigate.

Positive psychology studies extraordinary people who make a difference in their world. You've probably met the type of person who seems to have a knack for facilitating positive transformations. In fact, you most likely had someone who made a big difference in your life. Numerous studies show that nearly everyone who is successful has had someone take them under their wing, nourish them, and help them flourish. You may have even been lucky enough to work for an inspiring leader who fostered higher levels of satisfaction and success with staff members and patients.

## Christina's Story: The Problem

Christina was a slender, raven-haired woman who presents with a sweet smile and kind demeanor that belies her iron will. When Christina sets her mind to a goal, I discovered, she works tirelessly to achieve it.

I began working with Christina 4 months after she was appointed nurse manager of the Oncology Outpatient Treatment Center (OTC). She had quickly come to understand the OTC had serious problems. Most disturbing were the excessively long patient wait times; 7 hours was the norm, and 9 hours was not uncommon.

"Unacceptable," Christina told me. "I'm working hard to straighten out the nursing side of this problem. Then I'm going to figure out how to get the other departments to do their part to get patients through their chemotherapy treatment in a more reasonable amount of time."

"What have you been doing to make those improvements?" I wanted to know.

"Putting in long days…and nights. I'm here by 7:00 or 7:30 in the morning and I'm not leaving until 10:00 or 11:00 at night," Christina said wearily. "I've only been getting 3–4 hours of sleep a night over the last couple of months."

"That's alarming," I reacted. "Aren't you feeling a bit burnt out?"

"Yeah, well I'm somewhat short with people when they mess up," she confessed.

"Which, as their new manager, is getting you off to a rocky start with staff members. If people mostly hear about what's going wrong, they're not going to be eager to engage with you," I observed.

"That may explain why they want the problems fixed, but resist every suggestion I make," Christina commented.

"Absolutely right. You're alienating the people you need to help you improve the OTC. You're passionate about creating change, but personally obsessed with trying to make it happen. Doing too much and resenting that no one else is taking responsibility leads to physical and emotional exhaustion. Of course, that fuels more negativity and drives you further into a downward spiral."

"I'm tough," Christina told me. "I can handle it."

"Yes, you can. But at what price? How is this affecting your personal life?" I asked.

"What personal life?" she responded sarcastically. "I see what you mean. That part of my life's taken a real hit."

"I think there's another way for you to accomplish your goal," I offered, "and it's proven to be even more effective than your singlehandedly trying to take control of the situation."

"OK. You've got my attention," Christina said in her no-nonsense fashion.

"Have you taken one of the Strengths surveys?" I inquired.

"Yes, I took the Gallup StrengthsFinder 2.0," she said reaching into her desk drawer. "My top strengths are Achiever, Responsibility, Maximizer, Harmony, and Relator."

"That's a great set of strengths. Knowing which one to use in what situation is crucial. Here's a suggestion: It sounds like you're overusing Achiever, Responsibility, Maximizer, and underutilizing your strengths of Harmony and Relator," I observed. "What do you think it would look like if you used your relationship-building talents?"

"I guess I need to start including other people in the effort to get the wait times under control," she admitted.

"I'd suggest creating a PROPEL team," I advised. "In the next week or two, I'd like to meet with five to seven members of your staff members who are good problem solvers and well connected to their coworkers to discuss being on your PROPEL team. Let's find out who shares your passion for making a difference in how long patients have to wait for their treatment."

Kelly, Ellen, and Don were highly skilled veteran oncology nurses who were seriously demoralized. "I dread Mondays," Kelly said. "I used to love taking care of cancer patients. But now when I see them sitting in a waiting room all day long, I don't feel we're doing a very good job when it comes to alleviating their suffering."

"I get so frustrated having to tell our patients hour after hour that they have to continue to wait because we don't have a treatment bay ready for them," Ellen said. "These people are very sick and going through chemo is hard. We're doing them an injustice, in my opinion."

As Don explained, "It's hard to sort out the source of the problem but we regularly have patients waiting for 8 hours to get their chemo started. We need to figure it out. It's unfair to patients and it's causing tremendous dissatisfaction for all of us."

The problem, they explained, was multifaceted. The scheduling department needed to leave the fax machine behind and get up to speed with new computer software so that the patients could be given appointments based on their acuity. Phlebotomy could do a much better job of getting the patients' blood drawn and off to the lab quickly. The lab and pharmacy need to prioritize the patients participating in research trials over the less complex cases so that compounding specialized drugs didn't take the better part of a day—and stall all of the other patient treatments.

## The Research on Legacy

You probably once believed that you could be someone who empowers people to make a difference. How has that worked out? Have you risen to the challenges and grown into a leader who knows how to empower your staff members to perform at levels they never knew were possible? Are you teaching them to be transformative leaders as well? Or have you stalled, become disenchanted, and lapsed into wondering how healthcare systems got so screwed up?

Positive psychology researchers have discovered that people who leave a legacy attain the highest level of optimal functioning: flourishing. But some people languish, or worse, devolve into discouragement and dysfunctional behaviors. Before you can empower other people, however, you may need to know how to flourish in your *own* life. You can't help others to make a meaningful difference in the world if you haven't learned how to do so yourself.

## Flourishing and Languishing Defined

Sadly, many people are languishing in their lives. Corey Keyes, a famous researcher in the study of flourishing, has found that only 17.2 percent of Americans can be classified as flourishing. More than 80 percent of the general population is functioning at a suboptimal level, with 26.2 percent self-reporting symptoms of psychosocial impairment.[1]

Flourishing is defined by positive psychologists as "living within an optimal range of human functioning, one that connotes goodness, generativity, growth and resilience."[2] Languishing, on the contrary, falls toward the other end of the mental health continuum, just above mental illness.

According to Keyes, people who flourish demonstrate "three core components of positive mental health: feelings of happiness and satisfaction with life (emotional well-being), positive individual functioning in terms of self-realization (psychological well-being), and positive societal functioning in terms of being of social value (social well-being)."[3] Psychological well-being has six elements that enable individuals to realize their full potential[4]:

1. *Self-acceptance*: A positive and acceptant attitude toward aspects of self in past and present
2. *Purpose in life*: Goals and beliefs that affirm a sense of direction and meaning in life
3. *Autonomy*: Self-direction as guided by one's own socially accepted internal standards
4. *Positive relations with others*: Having satisfying personal relationships in which empathy and intimacy are expressed
5. *Environmental mastery*: The capability to manage the complex environment according to one's own needs
6. *Personal growth*: The insight into one's own potential for self-development

Social well-being, according to Keys, has five dimensions that characterize a person who functions optimally in society[4]:

1. *Social coherence*: An ability to make meaning of what is happening in the world
2. *Social acceptance*: A positive attitude regarding others while recognizing their shortcomings
3. *Social actualization*: The belief that the world in which they live has the potential to evolve positively
4. *Social contribution*: The feeling that their contributions will be valued by society
5. *Social integration*: A sense of belonging to the community in which they live and work

In summary, people who flourish first attain a high level of life satisfaction, develop a strong sense of personal mastery, and leave a legacy by making a meaningful difference in society.

## Strategies for Leaving a Legacy

### The Progress Principle

Teresa Amabile found in her research at Harvard that 25 percent of the time people have their best days at work when someone provided "nourishment" for them that day. Human beings have a primal need to feel a positive connection to those in their "tribe." "The primary way in which nourishers fuel inner work life and progress is by infusing the work with greater meaning. When we care about the people we work with, we want them to succeed. When our colleagues become a kind of family to us, work can take on a new meaning in our lives."[5]

There are four categories of nourishing factors that Amabile has identified:

1. *Respect*: Recognition of someone's good work is the most important action one can take to show respect. Giving a person's ideas serious attention and acknowledging that their insights are valuable also conveys respect. Lastly, treating someone in a civil manner, especially in contentious situations, signals respect. Incivility, however, is a strong sign of disrespect.
2. *Encouragement*: Enthusiasm is contagious. Expressing confidence in someone's ability to tackle an important assignment boosts the person's sense of effectiveness. Telling new employees they are capable of making a significant contribution creates a bond with their workgroup early on, minimizing the chance they will leave prematurely.
3. *Emotional support*: Members of highly functional teams excel at reading one another's emotions. Having one's feelings understood and validated is an essential component in a satisfying work life. Receiving empathy around struggles and sorrows builds bonds and is crucial for soothing negative emotions such as fear, frustration, and dejection.
4. *Affiliation*: The ultimate sign of high affiliation is when team members act to support the team rather than simply doing their jobs. Collaborating with coworkers to achieve a shared goal is a strong need, especially when people aren't working side by side. Actions indicating appreciation, trust, and even affection increase connectedness. Camaraderie is also built by finding ways to have fun together.

### Give and Take

Adam Grant of The Wharton School has found in his research that highly successful people have four things in common: motivation, ability, opportunity, and being a giver in interactions with other people. He points out that in every encounter with coworkers, people have a choice: claim as much value as they can or contribute value without worrying about what they receive in return.[6]

Grant writes that "takers have a distinctive signature: they like to get more than they like to give. They tilt reciprocity in their own favor, putting their own interests ahead of others' needs. Takers believe that the world is a competitive, dog-eat-dog place. They feel that to succeed, they need to be better than others. To prove their competence, they self-promote and make sure they get plenty of credit for their efforts. Garden-variety takers aren't cruel or cutthroat, they're just cautious and self-protective."

"Givers," Grant continues, "are a relatively rare breed. They tilt reciprocity in the other direction, preferring to give more than they get. Whereas takers tend to be self-focused, evaluating what other people can offer them, givers are other-focused, paying more attention to what other people need from them."

Grant found that most people operate somewhere in the middle of the spectrum. "Professionally, few of us act purely like givers or takers, adopting a third style instead. We become 'matchers,' striving to preserve an equal balance of giving and getting. Matchers operate on the principle of fairness: when they help others, they protect themselves by seeking reciprocity. If you're a matcher, you believe in tit for tat, and your relationships are governed by an even exchange of favors."[6]

If you think that people who are too caring, too trusting, and too willing to self-sacrifice for the benefit of others will burn out and fall to the bottom of the success ladder, you're correct. Yes, you read that right. When Grant closely examined the data on the drivers of success, he found that givers dominate both the top and the bottom to the performance continuum. Takers and matchers were more likely to fall in the middle of the spectrum.

What distinguishes ultra-successful givers from those who ultimately turn out to be poor performers? They always start out as givers because trust is hard to establish, but easy to damage. When the other individual clearly proves to be a taker rather than reciprocating as a giver, they switch to using matcher strategies. Even then, they return to being a giver in one out of every three exchanges, giving takers the opportunity to redeem themselves.

The trust-but-verify givers were generous in sharing their knowledge, ideas, energy, skills, and connections with colleagues who could benefit from them. Over time, they built an incredible reservoir of trust and goodwill, cultivating relationships and reputations that fueled their success. They established the most lucrative networks, the most effective collaborations, the best evaluations, and the greatest amount of influence.

## Multipliers

Liz Wiseman spent 17 years working at the Oracle Corporation as the vice president for global talent development. After observing distinct differences in the effectiveness of leaders, she devoted 2 years to studying why some leaders could create teams that vastly outperformed other groups. She identified a continuum of leaders defined at the end of the spectrum as either Multipliers or Diminishers.[8]

Those she identified as "Multipliers" bring out the best in their people, empowering their intelligence and capabilities to produce remarkable results. Their team meetings are a hotbed of ideas and debates about the best ways to solve tough problems. Their people report that they were able to give 100 percent and still leave work exhilarated. Recruits eagerly sought the opportunity to work with this kind of boss. But new people were rarely needed. When demands became heavier, Multipliers harnessed people's underutilized talents and brainpower. By cultivating their staff's strengths and intelligence, they're able to multiply capacity without costly investments of additional personnel.

A "Diminisher," by contrast, believes they are the smartest person in the room. So they do most of the talking. They ask questions to which they already have an answer. And they only listen to one or two of their right-hand staff members who affirm their positions. An employee who disagrees or offers an alternative possibility is belittled and undermined, creating an atmosphere in which staff members are loathe to offer any innovative ideas. As a result, their teams feel stifled and become disengaged. Diminishers can't do more with what they have. New challenges require additional resources and budget-busting expenses.

## What's Your Current Capacity for Making a Meaningful Difference?

The traits of Nourishers, Givers, and Multipliers offer an image of the type of person we all aspire to be. How did you feel as you read the descriptions of those who attain the highest level of optimal functioning?

- Do you recognize more undesirable qualities in yourself than you're comfortable admitting?
- Do you feel you're not making the progress you want to see for yourself, much less enabling your colleagues to achieve it?
- Do you mostly act more like a Matcher than like a Giver—and even behave like a Taker sometimes?
- Do you feel like you're alone and fighting a losing battle when facing the litany of problems involving patients and their families?
- Do you feel diminished by the people you report to and sense the contagious effects of disrespect being passed down the chain of command to other staff members?
- Do you frequently feel your work environment is not psychologically safe due to unrealistic demands, consequences for expressing opinions, and prioritizing finances over people?

You got into healthcare because you wanted to help people, but you probably discovered it is an enormously challenging career for a multitude of reasons. You're not alone. Remember that only one in three healthcare professionals feels engaged in the job, and far fewer than that would say they're functioning at an optimal level. If you've learned anything reading this book, it's that a growth mind-set will enable you to learn and improve. But to grow you need to be able to look at the inner obstacles that are blocking your development.

Maintaining a growth mind-set for yourself and mastering new skills for bringing out the best in people will bring you the highest level of life satisfaction—flourishing. Becoming an effective coach capable of guiding others through the growth process is immensely satisfying for all involved. Helping to create and maintain a psychologically safe culture is a contribution that will endure long past your tenure.

## Applying LEGACY Research: Developing Personal Mastery

### Coaching

Having a coach who possesses flourishing characteristics and is willing to help others develop is an incredibly effective way to create better leaders. Learning how to make a meaningful difference in other people's lives helps everyone become more successful.

You must consider, however, that if you're an authority figure in your workplace, you have a dual alliance—first to the organizational priorities and then to the individual's needs. This is particularly true if you are boss, but it applies to anyone who has an agenda that may conflict with someone's personal growth agenda. The key to knowing whether you can effectively coach someone is determining the extent of the competing values that will influence your thinking.

When you agree to start working with someone, see how the first session or two goes. You are looking to see if the two of you can establish a two-way communication channel: Are you comfortable giving feedback to the person you're coaching that will lead to some immediate progress? *And* as the coach, are you comfortable requesting feedback on what the person you're coaching believes you could do differently to enhance their learning?

Forty years of data have proven that the *client's rating* of the alliance is the best predictor of engagement and outcome. The *client's subjective experience of change* early in the process is the best predictor of whether a successful coaching relationship will be established. An alliance is forged by creating a formal agreement between the coach and the client on four factors[7]:

■ What the client wishes to achieve and why
■ The client's beliefs, values, and experiences

- What the client thinks should be the way their goals are achieved
- What the client thinks of the coach

As a coach, follow three steps that will lead to high performance:

1. Identify the individual's baseline.
2. Establish a formal, routine, ongoing two-way feedback loop.
3. Engage the person in "deliberate practice" activities.

"Deliberate practice" includes the following:

1. Working hard at overcoming old patterns of behavior that have become "automatic"
2. Becoming aware of fixed mind-sets that arrest people's development because they create discomfort with new ideas and ways of working
3. Planning, strategizing, tracking, reviewing, and adjusting the action plan and practice steps in each meeting
4. Consistently measuring and comparing performance to the individual's personal baseline or a national standard to measure progress

Deliberate practice must be accompanied by feedback. At the beginning of every meeting, an effective coach asks what progress has been made. If there has been no improvement, or there has been a decline in performance, the coach drills down to understand more about the situation and the internal obstacles that are holding the person back. After asking numerous questions, the coach offers a new or refined strategy to try. To solidify the plan for taking the next steps, the coach routinely employs the WOOP exercise.

It is important for the coach to ask for feedback regarding the individual's satisfaction with the session. A significant finding regarding effective coaching is that negative client feedback is associated with better outcomes. Clients who experience a problem but are extremely satisfied with the way it is handled are twice as likely to be engaged as those who never experience a problem. This type of client engagement is the best process-related predictor for helping someone achieve outstanding outcomes.[7]

Two-way feedback creates an alliance between the coach and the client. The coach's receptive attitude toward receiving feedback in order to improve his or her performance provides a growth mind-set model. A great coach realizes that no one strategy works for every person in every situation. Both parties continually learn how to be more effective in achieving the target goals.

## Applying LEGACY Research: Developing Team Mastery

Once again, the concept of mind-set explains the difference between how Multipliers and Diminishers think and act when they're trying to bring out the best in their team.[8]

The mind of the Diminisher holds the beliefs that

■ Intelligent people are rare and I'm one of them.
■ They'll never figure this out without me.
■ In meetings, I only listen to two people.
■ No one else really has anything to offer.
■ Intelligence is static—it can't change.
■ People who don't get it now, never will.
■ I'll have to do the thinking for everyone.

On the contrary, Multipliers believe that

■ Intelligence is continually developing.
■ People are smart, they'll figure it out.
■ Talented people can contribute at a higher level.
■ I can help them develop and grow abilities.
■ My job is to get the right people together and get out of the way.

In interviews with people who worked for Multipliers and Diminishers, Liz Wiseman asked what percent of their capability was derived from their boss. For Diminishers, the responses ranged from 20 percent to 50 percent. But for those who worked for Multipliers, the estimates ranged between 70 percent and 100 percent. Multipliers got 1.97 times as much out of their employees—nearly twice as much as Diminishers!

In subsequent studies across many different industries, Wiseman found that Multipliers consistently get twice as much from their employees. Their people hold nothing back, giving more than their job requires in terms of discretionary effort, energy, and resourcefulness. Their teams generate the best thinking, creativity, and ideas. In fact, people actively search for more valuable ways to contribute.

"Our research confirmed that Multipliers not only access people's current capability," Wiseman writes, "They stretch it. They get more from people than they knew they had to give. People reported getting smarter around Multipliers."[8]

# Applying LEGACY Research: Developing a Culture of Psychological Safety

Organizations that make a meaningful difference in people's lives create a culture of psychological safety. Employees in such organizations believe that they can respectfully express their thoughts, feelings, and suggestions without fear of reprisal. Harvard Professor Amy Edmondson has demonstrated that in psychologically safe workplaces, learning and innovation are enhanced—including in hospitals.[11]

Putting her hypothesis to the ultimate "life-and-death" test, Edmondson studied how eight hospital units handled medication errors. Some units enforced a zero-tolerance policy for making mistakes, sending the message they would not be tolerated. On other units, the healthcare professionals worked in a culture where their errors would be forgiven.

---

The American Psychological Association's meta-analysis of research results on the definition of forgiveness concluded: "Forgiveness is a process (or the result of a process) that involves a change in emotion and attitude regarding an offender. This process results in decreased motivation to retaliate or maintain estrangement from an offender despite their actions, and requires letting go of negative emotions toward the offender."[10]

Note that the function inherent in forgiving involves releasing negative emotions. As you've learned, negativity automatically focuses your brain on primitive fight–flight–freeze reactions when confronting dangerous situations, thereby restricting your mind's ability to envision adaptive solutions.

---

Based on the ratings of amount of psychological safety staff members perceived to be present, the number of medication errors reported was higher on those units where staff members felt safe to report their mistakes. Was this proof that tolerance caused the medical professionals to become complacent? Did safety for the staff members translate into unsafe conditions for the patients? No, and no.

Edmondson delved into the more objective, independent data reflecting the number of medication errors made. She found that the higher the level of psychological safety reported by staff members, the fewer mistakes they made. Those professionals felt it was safe to report errors, learning from them and preventing the same mistake from occurring in the future. The data demonstrated that higher psychological safety resulted in fewer mistakes, lowering the risk to patients of receiving ineffective treatment or experiencing adverse reactions.

Staff members on units with the lowest amount of psychological safety were hiding their errors in fear of retribution. Those units did not learn from mistakes, perpetuating their problem of preventable errors.

Edmondson states: "It appears that nurse manager behaviors are an important influence on unit members' beliefs about the consequences and 'discussability' of mistakes. In addition to the influence of what is said by the nurse manager, the ways past errors have been handled are noticed, and conclusions are drawn, which then are strengthened by ongoing conversations among unit members. In this way, perceptions may become reality, as the perception that something is not discussable leads to avoidance of such discussions. These kinds of perceptions, when shared, contribute to a climate of fear or of openness, which can be self-reinforcing, and which further influences the ability and willingness to identify and discuss mistakes and problems. These climates are characterized in part by the nature of relationships within and between professional identity groups."[12]

## Creating Psychological Safety with Teams and Organizations

Edmondson has identified five practices that build a psychologically safe environment. In her 2011 Harvard Business Review article, she illustrates how each practice was implemented by Julie Morath, the chief operating officer of Children's Hospital and Clinics of Minnesota, Minneapolis, Minnesota, from 1999 to 2009, when she led a highly successful effort to reduce medical errors.[12]

1. *Frame the work accurately.* Discuss the kinds of failures that are expected to occur. Explain why open, collaborative communication is important for surfacing and learning from them. Make it clear that to achieve optimal functioning, the focus of discussions needs to center on changing behavior *in the future.*

   "In a complex operation like a hospital, many consequential failures are the result of a series of small events. To heighten awareness of this system complexity, Morath presented data on U.S. medical error rates, organized discussion groups, and built a team of key influencers from throughout the organization to help spread knowledge and understanding of the challenge."

2. *Embrace messengers.* Staff members who report errors need to rewarded, not shot. Recognize the value of the information and the opportunity to figure out how to improve.

   "Morath implemented 'blameless reporting'—an approach that encouraged employees to reveal medical errors and near misses anonymously. Her team created a new patient safety report, which expanded on the previous version by asking employees to describe incidents in their own words and to comment on the possible causes. Soon after the new system was put in place, the rate of reported failures shot up. Morath encouraged her people to view the data as good

news, because the hospital could learn from failures—
and made sure that teams were assigned to analyze every
incident."

3. *Acknowledge limits.* Openly discuss the fact that everyone's perception of a
problem situation is limited because they only can see part of the picture.
By combining people's viewpoints, a much more accurate assessment of the
situation can be developed, enabling lessons to be learned and everyone to see
what their role needs to be in helping implement changes.

> "As soon as she joined the hospital, Morath explained
> her passion for patient safety and acknowledged that as a
> newcomer, she had only limited knowledge of how things
> worked at Children's. In group presentations and one-
> on-one discussions, she made clear that she would need
> everyone's help to reduce errors."

4. *Invite participation.* Create opportunities for sharing observations of factors
contributing to problems and encourage innovative ideas for making changes.
Rather than limiting the discussions and decision-making to a small group of
leaders, seek input from frontline staff members to learn what solutions they
believe will work.

> "Morath set up cross-disciplinary teams to analyze failures
> and personally asked thoughtful questions of employees at
> all levels. Early on, she invited people to reflect on their
> recent experiences in caring for patients: Was everything as
> safe as they would have wanted it to be? This helped them
> recognize that the hospital had room for improvement.
> Suddenly, people were lining up to help."

5. *Set boundaries and hold people accountable.* Staff members feel psychologically safer when they're clear about what acts are subject to disciplinary
action. When people are punished, explain exactly what happened and why
it warranted a consequence.

> "When she instituted blameless reporting, Morath explained
> to employees that although reporting would not be pun-
> ished, specific behaviors (such as reckless conduct, conscious
> violation of standards, and failing to ask for help when over
> one's head) would. If someone makes the same mistake three
> times and is then laid off, coworkers usually express relief,
> along with sadness and concern—they understand that
> patients were at risk and that extra vigilance was required
> from others to counterbalance the person's shortcomings."[12]

## Christina's Story: The Resolution

Christina's coaching focused on preparing her to be an effective participant on the PROPEL team she was forming. "How have you brought out the best in people in the past?" I ask.

"Well, to be honest, I do what my manager did for me. I was her assistant nurse manager for several years before she got promoted. More than showing me how to do the nuts and bolts stuff like payroll and scheduling, Anne encouraged me to do things I wasn't sure I could do—like sit down with the docs on the Safety Committee to discuss errors that had occurred. She trusted me to figure out how we could prevent a problem from reoccurring."

"Sounds like Anne was a multiplier," I reflected. "Have you done the same thing for some of your staff members in the few months since you took over as manager?"

"Somewhat. But what's a multiplier?" she wanted to know.

"It's someone who sees your talent—even more clearly than you do—and gives you stretch goals so you can expand the use of your strengths," I explained. "Give me an example of how you've done that."

"My assistant nurse manager, Nikki, is amazing. The staff members love her, even though she's the person who's supervising them all day long. But in the beginning, she was so shy. She was reluctant to take the position. I persuaded her by pointing out her capabilities and got her to try working with one of our treatment teams. She did a fantastic job, and the rest is history."

"I'm confused," I said with some hesitation. "If Nikki's done such a good job, why are the treatment teams refusing to change their practice model to better accommodate the needs of the patients?"

"Well, Nikki does what I do," Christina explained. "She jumps in and does what needs to be done herself."

"And that's self-limiting because you only have so much time and energy." I was having one of those 'Aha' moments. "Nikki's following the example you set. Is it possible that the two of you are compensating for the problems that the staff is creating by refusing to collaborate? Do you think the two of you may be overplaying your ability to take responsibility, thereby enabling staff members to stay in their silos rather than work as a team?"

"Oh, I get it," she said as the flash of insight instantly changed her mind-set.

Christina was a great learner, and her growth over the ensuing months was marvelous. She formed a PROPEL team and started to work with her most engaged staff members to create a more positive, teamwork-oriented environment.

The team started to meet every week and began by defining the outcome that the group was passionate about achieving. The team decided that the four values most important to them were caring, helping, inquiring, and recognizing. Their vision statement was as follows:

We have a culture of caring—for each other and for our patients. We help each other to get patients their treatment in a timely manner. We work for the good of the whole by asking how what we're doing impacts others. We recognize when a colleague has a problem and ask him or her to propose a solution.

The behaviors that described what it would look like if those values and that vision were being demonstrated daily were:

- Huddling every morning, including the techs, to plan the day
- Offering to help when we see someone's overloaded
- Remaining respectful—especially when stressed—by asking for what's needed
- Assuring that everyone gets a lunch break
- Convincing staff members to let someone else touch their patient's chemo pump
- Conducting regular debriefings to understand what worked
- Asking for suggestions to continue making progress

The PROPEL team worked hard to get the morning huddles to work well. The entire staff began to understand what they were expected to do to make it a good day. Christina rounded at the end of the day, asking each staff member what kind of day they had. She offered appreciation for their efforts and gave them an opportunity to make suggestions. One excellent idea emerged: to reduce the morning scramble to get patients' treatments started, the staff members would have everything prepared the day before their appointment.

"I discovered the wisdom of being a multiplier rather than trying to be super-woman," Christina reflected several months after forming her PROPEL team. "My strengths are achiever, responsibility, developer, empathy, and positivity. I was overusing my ability to take the responsibility for achieving positive outcomes. When I started using my talent for developing a team of people, they were able to accomplish much more than I ever could by pushing my agenda."

The PROPEL team had rave reviews to share as well. Ellen put it this way: "We developed goals—big goals. And then Christina got out of the way. She trusted us to figure out how to get the people in our treatment pods to work more collaboratively. The PROPEL team started to help other RNs when we saw opportunities to do so. 'Be the change you want to see' was our motto. And people were grateful for getting a helping hand when they needed it."

Don chimed in with his observations: "And it worked! First of all, I can personally attest it worked for the people on the PROPEL team. I was burned out and ready to take another job. But helping my colleagues have a good day gave me a lot more job satisfaction. I started coaching certain individuals on how to be at their best, and almost all of them came around to offering help as well. The few who didn't ended up moving on."

Kelly commented on achieving a tipping point with the staff members: "We had to create a culture in which our staff members felt safe to talk about problems. Rather than staying in their silos, we had to figure out how to help people join in the discussions. We began to routinely ask staff members what they saw as contributing to treatment delays, as well as what suggestions they had for making improvements.

"For example, we figured out that the staff members would benefit by going to 10-hour shifts because they were usually having to stay late anyhow. This change gave them an extra day off every week. The PROPEL team encouraged people to try the new schedule before passing judgment. And we set up an emergency plan so staff members knew it was safe to say they wanted to leave early. We arranged to have someone cover for them."

The OTC continued to develop a more collaborative, psychologically safe culture. Although that improved patient wait times somewhat, the staff members remained terribly frustrated by the long delays caused by interdepartmental issues. Staff members wanted to receive doctors' orders in a timely manner and get patients through phlebotomy quickly so labs could be completed and have the pharmacy mix the chemotherapy cocktail for that day's treatment.

Christina had learned a valuable lesson from creating a PROPEL team: It's essential to pull together a group of people who are willing to create a safe environment to solve complex problems. She put that lesson to use in approaching people in other departments.

Previously discussions with other departments had begun by bringing up the litany of problems that had recently occurred, which only evoked a defensive "it's not our fault" response. Christina learned to start conversations by focusing on ideas each of her counterparts had in mind for how their team could improve patient wait times. Only then did she ask what the other department leaders saw as impediments to change. She followed up by asking questions about how their department had overcome other obstacles in the past.

The medical director believed that reducing patient wait times required getting doctors to write their orders at least 48 hours ahead of the patient's appointment. He found several other physicians who were willing to join a team devoted to exploring this change. After several months, they had established a 48-hour rule as the new norm. A review board was established so doctors could request an exemption in case of an emergency. In the beginning physicians asked for an exception 70 percent of the time; most times they were denied. After a few months, the request rate was near zero.

Building on that win, Christina teamed up with champions in other areas to PROPEL new processes to speed up phlebotomy, lab work, and pharmacy chemo preparation time. The schedulers identified patients who were to receive a standard chemotherapy treatment and began to get their blood and lab work completed days before treatment. Following suit, the phlebotomists changed the schedule. Patients whose infusions would take the most time were scheduled at the start of the day.

Then the results of their blood work could be sent to the pharmacy and their chemo drugs could be compounded first.

*The result*: 18 months later nearly 50 percent of chemotherapy patients have no wait time whatsoever because their medications are waiting for them when they show up for their appointment. Patients who need special, complicated mixes of medications have seen their wait times cut in half. No one waits 9 hours anymore!

Knowing how to grow yourself into the best human being you can be will give you the perfect skill set to be able to do that for others—individuals, teams, and even larger groups who populate healthcare organizations.

In summary, people who leave a legacy:

- Nourish their coworkers with encouragement and emotional support.
- Pay attention to what other people need and give it to them.
- Switch to using matching tactics to deal with people who take advantage.
- Find and multiply people's talent by bringing out their best efforts—and then some.
- Create psychologically safe workplaces where employees have a voice in efforts to improve their organization.
- Empower others to make a meaningful difference in the world.

# TOOLKITS FOR INDIVIDUALS AND PROPEL TEAMS

# IV

The starting point for improving the quality of healthcare organizatons is to improve the quality of the lives of people who work in those systems. Chapters 13 and 14 provide practical guidance for applying the PROPEL Principles. These are the toolkits used by PROPEL coaches in a variety of healthcare settings.

The toolkit in Chapter 13 is for individuals who want to use an evidence-based methodology to improve their life. It is designed to be used over a period of several weeks. Think of it like being in a class on optimal functioning, acquiring one new skill at a time until you master the topic.

Chapter 14 is devoted to developing a PROPEL team in your workplace. You will discover how to align with like-minded individuals to create more a positive and engaged staff—just the ingredients you need to deliver higher quality healthcare. It is almost impossible for one person to significantly improve their healthcare organization. The stories in this book have demonstrated that working with other top performers makes achieving remarkable results possible.

---

Download a *free* copy of the PROPEL toolkit for individuals with space & write out answers when completing the exercises in Chapter 13 from my website:

**www.PROPELinstitute.com/toolkit**

# Your PROPEL Toolkit: Exercises for Elevating Your Level of Satisfaction and Success

## Introduction

The exercises in the PROPEL Toolkit for individual growth will help you develop personal mastery of the skills required to develop optimal functioning:

- *Passionately* pursuing desired goals, rather than dwelling on problems
- Enriching *Relationships*, rather than languishing in painful negativity when they go wrong
- Developing *Optimistic* thinking and a growth mind-set, rather than allowing discouragement to prevail
- *Proactively* responding to challenges by using hard-wired strengths, rather than disengaging
- Replenishing *Energy* and building resilience, rather than stressing out (or burning out)
- Leaving a *Legacy* by empowering others to make meaningful difference

You are strongly encouraged to use a journal to write down your answers when completing the following exercises. You can also download a copy of the PROPEL Toolkit on my website: www.PROPELinstitute.com/toolkit.

The PROPEL Toolkit for individuals follows a formula that has proven effective for facilitating change:

1. Increase awareness of your current level of functioning.
2. Develop a growth mind-set by identifying new ways of thinking.
3. Identify desired behaviors that will improve your performance.
4. Engage in daily deliberate practice to become competent and comfortable using your new skills.

*A key point to remember*: People who achieve satisfaction and success in life deliberately practice activities to improve their performance. Daily deliberate practice involves the following:

- Working hard to overcome old patterns of "automatic" thinking that arrest your development due to discomfort with new ideas and behaviors
- Overcoming internal obstacles that could potentially hold you back by routinely employing the wish, outcome, obstacle, and plan (WOOP) exercise
- Planning, strategizing, tracking, reviewing, and adjusting your daily practice activities to tailor new behaviors to your life circumstances
- Learning from setbacks by reviewing the research, asking questions, and developing a new or refined strategy to achieve your goals

## The Core of Optimal Functioning: Consistently Living Your Values

The first exercises in PROPEL Toolkit help you to identify your core values and to develop a vision of what it would look like if you were living an optimal life.

### Values Exercise 1: Peaks and Valleys[1]

*Part 1*: Using Figure 13.1 as a model, draw a line in the middle of page. Above the line indicate the top three to four peak experiences of satisfaction in your life. Below the line, note three to four low points, your worst moments.

*Part 2*

Step 1: Draw four columns as seen in Figure 13.2. In the first column, briefly describe the event.

Step 2: In the second column, write about the positive and negative feelings you associate with each experience.

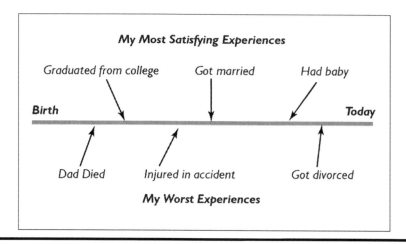

**Figure 13.1 Part 1 Example: Peaks and valleys.**

| Brief Description of Each Event | Feelings I Experienced | What stands out as most meaningful about this experience? | Core Values |
|---|---|---|---|
| Example: My father got cancer and died when I was in high school. | Sadness, Fear, Insecurity, Anger | Uncertainty about what would happen to my Mom, younger brother and myself. Feeling responsible for taking care of my family. Grateful for my Grandmother's reassurances. | Security Fairness Responsibility Gratitude |

**Figure 13.2 Part 2 Example: Discovering your core values.**

Step 3: In the third column note, what life lessons you took away from each experience. How did these events shape what is most important to you?

Step 4: In the fourth column, write down the fundamental values that were formed as a result of going through those experiences.

Step 5: When you've finished writing about one event, draw a line across the columns and repeat the exercise for the next event.

## Values Exercise 2: Prioritize Your Core Values

Step 1: Look at the words you used in Figure 13.2 to describe the values you've developed. Which ones have the strongest emotions attached to them? Which bring you the most joy? When violated, which values generate the greatest amount of anger?

Step 2: Draw a 4 × 4 table as seen in the example given in Figure 13.3. Review all of your values and choose your three most important—the ones that are core to your well-being. Write down why those stand out as most meaningful.

Step 3: Using a scale of 1–100 percent, guesstimate the percentage of the time you feel you are able to live your values because you get derailed by work demands, peer pressure, stressful situations, and so on.

Step 4: Write a short description of how inconsistencies are affecting your satisfaction and well-being.

| Core Value | What Makes this Value Meaningful? | Consistency Percentage | How Inconsistency Affects My Wellbeing |
|---|---|---|---|
| **Gratitude** | I appreciate people who step up and help during stressful times. | 33% | I get hyper-focused on getting things done. I feel ashamed when I don't take the time to thank people who helped me. |

**Figure 13.3  Example: How consistently are you living your values?**

---

### DELIBERATE DAILY PRACTICE

Pay attention to how increased awareness of your core values affects you each day. Use your insights to develop your "best self" vision in exercise 3.

## *Values Exercise 3: "WWILL" Power—How to Be Your Best Possible Self*

Ask yourself "What Will It Look Like?" (WWILL) if you were living your core values more consistently. Envisioning you at your best strengthens the pathways in your brain that support achieving optimal functionals.

Write a detailed, behaviorally based picture of the best possible version of yourself in the future. For example, if you want a stronger relationship with your boss, write about how you could set a mutually beneficial goal, work together to achieve it, and generate positive emotions along the way by expressing gratitude for his or her guidance. Describe how you would get his or her support, what the conversations might sound like, as well as how you will share your feelings of appreciation.

---

# PROPEL Principle 1: Nourishing Your Passion

Passion is the source of your inspiration and motivation. It drives you to engage in loving relationships. It enables you to invest time and energy in a job that you love. And it inspires you to master the skills required for an optimal personal and professional life.

## *Passion Exercise 1: Self-Assessment*

Most healthcare providers derive their passion from a desire to restore their patients to good health. But passion can wane over time, diminishing job enjoyment and engagement.[3] Do you find yourself having these types of inner conversations?

> Life is short. I spend too much of it at work rather than with family and friends.
>
> I'm trapped. After all the years of school and building my career, I can't walk away.
>
> I'm bored. I spend too much time taking care of paperwork rather than people.
>
> I'm not happy. All the frustrations and disappointments are making me miserable.
>
> I can't let it go. I constantly check my e-mails and ruminate on all of the problems.

Such thoughts signal it's time to regenerate your passion. It's time to reassess where you are and what's important to you.

## Passion Exercise 2: Your "WWILL" Power PROPEL Goal

To start moving toward your best possible self, identify a short-term PROPEL goal that moves you toward becoming your "best possible self." Write a "WWILL" (What Will It Look Like) statement that includes the following:

- The values that underlie your passion for attaining this goal.
- The activities you will actually be doing once the goal is attained. Be specific. What will you see, hear, and feel that's different from today?
- How you and others will benefit once you've realized your goal.
- Make the goal you wish to work toward over the course of the next several months SMART (specific, measurable, attainable, realistic, time-bound).
- Identify the smallest *first* step you can take that has a high probability of enabling you to make progress toward your goal.

## Passion Exercise 3: Wish, Outcome, Obstacle, and Plan[2]

WOOP (Wish, Outcome, Obstacle, and Plan) is a simple but effective method for significantly increasing your chances of success. It's helpful to record your answers in a 4 × 4 chart like the one in Figure 13.4.

Begin with the "W"—the *wish* of your goal. Picture yourself having achieved that positive outcome. What activities do you see yourself doing?

- You must be able to picture the positive behaviors you wish to be using as a starting point in the change process. *Literally picture yourself being in the situation to which you aspire* by asking "What Will It Look Like?"

Then, contemplate the first "O"—the positive *outcome* you'll experience by attaining your goal. What will you be feeling? What's the best part of having fulfilled your wish?

- Passion provides the motivation to begin the change process. Imagine the emotions you'll feel when someone you care about congratulates you. Think about how it will feel when you celebrate your success.

| W – WWILL? | O – Outcome |
|---|---|
| O – Obstacle | P - Plan |

**Figure 13.4   Example: WOOP exercise.**

Next, consider the second "O"—the *obstacle*. What is the obstacle within you that would prevent you from taking action? What's the insecurity, vulnerability, and uncertainty that's holding you back? Pay attention to what your inner critic is telling you about what could go wrong, why it's not possible, or what you're lacking to make it happen.

- Dig deeper to make sure you're identifying the real obstacle by asking yourself, "What else would stop me?" Is it a bad habit such as spending too much time watching TV or perusing Facebook? Or is it a more personal issue such as fearing what might happen if you asserted yourself or if your efforts failed?

Finally, reflect on the "P"—your *plan* for moving forward in the face of challenges. Once you have your obstacles in mind, formulate "if–then" statements: "If obstacle x occurs, then I'll do y." For example, "If I'm not taking my first step, then I'll select an even smaller behavior I feel I can take."

- If you have trouble figuring out your contingency plan, ask yourself: How have I overcome obstacles in the past? What have you seen others do when facing a similar challenge?

---

**DELIBERATE DAILY PRACTICE**

**Write down the best times to do mental rehearsals so you'll feel comfortable following through on your "if–then" plans. Review your "if–then" action plans whenever you get the chance—getting up in the morning, driving to work, and so on.**

---

# PROPEL Principle 2: Nourishing Your Relationships

It's nearly impossible to achieve our goals without support. People with the highest levels of success and satisfaction maintain high-quality connections. Despite the ups and downs of relationships, they remain committed to creating caring connections. Flourishing relationships have many more positive interactions than negative exchanges.

## *Relationship Exercise 1: Assessing Your Current Level of Positivity*

### *Positivity Self Test*[4]

What feelings have you had over the past 24 hours? Look back over the last day and, using the 0–4 scale that follows, indicate the greatest amount of each emotion that you experienced.

*0 = not at all   1 = a little bit   2 = moderate   3 = quite a bit   4 = extreme*

| Question | Score |
|---|---|
| 1. What is the most amused, fun-loving or silly you felt? | |
| 2. What is the most angry, irritated or annoyed you felt? | |
| 3. What is the most ashamed, humiliated or disgraced you felt? | |
| 4. What is the most wonder, awe or amazement you felt? | |
| 5. What is the most contemptuous, scornful or disdainful you felt? | |
| 6. What is the most disgust, distaste or revulsion you felt? | |
| 7. What is the most embarrassed, blushing or self-conscious you felt? | |
| 8. What is the most grateful, appreciative or thankful you felt? | |
| 9. What is the most guilty, repentant or blameworthy you felt? | |
| 10. What is the most hate, distrust or suspicion you felt? | |
| 11. What is the most hopeful, optimistic or encouraged you felt? | |
| 12. What is the most inspired, uplifted or elevated you felt? | |
| 13. What is the most interested, alert or curious you felt? | |
| 14. What is the most joyful, glad or happy you felt? | |
| 15. What is the most love, closeness or trust you felt? | |
| 16. What is the most proud, confident or self-assured you felt? | |
| 17. What is the most sad, down-hearted or unhappy you felt? | |
| 18. What is the most scared, fearful or afraid you felt? | |
| 19. What is the most serene, content or peaceful you felt? | |
| 20. What is the most stressed, nervous or overwhelmed you felt? | |

## Scoring

1. Circle the 10 items that reflect positivity: 1, 4, 8, 11, 12, 13, 14, 15, 16, 19.
2. Count the number of circled positivity items that you scored *two* or higher and write that number below.
3. Put a check by the 10 items that reflect negativity: 2, 3, 5, 6, 7, 9, 10, 17, 18, 20.
4. Count the number of check-marked negativity items that you endorsed as *one* or higher and write that number below.
5. Calculate the ratio by dividing your positivity tally by your negativity tally. If your negativity is zero for today, consider it instead to be a 1 to side-step the "can't-divide-by-zero" problem.
   Number of positive feelings scored 2 or higher _____
   Number of negative feelings scored 1 or higher _____
   Positive-to-negative ratio = _____:_____

It's been established that there is no "right" ratio that applies to everyone in every situation. Some researchers suggest that three positive interactions to every one negative exchange is a minimum. However, the number of positive emotions you need depends on several factors:

- The personal circumstances that are affecting your work life, and vice versa
- The amount of stress you experience when facing a challenge
- The degree to which your background has left you vulnerable to negativity
- The amount of positivity you require to sustain a growth mind-set
- The amount of recognition you need to maintain your motivation

## Relationship Exercise 2: "WWILL" Power for Increasing Your Positivity

Consider who you will need to support your efforts to accomplish your goal in Passion Exercise 1. What actions could you take to keep your positivity ratio high in those relationships? Write a "What Will It Look Like" statement that identifies how you will maintain good connections with the following:

- Loved ones
- Best friends
- Coworkers
- Boss
- Opponents

---

**DELIBERATE DAILY PRACTICE**

Identify 3 times a day to devote to increasing positive connections.
What's the best way to remind yourself that it's time to practice?
For example, set three reminders to yourself on your phone.

---

## *Relationship Exercise 3: WOOP Your Ability to Succeed*[2]

Step 1: Create another 4 × 4 WOOP chart and write down your "W"—What
are you *wishing* you'll be able to do in order to generate relationships that
can support accomplishing the PROPEL goal you wrote down in Passion
Exercise 2?

Step 2: For the first "O"—Imagine the positive *outcomes* any benefits you will
experience when you fulfill your wish.

Step 3: Consider the second "O"—It's often obstacles within us that hold us
back, including our feelings, thoughts, or actions. Identify the *obstacle* within
you that might hold you back from taking action.

Step 4: Reflect on the "P"—The WOOP model uses if–then *plans* to help us overcome our obstacles. Define your if–then plan using the formula: if [obstacle]
occurs, then I will [effective action].

---

# PROPEL Principle 3: Nourishing Your Optimism

So far, you have set goals and selected people to support you. But that will not prevent you from suffering setbacks as you work toward positive outcomes. By learning to challenge pessimistic attributions of negative events and explaining them in
optimistic terms, you can improve your ability to sustain hope, commitment, and
perseverance.

## *Optimism Exercise 1: Describe a Current Challenge*

- Write a description of a current work problem that is interfering with your
  ability to achieve your PROPEL goal.
- Write down the reasons why you think it has been a struggle to resolve this
  problem.

## *Optimism Exercise 2: Are You a Positive or Negative Thinker?*[5]

The following exercise is adapted from *Mind Tools* and used with permission:
https://www.mindtools.com/pages/article/newTCS_89.htm.

## Instructions

For each statement, circle the number that best describes your thinking as it relates to your PROPEL goal. Please answer questions as you actually are (rather than how you think you should be), and don't worry if some questions seem to score in the "wrong direction."

*1 = not at all   2 = rarely   3 = sometimes   4 = often   5 = very often*

1 2 3 4 5   1. When my boss, a coworker, or a patient asks to speak with me, I instinctively assume that he or she wants to discuss a problem or give me negative feedback.

1 2 3 4 5   2. When I experience real difficulty at work/home, I also feel negative about other parts of my life.

1 2 3 4 5   3. When I experience a setback, I tend to believe the obstacle will endure for the long term. For example, "I didn't get promoted. It doesn't seem like things will work out for me in this organization."

1 2 3 4 5   4. When a team I am on is functioning poorly, I believe that the cause is short term and has a straightforward solution. For example, "We're not working well at the moment. But when we fix this problem, then we'll do much better!"

1 2 3 4 5   5. When I'm not chosen for an assignment I really want, I tend to believe that I just don't have the specific skills they are looking for right now, as opposed to thinking I am generally unskilled.

1 2 3 4 5   6. When something happens that I don't like or appreciate, I tend to conclude that the cause is widespread in nature and will continue to plague me. For example, "I didn't get the e-mail. The poor communication around here will never change."

1 2 3 4 5   7. When I perform very well on an assignment, I believe that it's because I'm generally talented and smart, as opposed to thinking I am good in just one specific area.

1 2 3 4 5   8. When I receive a reward or recognition, I tend to assume that my talent and hard work play more of a role than luck or fate. For example, "They asked me to present at a conference next year. I guess they see how talented I am."

1 2 3 4 5   9. When I come up with a really good idea, I am surprised by my creativity. I figure it is my lucky day and caution myself not to get used to the feeling.

1 2 3 4 5   10. When something bad happens at work, I see the contributions that everyone made to the mistake, as opposed to thinking that I am incompetent or others are to blame.

1 2 3 4 5   11. After getting recognition, I believe it's because I am better at doing certain things than the competition. For example, "I won

that big award against two strong competitors. I simply have better skills in that area than they do."

1 2 3 4 5    12. When I'm in a leadership position and my team completes a project, I tend to attribute the success strictly to the hard work and dedication of the team members and downplay my leadership role.

1 2 3 4 5    13. When I make a decision that proves to be successful, it's because I have specialized expertise on that particular subject, as opposed to generally being a strong decision maker.

1 2 3 4 5    14. When I achieve a long-term and personally challenging goal, I congratulate myself and think about all the skills that I used in order to be successful.

## Scoring

Write your response to each of the questions in the grid that follows. Where a question is listed as a "Reverse Score" (*noted by an asterisk*), use the following key to calculate your score:

   *5 = 1    4 = 2    3 = 3    2 = 4    1 = 5*

In other words, if your answer to number 1 above was "4," record a "2" in the grid below for your score for that question.

| Question | Score | Question | Score | Question | Score | Question | Score | Question | Score |
|----------|-------|----------|-------|----------|-------|----------|-------|----------|-------|
| 1*       |       | 4        |       | 7        |       | 10       |       | 13*      |       |
| 2*       |       | 5        |       | 8        |       | 11       |       | 14       |       |
| 3*       |       | 6*       |       | 9*       |       | 12*      |       |          |       |

Overall score (add individual scores for questions 1 through 14): _____

## Score Interpretation

*Be sure you reverse scored (5 = 1, 4 = 2, 2 = 4, 1 = 5) questions 1, 2, 3, 6, 9, 12, and 13.*

*14–31* You have developed the habit of personalizing the cause of problems—attributing them to yourself or others—rather than looking at the multitude of other factors that can contribute to the situation. You've learned to give up your control in many situations. Taking this quiz is the first step toward turning your pessimism around.

*32–50* You try to be optimistic and positive, but some situations get the better of you. Identify your triggers for negative thinking—such as assuming a problem is permanent or will contaminate many aspects of your life. Learning to explain problems as temporary and contained to one facet of your life will enable you to become more optimistic.

*51–70* You have a generally positive and optimistic outlook on life. You don't make problems personal and you are able to see that setbacks won't ruin the rest of your life.

---

### DELIBERATE DAILY PRACTICE

You deal with problems almost every day. Use the optimism filter to determine how you're explaining them if you find yourself struggling:

- Are you making the problem permanent versus temporary?
- Are you focusing on the specific issue or speculating the problem will adversely affect everything else?
- Are you making the problem personal rather than focusing on changing the situation?

Pick a time that you could routinely practice how you are thinking about problems.

---

## *Optimism Exercise 3: Turn Negative Thinking into Optimistic Thinking*

Review the explanation you gave in Optimism Exercise 1 regarding how you've been thinking about a problem you are currently facing in your efforts to attain your PROPEL goal. *Based on what you've learned about optimistic thinking, rewrite your explanation.*

---

# PROPEL Principle 4: Nourishing Your Proactivity

In the following exercises, you will learn how to identify and use behaviors that will enable you to perform at your best when tackling a challenge.

## *Proactivity Exercise 1: Identify Your Strengths*

Go to the website at www.viacharacter.org and take the *free* Character Strengths Survey. Or discover your business-related strengths by paying for the StrengthsFinder Survey at the Gallup website: https://www.gallupstrengthscenter.com.

When you have your results, write your top five strengths at the top of a page in your journal or on the Proactivity page of the PROPEL Toolkit you downloaded. From my website: www.PROPELinstitute.com/toolkit.

## *Proactivity Exercise 2: Strengths Spotting[6]*

Recall a time when you were functioning at your best, enjoying the activity, feeling confident and energized. Write about how you used some or all of your top five strengths to attain this level of performance in the past.

## *Proactivity Exercise 3: The 11-Minutes-a-Day Ritual*[7]

Deliberately using your strengths for just 11 minutes a day, every day, will enable you to become a more proactive person. This exercise will enhance your ability to achieve your PROPEL goal as you become better at using your best qualities. Follow these three steps to become more effective at using your strengths:

- *30 Seconds to activate your new habit*—Start using one of your strengths to work on your PROPEL goal immediately following a habit you already have established. Use a "when–then" statement to program your brain. For example, "When I get up from my computer, then I'll use my social IQ strengths to create a positive exchange with a coworker."
- *10 Minutes to practice*—Devote 10 minutes to practice using one of your strengths.
- *30 Seconds to celebrate*—Reward yourself. Habits are formed more quickly if you give yourself positive reinforcement by doing something like checking it off your to-do list or getting a cup of coffee.

---

**DELIBERATE DAILY PRACTICE**

**Set aside 11 minutes in your daily calendar to practice using *one* of your strengths to help you achieve your PROPEL goal.**

---

## PROPEL Principle 5: Renewing Your Energy

Pursuing your personal and professional goals takes energy that must be replenished. If you do not take time to take care of yourself, you will run out of energy. When you become so consumed by your work that you fail to replenish your energy, you become physically exhausted, mentally drained, emotionally spent, and spiritually depleted. You burn out.

### *Energy Exercise 1: Self-Assessment*[8]

Check the statements that are true for you.

### *Body*

- ❒ I don't regularly get at least 7–8 hours of sleep. I often wake up feeling tired.
- ❒ I frequently skip breakfast, or I settle for something that isn't nutritious.
- ❒ I don't work out enough (meaning cardiovascular training at least 3 times/week and strength training at least once/week).
- ❒ I don't take regular breaks during the day to truly renew and recharge, or I often eat lunch at my desk if I eat at all.

## Emotions

- ❏ I frequently find myself feeling irritable, impatient, or anxious at work, especially when work is demanding.
- ❏ I don't have enough time with my family and loved ones, and when I'm with them, I'm not always really with them.
- ❏ I have too little time for the activities that I most deeply enjoy.
- ❏ I don't stop frequently enough to express my appreciation to others or to savor my accomplishments and blessings.

## Mind

- ❏ I have difficulty focusing on one thing at a time, and I am easily distracted during the day, especially by e-mail.
- ❏ I spend much of my day reacting to immediate crises and demands rather than focusing on activities with longer term value and high leverage.
- ❏ I don't take enough time for reflection, strategizing, and creative thinking.
- ❏ I work in the evenings or weekends. I rarely take an e-mail-free vacation.

## Spirit

- ❏ I don't spend enough time at work doing what I do best and enjoy most.
- ❏ There are significant gaps between what I say is most important to me in my life and how I actually allocate my time and energy.
- ❏ My decisions at work are more often influenced by external demands rather than a strong, clear sense of my own purpose.
- ❏ I don't invest enough time and energy in making a positive difference to others or to the world.

## Scoring

| How is your overall energy? Total number of statements checked | Guide to total score 0–3: Excellent energy management skills 4–6: Reasonable energy management skills 7–10: Significant energy management deficits 11–16: Full-fledged energy management crisis |
|---|---|
| **Number of checks in each domain** Body _____ Mind _____ Emotions _____ Spirit _____ | **Guide to domain scores** 0: Excellent energy management skills 1: Strong energy management skills 2: Deficits 3: Poor energy management skills 4: A full-fledged energy crisis |

---

**DELIBERATE DAILY PRACTICE**

Schedule times in your calendar to implement each of your new daily rituals for replenishing energy while you're working toward your PROPEL goal.

---

## Energy Exercise 2: Action Plan

After reflecting on your Energy Self-Assessment, you probably have a lot of ideas about how you could take better care of yourself. Start small. Pick just one daily ritual that will begin to give you better energy in each of the four domains: Body, Mind, Emotions, and Spirit.

---

# PROPEL Principle 6: Fulfilling Your LEGACY

You're learning how to optimize your performance and wellbeing. But the highest level of life satisfaction comes from empowering others to make making a meaningful difference in the world.[6] You've become well versed in the science of what is required to become an optimally functioning individual. Now it's time to teach others what you've learned.

## Legacy Exercise 1: Lessons from People Who Brought Out the Best in You?

Think of those individuals who have had a positive impact on your life. Write a description in your journal or downloaded PROPEL Toolkit about what you learned from those people. How did they empower you? Reflect on their qualities and how their coaching brought out the best in you. Then describe what it would it look like if you developed those coaching capabilities.

## Legacy Exercise 2: Establishing a Coaching Relationship

Think of someone you know who has unrealized potential. Explore whether they may interested in getting some coaching to learn about what optimal functioning could look like in their life. Express your belief that he or she could develop into an even higher functioning performer. Specifically, ask questions such as the following:

Would you like to learn more about how to

■ Maintain passion for achieving positive outcomes?
■ Develop more collaborative relationships?

- Persevere when you get discouraged?
- Identify and use your best qualities?
- Convert stress into constructive energy?
- Empower others to be at their best?

## *Legacy Exercise 3: Developing a Coaching Relationship*

---

### DELIBERATE DAILY PRACTICE

**To be an effective coach you must practice what you preach. What is the goal you're striving to achieve? What do you need to learn in order to be able to grow your capabilities? Are you deliberately practicing a new behavior every day?**

---

After working with someone for several sessions, evaluate the coaching relationship. Here are some criteria to judge whether or not you're off to a solid start:

- Did you agree on what goal the two of you will work toward?
- Did you discuss how a growth mind-set enables goal attainment?
- Did you agreed on new behaviors to be deliberately practiced?
- Did those new behaviors result in making progress toward the goal?
- Did you as the coach ask for feedback on how to improve the coaching process?

If these elements are established early, then the coaching has a high probability of success. Establish a routine of starting every meeting with a progress report and ending with a homework assignment.

For more information on how to apply the PROPEL Principles, visit: www. PROPELinstitute.com.

# Toolkit for Developing a PROPEL Team: Creating a Highly Effective Team to Facilitate Change

You have probably been struggling with problems in your healthcare organization. Like the people in the stories, you have discovered that you cannot solve complex issues on your own. This chapter provides the information you need to create and develop a high-functioning PROPEL team. Here you will find evidence-based methods for motivating these small groups of highly engaged staff members to work with you to achieve extraordinary results. PROPEL teams create "tipping points" to engage the vast majority of staff members in the process of making improvements—immediately and long term.

## Assess Your Workplace

To begin the performance improvement process, complete the short assessment that follows to help you identify areas that a PROPEL team could target for improvement.

## *Workplace Assessment Questions*

Using the following five-star ratings, assess the areas of opportunity to enhance optimal functioning in your unit, clinic, provider group, leadership team, etc. Circle the number of stars that describe your workgroup.

★ Dysfunctional ★★ Languishing ★★★ Average
★★★★ Superior ★★★★★ Optimal

### Values

★★★★★ I can describe at least three core values I share with others in my workgroup.

★★★★★ Most of the time my coworkers and I live by our shared values.

★★★★★ People in my workgroup feel valued for their contributions.

★★★★★ I know what's most important to the leaders of our workgroup.

★★★★★ I think the senior leaders in my organization usually understand what is most important to my workgroup.

### Passion

★★★★★ My workgroup has identified a specific outcome for improving our working environment.

★★★★★ At least two-thirds of my workgroup seem committed to achieving that outcome.

★★★★★ We don't allow just one or two people to control what our workgroup needs to do to attain our goals.

★★★★★ I personally feel a strong desire to perform at my best.

★★★★★ My coworkers work hard to help achieve our organization's overall goals.

### Relationships

★★★★★ I leave work most days feeling good about almost everyone in my workgroup.

★★★★★ When negative feelings are aroused, we almost always find a way to resolve them quickly and satisfactorily.

★★★★★ Our workgroup has enough people generating positive feelings to offset the negative emotions that are automatically aroused when problems surface.

★★★★★ Someone helps me get my job done almost every day.

★★★★★ Most days I receive appreciation for my efforts to help my coworkers.

## Optimism

★★★★★ When dealing with challenges, my coworkers and I quickly get past complaining and move on to brainstorming solutions.

★★★★★ Most of my coworkers pitch in to help overcome problems.

★★★★★ Our group rarely blames a particular person when things go wrong.

★★★★★ People in my workgroup persevere when we experience a setback.

★★★★★ Most of my coworkers typically support organizational change initiatives.

## Proactivity

★★★★★ People in my workgroup recall their top strengths when they need to enable themselves to be at their best.

★★★★★ My coworkers routinely talk about who has the most appropriate strengths to accomplish a positive outcome.

★★★★★ The manager of our team routinely talks to individual staff members about how they could more effectively apply their strengths.

★★★★★ My organization provides coaching or education to improve people's ability to use their strengths.

★★★★★ My organization's annual performance reviews include assessments of people's ability to use their strengths.

## Energy

★★★★★ Most of my coworkers have good energy to invest in people as well as projects.

★★★★★ Our workgroup makes sure that everyone gets time for a lunch break.

★★★★★ Our group rallies to take care of each other when problems occur or staffing is short.

★★★★★ People I work with believe that our workgroup can come out of a challenging situation stronger and wiser.

★★★★★ My organization provides plenty of opportunities for people to learn and grow.

## Legacy

★★★★★ The more senior people in our workgroup usually have one or two people they are actively mentoring.

★★★★★ Managers and staff members have effective two-way communication about what is working well and what needs improvement.

★★★★★ When our workgroup must learn something new, we are provided with training or education sessions to practice new skills.

★★★★★ I am routinely given a goal and asked to figure out how to achieve it.

★★★★★ My organization encourages people to point out and discuss problems—no matter who is involved—in order to get them resolved.

Where does your team and organization come out overall on this sampling of optimal functioning qualities? What are your strongest qualities? Where do you see a need for improvement? You cannot achieve optimal functioning in your workgroup without having support. As you have learned, PROPEL teams can be a major force in helping healthcare organizations move closer to performing a five-star level.

## Select the Team Members

PROPEL teams need to be small, typically no more than seven people. The reason for limiting the size of the group is to assure that everyone on the team has a chance to fully discuss their observations, concerns, and suggestions. If seven people meet for an hour, that only allows 8.5 minutes per person of airtime—not much when you're trying to resolve complex issues.

Identify who *you* think are the most positively engaged staff members. Then do a survey with staff members to identify who *they* believe are most helpful, have the best relationships, and are most optimistic. You're likely to find some surprises. There will be some new names to consider. And some people who relate well to you may not do so well with other staff members.

## Guidelines for Leading a PROPEL Team

Leaders function differently on a PROPEL team. The most effective leaders have an egalitarian mind-set. In her book, *Multipliers: How the Best Leaders Make Everyone Smarter*, Liz Wiseman presents five factors that leaders use to accelerate team performance[1]:

1. Find each team member's genius and turn them loose to work on a project rather than having them report to you every step of the way.
2. Assume that your team members' best thinking will occur when encouraged rather than pressured.
3. Believe that your team's collective wisdom will generate better ideas than if you try to figure out all the answers.
4. Populate teams with people with a variety of perspectives and challenge them to find spectacular solutions.
5. Let the "smart" people you put on your team figure out solutions by getting out of their way.

# Guidelines for PROPEL Team Members

To help your PROPEL team get off to a great start, schedule a 2- to 3-hour initial "kickoff" meeting. Introduce guidelines for optimal team functioning at the beginning of the meeting:

- Explain the PROPEL team's purpose: to identify possibilities for overcoming complex challenges *and* to engage coworkers in helping to implement solutions.
- Ask the team members to commit to adopting the rules of "smart" teams:
    - Everyone contributes equally to discussions, ensuring an equal voice for men and women, doctors and nurses, and so on.
    - Teammates read each other's emotional state to ensure that more positive than negative interactions are occurring.
    - People ask questions to understand different points of view before advocating for a solution.
    - Leaders offer opinions last during discussions to encourage those with less power to express their opinions.
- Request that PROPEL team members practice courageous communication:
    - When people speak in generalities, teammates ask for specific behavioral descriptions. For example, if they hear "people on the unit will be happy," ask "What behaviors would I see if that were occurring?" (A good answer: "more smiles.")
    - If people offer solutions containing the words "not" or "no" (such as "no complaining"), teammates ask, "What would I see instead?"
    - When a team member hears a solution they would like to explore, they respond with enthusiasm: "I really like that idea. How we could make that work?"
    - When people offer solutions that teammates believe may be problematic, they're required to use the "yes, and ..." method: "Yes I understand what you're suggesting, and have you considered _____?"
- Insist that the PROPEL team members create psychological safety by:
    - Committing to do their part to make progress toward the team's goal.
    - Accepting that change is a trial and error process; therefore, reporting problems is rewarded and recommending solutions is reinforced.
    - Maintaining a growth mind-set to encourage people who are struggling to learn and use new skills to build positive relationships, develop strengths, and so on.
    - Agreeing to establish, publicize, and support consequences for coworkers who violate rules or don't meet expectations for appropriate behavior.

# The Kickoff Meeting Exercises

## Discuss Past Performance

*When has our team been at its very best?*
1. What were the specific behaviors we demonstrated?
2. How did it feel at the end of the day?
3. What was most valuable about that experience?

*When have we been at our worst?*
1. What did that look like?
2. What are the valuable takeaways from that experience?

*What core values were forged as result of those previous experiences?*
1. What feelings did people experience during those times?
2. What does our team care about the most?
3. What core values do we share when we're at our best?

## Create a Vision for the Future

*What would it look like if we were living our values more consistently?*
1. What specific behaviors would we see if we were functioning at our best?
2. What feelings would people have at the end of the day?
3. What immediate impact would being at our best consistently produce?
4. What ripple effects would occur?
5. How would being at our best contribute to our organization's ultimate destiny?
6. How would it effect what patients and their families care deeply about?

*What is the best possible outcome that we can imagine?*
1. What's a vision we can all agree would represent our team at its best?
2. How can we condense our vision into three to four sentences we can all remember?

## Establish a Specific Goal

*What SMARTER goal will lead us closer to our vision?*
1. What will we need to do to achieve our vision?
2. What's the first step we could take?
   a. What would give us an early "win"?
   b. What would garner the most staff support?
3. How can we make it a SMARTER goal?
   a. Specific actions
   b. Meaningful results

   c. Attainable milestones

   d. Time line for success

   e. Evaluation of progress

   f. Readjustments based on lessons learned

## Commit to Taking First Steps

*What can the group count on each person to do as a first step?*

1. Ask each person to identify an action they could take in the next 2–3 weeks that would enable the team to begin making progress.
2. Have team members publicly state their intention, indicating exactly what actions they'll take, when and where they'll occur, and the results that they're committed to achieving.
3. To prevent people from going down the road of "good intentions" that were never realized, ask each person to complete the WOOP[2] exercise:
   a. Wish—what do want to do to help make progress?
   b. Outcome—how it will feel when you have taken that action?
   c. Obstacle—what is it within you that might hold you back?
   d. Plan—*if* you experience that obstacle, *then* what's your plan for overcoming it.
4. Determine times that will work best to hold regularly scheduled meetings.
5. Give team members instructions for taking either the VIA Character Strengths survey or the Gallup StrengthsFinder test.

# Conduct Regular PROPEL Team Meetings

Following the kickoff meeting, your PROPEL team should meet every week or two. Agenda items should include the following:

*Reporting the progress that's being made toward the values-based vision and the specific SMARTER goal that the team has agreed to work toward:*

1. Each team member comes prepared to give a brief progress report on the actions he or she had committed to take.
2. An active, constructive response is given to each person to build positivity among team members.

*Determining what the team thinks should be the next step toward the SMARTER goal:*

1. Possibilities are discussed, with each team member encouraged to express their ideas.

2. A consensus decision is reached that every team member is willing to support.
3. Strengths are reviewed to see who would be best suited to take on specific tasks.
4. Team members publicly commit to taking action prior to the next meeting.
5. Each person works through the WOOP exercise to boost their motivation.

*Deciding how team members will support each other's efforts between now and the next meeting:*

1. Who may need help?
2. Who may need encouragement?
3. How will we check in on each other between meetings?

## Using the PROPEL Team's Strengths

### Create a Strengths Matrix

Ask each of the PROPEL team members to give you their top five strengths. Depending on which of the strengths tests you ask them to complete at the end of the kickoff meeting, use one of the following matrices to display the results for the entire team. Here are two examples of strengths matrices. One displays the Gallup StrengthsFinder test[3] (Figure 14.1) and the other the VIA Character Strengths survey[4] (Figure 14.2).

### Assign Tasks Using Strengths Matrix

As you consider the steps required for your team to achieve the SMARTER goal that you've established, use strengths to assign the best suited people to work on specific tasks. Begin by outlining the tasks the team is pursuing on a whiteboard or poster board. Have each team member write their name and each of their top five strengths on Post It notes. Place the notes on a table with an area designated for each of the strength domains. Then have the team decide what strengths are needed to complete the tasks and put the notes of the board surrounding that task.[5] See Figure 14.3 for an example.

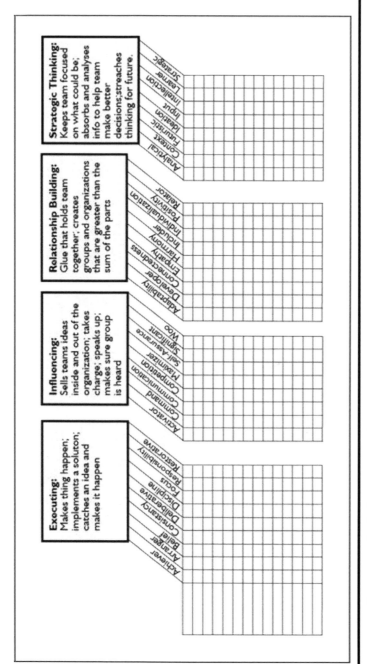

**Figure 14.1   Gallup StrengthsFinder team matrix.**

| Virtue | Character Strength | Team Members | | | | | |
|---|---|---|---|---|---|---|---|
| | | TRE | JUL | RAC | SAS | GEM | KEL |
| **Wisdom** | CREATIVITY | | ● | | | ● | ● |
| | CURIOSITY | | | ● | | | |
| | JUDGMENT | ● | ● | | | | |
| | LOVE OF LEARNING | | | | | ● | |
| | PERSPECTIVE | ● | | ● | | | ● |
| **Courage** | BRAVERY | | | | | | ● |
| | PERSERVERANCE | | ● | | | ● | |
| | HONESTY | | ● | | | | |
| | ZEST | | | | | | |
| **Humanity** | LOVE | | | | ● | ● | |
| | KINDNESS | | ● | | ● | | ● |
| | SOCIAL INTELLIGENCE | ● | | | ● | | |
| **Justice** | TEAMWORK | | | | | | |
| | FAIRNESS | | | | | | |
| | LEADERSHIP | | | | | | ● |
| **Temperance** | FORGIVENESS | ● | | | | | |
| | HUMILITY | | | | | | |
| | PRUDENCE | ● | | | | | |
| | SELF-REGULATION | | | | | | |
| **Transcendence** | APPREC BEAUTY/EXCEL | | | ● | | | |
| | GRADITUDE | | | | ● | | ● |
| | HOPE | ● | | ● | | | |
| | HUMOR | | | | | | |
| | SPIRITUALITY | | | | | | |

Figure 14.2   VIA Character Strengths team matrix.

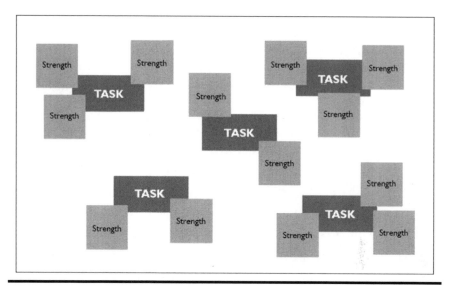

**Figure 14.3   Strengths SNOW (Sticky Note On Wall) board.**

## Dealing with Resistance and Setbacks

Your PROPEL team will encounter resistance from the staff members that can cause setbacks. Many of the staff members may be disengaged. In addition, there will probably be a small group who oppose any change efforts. Your team will need to use multiple sources of influence to achieve a "tipping point" in which two-thirds of your staff members are engaged in helping to achieve your SMARTER goal.

To generate a tenfold increase in the team's chance of success, it will be essential that they harness at least four of the six sources of Influence[6]:

*Source 1*: To motivate staff members—especially those who are disengaged—the team will need to find a way to link the behaviors they want to see with the values they know their coworkers already have. For example, they can share stories that illustrate the consequences of continuing the old behaviors, putting a human face on the challenge they are working to overcome. When staff members see that their past choices have caused harm to patients and/or coworkers, they will realize they can help make a difference by adopting new behaviors.

*Source 2*: To improve people's ability to act differently, the team will offer opportunities for staff members to practice building their skills in simulations that are as tough and realistic as possible.

*Source 3*: To create peer support, each team member will work with two people on staff members who they feel can be easily recruited. As those staff members experience the benefits of adopting new behaviors, they too can become social influencers.

*Source 4*: The team asks the staff member they recruited to help encourage even more staff members to become actively engaged in supporting the change initiative. This strategy exponentially expands the number of people who are working to achieve the team's SMARTER goal.

*Source 5*: Rewarding the right behaviors and creating clear accountability expectations will provide another level of motivation. Leaders will need to create external incentives and consequences. They will have to make sure that the rewards/consequences will be important enough to matter, even to the most resistant coworkers.

*Source 6*: To change people's mind-sets, the team will have to change the information being presented to the staff members. The team must measure progress toward achieving the SMARTER goal and give feedback to the staff members as frequently as possible.

## Recognize, Reward, and Celebrate

Celebrate the PROPEL team's success all along the way to achieving the SMARTER goal. Every time measurable progress is made, have a ceremony where you gather the team around to put a mark on a chart, drop a marble in a jar, or read a gratitude letter from a patient. Have team members identify teammates who helped them and express appreciation to them.

It is important to recognize the PROPEL team's efforts. Not with a "good job everybody." But with specific, individual feedback: "Carole, you were terrific at communicating our goal to the staff." Share your comments in a public setting— an awards ceremony, a staff meeting, or on a kudos board in the break room.

When the SMARTER goal has finally been accomplished, hold a victory celebration. We all like to feel we are a part of a winning team. Everyone can feel proud working in a healthcare organization that is able to make a meaningful difference in the lives of staff members and patients alike. And the staff's confidence in their ability to continue making improvements will soar.

Reward people for the time and energy they put into helping achieve the SMARTER goal. Give them great ratings on the performance reviews. Put them up for promotion. Buy lunch for the team; food always seems to be a welcome reward!

The PROPEL research has proven that forming teams of five to seven thought leaders who are well respected in a variety of disciplines can be a potent force for improving performance. PROPEL teams can work with leaders and staff members to find solutions to the challenges your organization is facing.

Optimal teamwork needs to start somewhere, and PROPEL teams are the perfect incubator for people to learn how to flourish. Once that group has mastered the requisite skills, they're well positioned to teach others. And that's how PROPEL teams improve patient care, staff engagement, and the bottom line.

## HELP IMPROVE HEALTHCARE BY SHARING HOW YOU LEAVE A LEGACY

Share what you've discovered that makes a difference in your workplace with other healthcare professionals in the community forum section at www.PROPELinstitute.com

# References

## Chapter 1

1. James, J.T. 2013. A new, evidence-based estimate of patient harms associated with hospital care. *Journal of Patient Safety* 9(3): 122–128, (July).
2. Gallup. 2013. The American Workplace: Employee Engagement Insights for U.S. *Business Leaders*. http://employeeengagement.com/wp-content/uploads/2013/06/Gallup-2013-State-of-the-American-Workplace-Report.pdf (accessed on February 25, 2017).
3. Becker's Hospital Review. 2013. 70% of Employees Aren't Engaged at Work. http://www.beckershospitalreview.com/human-capital-and-risk/70-of-employees-aren-t-engaged-at-work.html.
4. American Nursing Association. 2011. ANA Health and Safety Survey. http://www.nursingworld.org/MainMenuCategories/WorkplaceSafety/Healthy-Work-Environment/Work-Environment/2011-HealthSafetySurvey.html.
5. Medscape. 2016. Lifestyle Report: Bias and Burnout. http://www.medscape.com/features/slideshow/lifestyle/2016/public/overview.
6. NSI Nursing Solutions. 2016. National Healthcare Retention & RN Staffing Report. http://www.nsinursingsolutions.com/Files/assets/library/retention-institute/NationalHealthcareRNRetentionReport2016.pdf.

## Chapter 2

1. Seligman, M.E.P. 2011. *Flourish: A Visionary New Understanding of Happiness and Well-being.* New York: Free Press.
2. The Harris Poll. 2016. Latest Happiness Index Reveals American Happiness at All-Time Low. http://www.theharrispoll.com/health-and-life/American-Happiness-at-All-Time-Low.html (accessed on February 25, 2017).
3. Gallup. 2013. The American Workplace: Employee Engagement Insights for U.S. *Business Leaders.* http://employeeengagement.com/wp-content/uploads/2013/06/Gallup-2013-State-of-the-American-Workplace-Report.pdf (accessed on February 25, 2017).
4. Harter, J., Schmidt, F., Killham, E., and Agrawal, S. 2009. Q$^{12}$ Meta-Analysis: The Relationship between Engagement at Work and Organizational Outcomes. Gallup White Paper. https://strengths.gallup.com/private/resources/q12meta-analysis_flyer_gen_08%2008_bp.pdf.

5. NSI Nursing Solutions. 2016. National Healthcare Retention & RN Staffing Report. http://www.nsinursingsolutions.com/Files/assets/library/retention-institute/NationalHealthcareRNRetentionReport2016.pdf.

6. Muha, T., and Manion, J. 2010. Using positive psychology to engage your staff during difficult times. *Nurse Leader* 8: 1.

7. Fredrickson, B. 2009. *Positivity: Top-Notch Research Reveals the Upward Spiral That Will Change Your Life.* New York: Three Rivers Press.

8. Achor, S. 2010. *The Happiness Advantage: The Seven Principles of Positive Psychology That Fuel Success and Performance at Work.* New York: Crown Publishing.

9. Cameron, K. 2013. *Practicing Positive Leadership: Tools and Techniques That Create Extraordinary Results.* San Francisco, CA: Berrett-Koehler Publishers.

10. Cameron, K., Mora, C., and Leutscher, T. 2011. Effects of positive practices on organizational effectiveness. *Journal of Applied Behavioral Science* 47: 1–43.

# Chapter 3

1. Modern Healthcare. 2012. Top 100 hospitals. http://www.modernhealthcare.com/section/awards-and-recognition?module=900&id=3205974 (accessed on February 25, 2017).

2. Nicks, B.A., and Manthey, D.M. 2012. The impact of psychiatric patient boarding in emergency departments. *Emergency Medicine International* 2012: 306–308.

# Chapter 7

1. Vallerand, R.J., and Houlfort, N. 2003. Passion at work: Toward a new conceptualization. In S.W. Gilliland, D.D. Steiner, and D.P. Skarlicki (Eds.), *Emerging Perspectives on Values in Organizations* (pp. 175–204). Greenwich, CT: Information Age Publishing.

2. Vallerand, R.J., Blanchard, C.M., Mageau, G.A., Koestner, R., Ratelle, C., Léonard, M., Gagné, M., and Marsolais, J. 2003. Les passions de lame: On obsessive and harmonious passion. *Journal of Personality and Social Psychology* 85: 756–767.

3. Deci, E.L., and Ryan, R.M. 2000. The "what" and "why" of goal pursuits: Human needs and the self-determination of behavior. *Psychological Inquiry* 11: 227–268.

4. Gousse-Lessard, A.S., Vallerand, R.J., Carbonneau, N., and LaFreniere, M.-A.K. 2013. The role of passion in mainstream and radical behaviors: A look at environmental activism. *Journal of Environmental Psychology* 35: 18–29.

5. Mageau, G., Carpentier, J., and Vallerand, R.J. 2011. The role of self-esteem contingencies in the distinction between obsessive and harmonious passion. *European Journal of Social Psychology* 41: 720–729.

6. Vallerand, R.J., Houlfort, N., and Forest, J. 2014. Passion for work: Determinants and outcomes. In M. Gagne (Ed.), *The Oxford Handbook of Work Engagement, Motivation, and Self-Determination Theory.* Oxford: Oxford Library of Psychology.

7. Carbonneau, N., Vallerand, R.J., Fernet, C., and Guay, F. 2008. The role of passion for teaching in intra and interpersonal outcomes. *Journal of Educational Psychology* 100: 977–988.

8. Belanger, J.J., Lafreniere, M.K., Vallerand, R.J., and Kruglanski, A.W. 2013. When passion makes the heart grow colder: The role of passion in alternative goal suppression. *Journal of Personality and Social Psychology* 104: 126–147.

9. Houlfort, N., and Rinfret, N. 2010. *Human Management in Organizations*. Paris, France: Éditions L'Harmattan.

10. Vallerand, R.J. 2012. The role of passion in sustainable psychological well-being. *Psychological Well-Being: Theory, Research and Practice* 2: 1–21.

11. Waugh, C.E., and Fredrickson, B.L. 2006. Nice to know you: Positive emotions, self-other overlap, and complex understanding in the formation of new relationships. *Journal of Positive Psychology* 1: 93–106.

12. Lavigne, G.L., Forest, J., and Crevier-Braud, L. 2012. Passion at work and burnout: A two-study test of the mediating role of flow experiences. *European Journal of Work and Organizational Psychology* 21: 518–546.

13. Garland, E.L., Fredrickson, B., Kring, A., Johnson, D.P., Meyer, P.S., and Penn, D.L. 2010. Upward spirals of positive emotions counter downward spirals of negativity: Insights from the broaden-and-build theory and affective neuroscience on the treatment of emotion dysfunctions and deficits in psychopathology. *Clinical Psychology Review* 30: 849–864.

14. Vallerand, R.J., Paquet, Y., Philippe, F.L., and Charest, J. 2010. On the role of passion in burnout: A process model. *Journal of Personality* 78: 289–312.

15. Holdren, P., Paul III, D.P., and Coustasse, A. 2015. Burnout syndrome in hospital nurses. *Paper Presented at Business and Health Administration Association International Conference*, Chicago, IL. http://mds.marshall.edu/cgi/viewcontent.cgi?article=1141&context=mgmt_faculty.

16. Cimiotti, J.P., Aiken, L.H., Sloane, D.M., and Wu, E.S. 2012. Nursing staffing, burnout, and health care-associated infection. *American Journal of Infection Control* 40: 486–490.

17. McHugh, M.D., Kutney-Lee, A., Cimiotti, J.P., Sloane, D.M., and Aiken, L.H. 2011. Nurses' widespread job dissatisfaction, burnout, and frustration with health benefits signal problems for patient care. *Health Affairs* 30(2): 202–210.

18. Peckham, C. 2016. Medscape lifestyle report 2016: Bias and burnout. *Medscape Family Medicine*. http://www.medscape.com/features/slideshow/lifestyle/2016/public/overview.

19. Shanafelt, T.D., Boone, S., Tan, L., Dyrbye, L.N., Sotile, W., Satele, D., West, C.P., Sloan, J., and Oreskovich, M.R. 2012. Burnout and satisfaction with work-life balance among US physicians relative to the general US population. *Archives of Internal Medicine* 172: 1377–1385.

20. Brown, B. 2012. *Daring Greatly: How the Courage to Be Vulnerable Transforms the Way We Live, Love, Parent, and Lead*. New York: Gotham.

21. Morris, D., and Garrett, J. 2010. Strengths: Your leading edge. In P.A. Linley, S.A. Harrington, and N. Garcea (Eds.), *Oxford Handbook of Positive Psychology and Work*. Oxford: Oxford University Press.

22. Kruger, J., and Dunning, D. 1999. Unskilled and unaware of it: How difficulties in recognizing one's own incompetence lead to inflated self-assessments. *Journal of Personality and Social Psychology* 77: 1121–1134.

23. Lewis, S. 2011. *Positive Psychology at Work*. Chichester, England: Wiley-Blackwell.

24. Kaplan, R.E., and Kaiser, R.B. 2010. Towards a positive psychology for leaders. In P.A. Linley, S.A. Harrington, and N. Garcea (Eds.), *Oxford Handbook of Positive Psychology and Work*. Oxford: Oxford University Press.

25. Neff, K. 2015. *Self-Compassion: The Proven Power of being Kind to Yourself*. New York: HarperCollins.

26. Simon, S., Howe, L., and Kirschenbaum, H. 1995. *Values Clarification*. New York: Warner.

27. Oettingen, G. 2014. *Rethinking Positive Thinking: Inside the New Science of Motivation*. New York: Penguin Random House.

28. Gollwitzer, P.M., and Oettingen, G. 2013. Implementation intentions. In M. Gellman and J.R. Turner (Eds.), *Encyclopedia of Behavioral Medicine* (Part 9). New York: Springer-Verlag.

29. Kappes, H.B., and Oettingen, G. 2011. Positive fantasies about idealized futures sap energy. *Journal of Experimental Social Psychology* 47: 719–729.

30. Gollwitzer, P., and Sheeran, P. 2006. Implementation intentions and goal achievement: A meta-analysis of effects and processes. *Advances in Experimental Psychology* 38: 69–119.

31. Oettingen, G. 2014. Stop being so positive. *Harvard Business Review* 92(10): 92–99.

32. Fredrickson, B.L., and Losada, M. 2005. Positive affect and the complex dynamics of human flourishing. *American Psychologist* 60(7): 678–686.

33. Woolley, A.W., Chabris, C.F., Pentland, A., Hashmi, N., and Malone, T.W. 2010. Evidence for a collective intelligence factor in the performance of human groups. *Science* 330(6004): 686–688.

34. Hagel, J., Brown, J.S., Ranjan, A., and Byler, D. 2014. Passion at work: Cultivating worker passion as a cornerstone of talent development. Westlake, TX: Deloitte University Press.

35. Blizzard, R. 2005. Nurse engagement key to reducing medical errors. *Gallup Business Journal.* http://www.gallup.com/poll/20629/nurse-engagement-key-reducing-medical-errors.aspx.

# Chapter 8

1. Gottman, J., and Silver, N. 1999. *The Seven Principles for Making Marriage Work*. New York: Crown (Three Rivers Press).

2. Adkins, A. 2015. Majority of U.S. employees not engaged despite gains in 2014. *Gallup Employee Engagement Poll.* http://www.gallup.com/poll/181289/majority-employees-not-engaged-despite-gains-2014.aspx.

3. Robison, J. 2008. Turning around employee turnover. *Gallup Business Journal.* http://www.gallup.com/businessjournal/106912/turning-around-your-turnover-problem.aspx.

4. Blizzard, R. 2005. Nurse engagement key to reducing medical errors. *Gallup Health and Healthcare.* http://www.gallup.com/poll/20629/nurse-engagement-key-reducing-medical-errors.aspx.

5. Blizzard, R. 2005. Nurturing hospital employee engagement: Registered nurses. *Gallup Business Journal.* http://www.gallup.com/poll/17398/nurturing-hospital-employee-engagement-registered-nurses.aspx.

6. Harter, J. 2015. Who drives employee engagement—Manager or CEO? *Gallup Blog.* http://www.gallup.com/opinion/gallup/186503/drives-employees-engagement-manager-ceo.aspx.

7. Sirota, T. 2008. Nursing2008 nurse/physician relationships survey report. *Nursing* 38(7): 28–31.

8. Manojlovich, M., and De Cicco, B. 2007. Healthy work environments, nurse-physician communication and patients' outcomes. *American Journal of Critical Care* 16(6): 536–543.

9. Ayd, M.A. 2004. A remedy of errors. *Hopkins Medicine Magazine*, Spring/Summer.

10. Pronovost, P., Berenholtz, S., Dorman, T., Lipsett, P.A., Simmonds, T., and Haraden, C. 2003. Improving communication in the ICU using daily goals. *Journal of Critical Care* 18(2): 71–75.

11. Patterson, K., Grenny, J., McMillan, R., and Switzler, A. 2012. *Crucial Conversations: Tools for Talking When the Stakes are High,* 2nd ed. New York: McGraw-Hill.

12. Ancona, D., and Isaacs, B. 2009. Structural balance in teams. In J. Dutton and B.R. Ragins (Eds.), *Exploring Positive Relationships at Work: Building a Theoretical and Research Foundation.* New York: Psychology Press.

13. McMains, V. 2016. Johns Hopkins study suggests medical errors are third-leading cause of death in U.S. *Johns Hopkins HUB.* https://hub.jhu.edu/2016/05/03/medical-errors-third-leading-cause-of-death/.

14. Seligman, M.E.P. 2012. *Flourish: A Visionary New Understanding of Happiness and Well-Being.* New York: Free Press.

15. Fredrickson, B.L. 2013. *Love 2.0: Finding Happiness and Health in Moments of Connection.* New York: Hudson Street Press (Penguin).

16. Brown, B. 2015. *Rising Strong.* New York: Spiegel and Grau.

17. Gable, S., Reis, H.T., Impett, E.A., and Asher, E.R. 2004. What do you do when things go right? The intrapersonal and interpersonal benefits of sharing positive events. *Journal of Personality and Social Psychology* 87(2): 228–245.

18. Seligman, M.E.P. 2004. *Authentic Happiness: Using the New Positive Psychology to Realize Your Potential for Lasting Fulfillment.* New York: Atria.

19. Kashdan, T., and Biswas-Diener, R. 2014. *The Upside of Your Dark Side: Why Being Your Whole Self—Not Just Your "Good" Self—Drives Success and Fulfillment.* New York: Hudson Street Press.

20. Grossman, D. 2012. *On Combat: The Psychology and Physiology of Deadly Conflict in War and in Peace,* 3rd ed. Belleville, IL: PPCT Research Publications.

21. Davidson, R. 2012. *The Emotional Life of Your Brain: How Its Unique Patterns Affect the Way You Think, Feel, and Live—and How You Can Change Them.* New York: Penguin.

22. Cuddy, A. 2015. *Presence: Bringing Your Boldest Self to Your Biggest Challenges.* New York: Little, Brown.

23. Cialdini, R.B. 2006. *Influence: The Psychology of Persuasion.* New York: Harper Business.

24. Gottman, J. 2001. *The Relationship Cure: A 5 Step Guide to Strengthening Your Marriage, Family, and Friendships.* New York: Three Rivers Press.

25. Amabile, T., and Kramer, S. 2011. *The Progress Principle: Using Small Wins to Ignite Joy, Engagement and Creativity at Work.* Boston, MA: Harvard Business Review Press.

# Chapter 9

1. Watson, T. How the fundamentals have evolved and the best adapt. *2013-2104 Change and Communication ROI Study Report.* https://www.towerswatson.com/en-US/Insights/IC-Types/Survey-Research-Results/2013/12/2013-2014-change-and-communication-roi-study (accessed on February 25, 2017).

2. Blanchard, K. 2010. *Mastering the Art of Change.* http://www.kenblanchard.com/img/pub/Blanchard_Mastering_the_Art_of_Change.pdf.
3. Paul, A.M. 2011. The uses and abuses of optimism and pessimism. *Psychology Today.* https://www.psychologytoday.com/articles/201111/the-uses-and-abuses-optimism-and-pessimism.
4. Weiner, B. 1985. An attributional theory of achievement motivation and emotion. *Psychological Review* 92: 548–573.
5. Kahneman, D. 2011. *Thinking, Fast and Slow.* New York: Farrar, Straus and Giroux.
6. Seligman, M. 2006. *Learned Optimism: How to Change Your Mind and Your Life.* New York: Vintage Books.
7. Blackburn, E., and Epel, E. 2017. *The Telomere Effect: A Revolutionary Approach to Living Younger, Healthier, Longer.* New York: Grand Central Publishing.
8. Korb, A. 2015. *The Upward Spiral: Using Neuroscience to Reverse the Course of Depression, One Small Change at a Time.* Oakland, CA: New Harbinger Publications.
9. Dweck, C. 2008. *Mindset: The New Psychology of Success.* New York: Ballantine.
10. Duckworth, A. 2016. *Grit: The Power of Passion and Perseverance.* New York: Scribner.
11. Fredrickson, B.L., and Dutton, J.E. 2008. Unpacking positive organizing: Organizations as sites of individual and group flourishing. *The Journal of Positive Psychology* 3: 1–3.
12. Aon Thought Leadership. 2016. Trends in global employee engagement. http://www.aon.com/human-capital-consulting/thought-leadership/talent/2016-Trends-in-Global-Employee-Engagement.jsp.
13. Grenny, J., Patterson, K., Maxfield, D., McMillan, R., and Switzler, A. 2013. *Influencer: The New Science of Leading Change,* 2nd ed. New York: McGraw-Hill.

# Chapter 10

1. Augustine, J.J. 2013. The True Cost of Ambulance Diversion. *Emergency Physicians Monthly.* http://epmonthly.com/article/the-true-cost-of-ambulance-diversion/ (accessed on February 25, 2017).
2. McQuaid, M., and Lawn, E. 2014. *Your Strengths Blueprint: How to Be Engaged, Energized, and Happy at Work.* Australia: Self-published.
3. Linley, A. 2008. *Average to A+: Realizing Strengths in Yourself and Others.* Coventry, England: CAPP Press.
4. Rath, T. 2007. *StrengthsFinder 2.0.* New York: Gallup Press.
5. Clifton, D.O., and Harter, J.K. 2003. Investing in strengths. In K.S. Cameron, J.E. Dutten, and R.E. Quinn (Eds.), *Positive Organizational Scholarship* (pp. 111–121). San Francisco, CA: Berrett-Koehler Publishers.
6. Seligman, M. 2006. *Authentic Happiness: Using the New Positive Psychology to Realize Your Potential for Lasting Fulfillment.* London: Nicholas Brealey.
7. VIA Institute on Character. VIA Classification of Character Strengths and Virtues. http://www.viacharacter.org/www/Character-Strengths/VIA-Classification.
8. Sorenson, S. 2014. How employees' strengths make your company stronger. *Gallup Business Journal.* February 20, 2014. http://www.gallup.com/businessjournal/167462/employees-strengths-company-stronger.aspx.
9. Rath, T., and Conchie, B. 2008. *Strength Based Leaderships: Great leaders, Teams, and Why People Follow.* New York: Gallup Press.

10. Harter, J., Schmidt, F., and Hayes, T. 2002. Business-unit-level relationship between employee satisfaction, employee engagement, and business outcomes: A meta-analysis. *Journal of Applied Psychology* 87: 268–279.

11. Burger, J., and Sutton, L. 2014. How employee engagement can improve a hospital's health. *Gallup Business Journal.* April 3, 2014. http://www.gallup.com/businessjournal/168149/employee-engagement-improve-hospital-health.aspx.

12. Buckingham, M. 2007. *Go Put Your Strengths To Work: 6 Powerful Steps To Achieve Outstanding Performance.* New York: Free Press.

13. Manning, J. 5 Surprising facts about willpower. *WebMD.* http://www.webmd.com/diet/features/willpower-facts#1.

14. Neal, D.T., Wood, W., and Quinn, J.M. 2006. Habits—A repeat performance. *Current Directions in Psychological Science* 15(4): 198–202.

15. Graybel, A.M. 1998. The basal ganglia and chunking of action repertories. *Neurobiology of Learning and Memory* 70(1): 119–136.

16. Corporate Leadership Council. 2004. *Driving Performance and Retention through Employee Engagement.* Washington, DC: Corporate Executive Board.

17. Hodges, T., and Asplund, J. 2010. Strengths development in the workplace. In A. Linley, S. Harrington, and N. Garcea (Eds.), *Oxford Handbook of Positive Psychology and Work* (pp. 213–220). Oxford: Oxford University Press.

18. Groscurth, C. 2014. Hospitals' performance management must be improved fast. *Gallup Business Journal.* http://www.gallup.com/businessjournal/182195/hospitals-performance-management-improved-fast.aspx.

19. Gallup's Employee Engagement Science. https://q12.gallup.com/Help/en-us/About.

20. Sorenson, S. 2014. How employees strengths make your company stronger. *Gallup Business Journal.* http://www.gallup.com/businessjournal/167462/employees-strengths-company-stronger.aspx.

# Chapter 11

1. Peckham, C. 2016. *Medscape Lifestyle Report 2016: Bias and Burnout.* http://www.medscape.com/features/slideshow/lifestyle/2016/public/overview (accessed on February 25, 2017).

2. Shanafelt, T.D., Hasan, O., Dyrbye, L.N. et al. 2015. Changes in burnout and satisfaction with work-life balance in physicians and the general US working population between 2011 and 2014. *Mayo Clinic Proceedings* 90(12): 1600–1613.

3. American Foundation for Suicide Prevention. *Physician and Medical Student Depression and Suicide Prevention.* https://afsp.org/our-work/education/physician-medical-student-depression-suicide-prevention/.

4. American Nursing Association. 2011. http://www.nursingworld.org/MainMenuCategories/WorkplaceSafety/Work-Environment/2011-HealthSafetySurvey.html.

5. Dall'Ora1, C., Griffiths, P., Ball, J., Simon, M., and Aiken, L.H. 2015. Association of 12h shifts and nurses' job satisfaction, burnout and intention to leave: Findings from a cross-sectional study of 12 European countries. *BMJ Open.* 5: e008331.

6. Cimiotti, J.P., Aiken, L.H., Sloane, D.M., and Wu, E.S. 2012. Nurse staffing, burnout, and health care–associated infection. *American Journal of Infection Control* 40(6): 486–490.

7. NPR/Robert Wood Johnson Foundation/Harvard School of Public Health. 2014. *The Burden of Stress in America.* http://www.rwjf.org/en/library/research/2014/07/the-burden-of-stress-in-america.html.

8. American Psychological Association. 2015. *Stress in America.* http://www.apa.org/news/press/releases/stress/2015/snapshot.aspx.

9. Loehr, J., and Schwartz, T. 2003. *The Power of Full Engagement: Managing Energy, Not Time, Is the Key to High Performance and Personal Renewal.* New York: The Free Press.

10. Keller, A., Litzelman, K., Wisk, L.E., Maddox, T., Cheng, E.R., Creswell, P.D., and Witt, W.P. 2012. Does the perception that stress affects health matter? The association with health and mortality. *Health Psychology* 31(5): 677–684.

11. McGonigal, K. 2015. *The Upside of Stress: Why Stress Is Good for You, and How to Get Good at It.* New York: Avery Publishing.

12. Crum, A., Salovey, P., and Achor, S. 2013. Rethinking stress: The role of mindsets in determining the stress response. *Journal of Personality and Social Psychology* 104(4): 716–733.

13. Cameron, K. 2013. *Practicing Positive Leadership: Tools and Techniques That Create Extraordinary Results.* San Francisco, CA: Berrett-Koehler Publishers.

14. Cameron, K. 2009. Positive psychology leaders series. *International Positive Psychology Association.* http://www.ippanetwork.com/leader-series/kim-cameron/.

# Chapter 12

1. Keyes, C.L.M. 2002. The mental health continuum: From languishing to flourishing in life. *Journal of Health and Social Behavior* 43: 207–222.

2. Fredrickson, B.L., and Losada, M.F. 2005. Positive affect and complex dynamics of human flourishing. *American Psychologist* 60: 678–686.

3. Westerhol, G.J., and Keyes, C.L. 2010. Mental illness and mental health: The two continua model across the lifespan. *Journal of Adult Development* 17(2): 110–119.

4. Ryff, C.D., and Keyes, C.L.M. 1995. The structure of psychological well-being revisited. *Journal of Personality and Social Psychology* 69: 719–727.

5. Amibile, T., and Kramer, S. 2011. *The Progress Principle: Using Small Wins to Ignite Joy, Engagement and Creativity at Work.* Boston, MA: Harvard Business School Publishing.

6. Grant, A. 2013. *Give and Take: A Revolutionary Approach to Success.* New York: Viking.

7. Duncan, B., Miller, S., Wampold, B., and Hubble, M. (Eds.) 2009. *The Heart and Soul of Change,* 2nd ed. Washington, DC: APA Press.

8. Wiseman, E. 2010. *Multipliers: How the Best Leaders Make Everyone Smarter.* New York: HarperCollins.

9. Edmondson, A. 2012. *Teaming: How Organizations Learn, Innovate, and Compete in the Knowledge Economy.* San Francisco, CA: Jossey-Bass.

10. American Psychological Association. 2006. *Forgiveness: A Sampling of Research Results.* Washington, DC: Office of International Affairs.

11. Edmondson, A. 1996. Learning from mistakes is easier said than done: Group and organizational influences on the detection and correction of human error. *Journal of Applied Behavior Science* 32: 5–28.

12. Edmondson, A. 2011. Strategies for learning from failure. *Harvard Business Review* 89(4): 48–55.

# Chapter 13

1. Bergquist, J. 2011. *Core Values Exercises.* Culture Sync. http://www.triballeadership. net/core-values/core-values-exercises (accessed on February 25, 2017).
2. Oettingen, G. 2014. *Rethinking Positive Thinking: Inside the New Science of Motivation.* New York: Penguin Random House.
3. Adkins, A. 2015. Gallup Employee Engagement. *Majority of U.S. Employees Not Engaged Despite Gains in 2014.* http://www.gallup.com/poll/181289/majority-employees-not-engaged-despite-gains-2014.aspx.
4. Fredrickson, B. 2009. *Positivity: Top-Notch Research Reveals the Upward Spiral That Will Change Your Life.* New York: Three Rivers Press.
5. MindTools. https://www.mindtools.com/pages/article/newTCS_89.htm.
6. Seligman, M. 2006. *Learned Optimism: How to Change Your Mind and Your Life.* New York: Vintage Books.
7. McQuaid, M. Use *Your Strengths Each Day At Work.* http://www.michellemcquaid. com/strengths-habit.
8. Schwartz, T., and McCarthy, C. 2007. Manage your energy, not your time. *Harvard Business Review.* https://hbr.org/2007/10/manage-your-energy-not-your-time?cm_sp=Article-_-Links-_-Comment.

# Chapter 14

1. Wiseman, E. 2010. *Multipliers: How the Best Leaders Make Everyone Smarter.* New York: HarperCollins.
2. Grenny, J., Patterson, K., Maxfield, D., McMillan, R., and Switzler, A. 2013. *Influencer: The New Science of Leading Change,* 2nd edition. New York: McGraw-Hill.
3. Rath, T., and Conchie, B. 2008. *Strength Based Leaderships: Great Leaders, Teams, and Why People Follow.* New York: Gallup Press.
4. VIA Institute on Character, VIA Pro Team Report: www.viacharacter.org/www/Reports-Courses-Resources/Reports/The-VIA-Pro-Team-Report (accessed on February 25, 2017).
5. Pennock, S., and Alberts, H. Positive Psychology Practitioner's Tools. http://www.positivepsychologyprogram.com.
6. Crum, A., and Crum, T. 2015. Stress can be a good thing if you know how to use it. Harvard Business Review. https://hbr.org/2015/09/stress-can-be-a-good-thing-if-you-know-how-to-use-it.

# Index

Note: Page numbers followed by f refer to figures.